JOHN QUINCY ADAMS

SLAVERY AND ABOLITION

1831–1841

BY

ALBERT BUSHNELL HART, LL.D.
PROFESSOR OF HISTORY IN HARVARD UNIVERSITY

WITH MAPS

NEGRO UNIVERSITIES PRESS
NEW YORK

TO

JAMES FORD RHODES

CANDID HISTORIAN
VALUED FRIEND
PROMOTER OF TRUTH

CONTENTS

CONTENTS

MAPS

AUTHOR'S PREFACE

EXCEPT perhaps the struggle between patriots and tories at the outbreak of the Revolution, no controversy in the history of the United States has aroused such passion and led to such momentous results as that between the advocates and the opponents of slavery. Yet in its initial movement the organized propaganda, to which the term abolition is usually applied, was disassociated from political parties; and nearly a quarter of a century passed before a national election turned upon the issue of the farther territorial extension of slavery. It is therefore possible to separate from the party questions which arose during the administrations of Jackson and Van Buren the elements of the slavery contest; to sketch the conditions of the slave, of the master, and of the anti-slavery agitator; and to trace the controversy from the press and public meetings to the state governments, and thence to Congress. The book has the double purpose of describing the conditions of slavery and the state of mind of those interested for it or against it, and at the same time of recording the events which mark the anti-slavery agitation. The conditions of the plantations were little changed down to the Civil War, and I have therefore frequently illustrated them by the testimony of observers later than 1840; the events, however, are followed out only to about 1841; and later causes of excitement will appear in their proper setting, in subsequent volumes of the series.

The first three chapters of this volume describe the social and economic background of the struggle. Chapters v. to ix. are devoted to a description of the master and slave as they lived together in a social combination which could be shaken apart only by a great convulsion. Chapters x. to xvii. take up the obverse of the medal, the abolitionists and their methods and relation to master, slave, and government. Chapters xviii. and xix. carry the controversy into the national government. Chapter xx. is on the political events of Van Buren's administration. Chapter xxi. is a summary of the actual effects of the movement. The authorities upon which the volume is based are in part enumerated in chapter xxii. But such references cannot include the personal impressions gained from association with southern whites, with the descendants of slaves, and with military and civil actors in the great drama on both sides.

I am under obligations to Dr. Albert Gaillard Hart, to Colonel Thomas Wentworth Higginson, and to Mr. William Roscoe Thayer for reading the proofs and making valuable suggestions, but I

cannot lay to their charge any errors in point of
view or statement of fact which may appear in
this volume.

It is hard for a son and grandson of abolitionists
to approach so explosive a question with imparti-
ality; but the book is intended to show that there
was more than one side to the controversy, and
that both the milder form of opposition called anti-
slavery and the extremer form called abolition were
confronted by practical difficulties which to many
public-spirited and conscientious men seemed insurmountable. It is for later writers in the series
to show how those difficulties were finally sur-
mounted.

ALBERT BUSHNELL HART.

SLAVERY AND ABOLITION

SLAVERY AND ABOLITION

CHAPTER I

AMERICAN SOCIAL CHARACTERISTICS
(1830–1860)

IN most periods of American history a central thread can be discovered about which are arranged the events of the times; but in the administrations of Jackson and Van Buren a variety of questions struggled for precedence. A previous writer in this series has undertaken to disentangle the political and economic controversies of that interesting time, leaving the complexities of the anti-slavery movement for this separate treatment; but it must not be supposed that in the people's minds slavery was disconnected from other economic problems which pressed upon the country, or that abolition was entirely different from the other social agitations of the period, or that even the agitators realized that slavery had the latent power of dividing the Union and bringing about civil war.

Many other sectional problems arose in that period: the seaboard and the interior squabbled over internal improvements; east and west were sometimes in antagonism over public lands; north and south were at odds on nullification. Why should not the slavery conflict also come up and go down again like other passionately disputed questions? Why did the controversy, once fairly started, grow fiercer every year and bring in new and still more divisive issues? Why was the national government, which did its best to keep out of the controversy, drawn in deeper and deeper, till Congress became the forum of an excited discussion over slavery? These questions involve many disputed points which still perplex people, states, sections, and the Union; and the only way to answer them is to make clear the moral, social, and economic conditions peculiar to slavery which caused the rising feeling of sectional bitterness and distrust; to reconstruct a vanished civilization; to breathe the breath of life into master, slave, and abolitionist, years since in their graves.

No American in the thirties undertook to analyze and describe the standards and aspirations of his countrymen; for the social life of the period we must depend on the testimony of many observers, each of whom saw only a part. Several foreigners undertook a more general task. Mrs. Trollope's book[1] was accepted by many people in England as a typical account of a disagreeable people. This

[1] Trollope, *Domestic Manners of the Americans*.

Englishwoman in 1827 dropped into a boarding-house in Cincinnati, saw the crude side of a frontier community—the "quick feeders," the empty-headed young women, and the tobacco chewers—and too late discovered a more refined and intellectual society in the east. Of characteristic American life she saw far less than Harriet Martineau, who came over in 1834, and in her two years' stay travelled widely north and south. She found plenty to criticise in American life, yet appreciated the vigor and the advance of the nation.[1] A third foreigner, accepted as one of the most far-seeing observers and critics of American character and statecraft, was Alexis de Tocqueville, a Frenchman, who came over in 1831, with the express purpose of studying the institutions of the Americans, and in 1835 and 1840 published his *Democracy in America*. This was the first scientific estimate of popular government in America, going beneath the self-satisfaction of a successful republic to discover the real forces which animated it, and to find out how far it swerved from its own standards. He saw in America a big, bustling community, intensely self-conscious, yet in general sticking to its basal principle of equality of opportunity and encouraging the individual to make the most of himself.

All three of these critics noticed the lack of harmony between free democratic government and slavery, and Tocqueville foresaw a menace to Amer-

[1] Martineau, *Society in America*, passim.

ican democracy in the presence of a servile race, so that, even if slavery were to disappear, the prejudices to which it had given birth would remain; and his final generalization was that slavery, which is "unjust and by political economy is prejudicial, and which is now contrasted with democratical liberties and the information of our age, cannot survive." [1]

No foreign or home-grown criticism could much affect either the vigorous growing democracy or the slave-holder; but their attention was caught by the sectional rivalry of the north and south. For this rising hostility new material was furnished by the censuses of 1830 and 1840, which revealed the fact that the free states had permanently forged ahead of the slave-holding communities in numbers: from about 2,000,000 each in 1790, the north in fifty years rose to 9,100,000 natives, besides 600,000 immigrants, a gain of 40 per cent. over 1830; while the south showed 7,300,000, a gain of 27 per cent. The main difference was the rapid birth-rate in the northeastern and northwestern states, where cheap land and variety of employment made the conditions of life easy. New York state increased in ten years by more than half a million; while Maryland, Virginia, and North Carolina were nearly at a stand-still.

The urban population was growing faster than the average, but most of it was in the north. Boston, New York, and Philadelphia were still big, sprawling

[1] Tocqueville, *Democracy in America* (Reeves' translation), I., 364, 388.

towns, ill-paved, faintly lighted, and miserably policed, and outside of half a dozen places the south had no cities at all; even Washington was still a dirty country town, where hogs ran at large. Charleston seemed more to "resemble a city of the European continent, at least in the style of its houses, than either Boston or New York." [1] Savannah was a winter resort for southerners, and some people foresaw a migration of invalids and winter visitors from the north. New Orleans was the southern city *par excellence*, and the only one in the lower south except Charleston which had a lively commerce and direct relation with the old world. Most visitors were interested in the old French town, and the St. Charles Hotel, "with its large and elegant Corinthian portico, and the lofty swelling dome which surmounts it." [2]

Social life in the United States was much influenced by the prosperity of the decade from 1827 to 1837, but as yet there were few men of large fortune in the country: the richest planters probably had net incomes of less than fifty thousand dollars a year; and Stephen Girard, of Philadelphia, and John Jacob Astor, of New York, were almost the only reputed millionaires. In the north there were few owners of large estates divided into farms; most of the northern money came from trade and manufacturing, although the foundations of some great fortunes,

[1] Bremer, *Homes of the New World*, I., 263.
[2] Mackay, *Western World*, II., 78.

such as the Astor's, were being laid by the purchase of real-estate in growing cities. In the north, new individuals were constantly pushing to the front, and society was in a state of flux; in the south, hereditary family dignities were better established, and it was hard to break into the charmed circle.

Social life in 1830 was not essentially different from that of 1820.[1] The most significant thing was the contrast within the same nation, and even the same state, between the traditional civilization derived from England and the robust life of the frontier: in wealth, in the appliances of trade and manufactures, in education and in literature, the Atlantic coast was closely allied with Europe; but the west and southwest was almost all frontier, and in northern New England and New York, in central Pennsylvania, and in the heart of all the southern states were large areas with a population of hundreds of thousands still in the rude conditions of the early eighteenth century.

These conditions were reflected in an impatience with orderly government. Though laws and constitutions were changed with amazing rapidity, people could not wait for the law to take its effect. No yellow journal of to-day has a more revolting list of crimes than could be made up from the press of that time.[2] The duello had not yet disappeared from any part of the country, and in 1838 Jonathan Cilley, a

[1] See Turner, *New West* (*Am. Nation*, XIV.), chaps. ii.–vi.
[2] See extracts in Brothers, *United States*, 261–385.

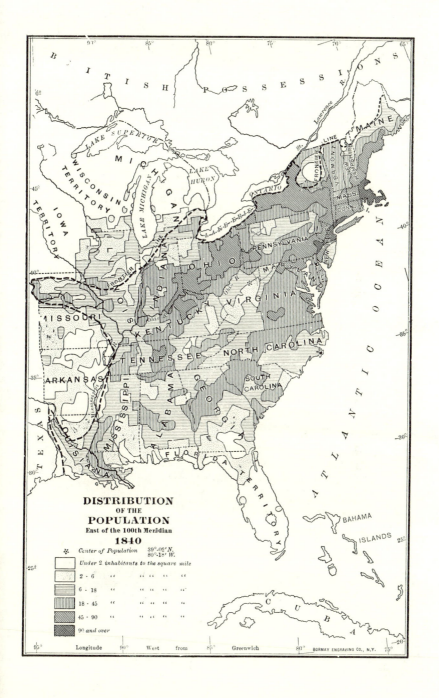

DISTRIBUTION
OF THE
POPULATION
East of the 100th Meridian
1840

✳ *Center of Population*   39°·02′N.
                           80°·18′W.

Under 2 inhabitants to the square mile

2 - 6   "   " " " "

6 - 18 "   " " " "

18 - 45 "   " " " "

45 - 90 "   " " " "

90 *and over*

Longitude   West   from   Greenwich   BORMAY ENGRAVING CO., N.Y.

member of Congress from New Hampshire, provoked a quarrel which resulted in his being challenged and killed by Graves, a member from Kentucky.[1] Altercations in the legislature and in Congress were not uncommon. Elections were frequently scenes of petty civil war.[2] Fires were regular occasions for a fight between rival fire companies, who often let the buildings burn while they were settling their differences. In 1834 came the burning of the Ursuline Convent, within sight of Bunker Hill monument, by an anti-Catholic mob, who drove out the nuns and their pupils, with the eventual loss of two lives; and the only prisoner convicted for a share in the outrage was pardoned by the governor.[3] The negroes in the northern cities, as the poorest and most friendless of the population, usually suffered from any mob, no matter what had been its original occasion; and the abolitionists came in for the most determined assaults of these lawless efforts to secure law and order.[4] Foreign immigration, which pushed men out of previous employment, organization of strikes on a larger scale than had been known before, attempts to get political control of city governments, all contributed to this reign of misrule. Perhaps the most decisive reason for it was the weakness of the local governments: not a single city had a disciplined

[1] Mass. Hist. Soc., *Proceedings*, 2d series, XII., 287–292.
[2] Brothers, *United States*, 297–316, 422–432.
[3] *Ibid.*, 503–508; Mrs. Whitney, *Burning of the Convent*.
[4] See chap. xvii., below.

police force, and the state militia could not be relied upon to fight a mob.

In the south the few cities were no better governed than those of the north, and there was a greater indifference to human suffering, and brutal treatment of prisoners and other defenceless people. Alongside the strength, vigor, and hopefulness of the frontier was the uncouthness, the ignorance, the prejudice, and the latent barbarism of the man who spent his life in conquering nature and the savage.[1]

This was shown in the ordinary administration of the criminal law: at a time when the Pennsylvania separate-cell penitentiary was known throughout the world as a model of humane treatment, the Georgia state-prison was a dirty place where "a piece of cooked meat was laid on the table for each prisoner without knives, forks, or plates."[2] An abolitionist inmate of the Missouri penitentiary from 1841 until 1845 found it an awful place of cruelty and wretchedness, in which the warden came home drunk at midnight to drag white men out of their cells to be whipped before him, and where white women prisoners were sometimes chained to the wall.[3] As late as 1854 a traveller saw a pillory and stocks in a Mississippi town, and was told that "a white man had been recently stripped, whipped and

[1] See Turner, *New West* (*Am. Nation*, XIV.), chaps. iv.–viii.
[2] Saxe-Weimar, *Travels*, II., 20.
[3] Thompson, *Prison Life*, passim.

branded with a red hot iron by officers of the law." [1]

The worst prison, however, was more merciful than lynch law. During the Revolution there was an actual Judge Charles Lynch in Virginia who took the responsibility of whipping loyalists, and gave his name to a system; but after 1830 the term "Lynch Law" came to be applied also to killings.[2] The one justification of such a system is that frontier communities which have not provided themselves with the machinery of the law are subject to desperate and organized malefactors, and hence the practice gained headway in the west and southwest; but in the south the thing grew while the chief reason for it was disappearing. At first applied to ordinary criminals, such as murderers and gamblers,[3] it soon began to reach negroes: one was burned alive by a mob near Greenville, South Carolina, in 1825, and fifty-six ascertained cases of lynching negroes occurred between 1823 and 1860.

If one looks for the most distinctive feature of the American people in 1830, it will not be home life or social disorder, but the religious and philanthropic life and experiences of the time. Depravity and crime were common enough from end to end of the Union, and though people were squeamish about theatres and dancing, social life was in most ways

[1] Olmsted, *Back Country*, 246.
[2] Cutler, *Lynch Law*, 23–40, 116.
[3] Stuart, *North America*, II., 169; Cutler, *Lynch Law*, 98–100.

grosser and ruder than at present; but in most communities, next to getting a living, the most important thing in life was religion, or at least religious observances. Puritanism, as a political force, was not yet dead in New England; not until 1835 was the Congregational church disestablished in Massachusetts, its last stronghold; and a severe type of piety was common throughout the country. For the ruder element, Sunday might be a period of carousal or of cock-fighting, according to the latitude, but to most respectable people it was a serious and depressing day. A morning and an afternoon sermon were the ordinary provision, combined in many communities with a "Thursday Lecture," which was a third sermon; and on Sundays and week-days was added a variety of religious exercises—prayer meetings, conference meetings, class meetings, and love-feasts. For the children a door of hope was opened in the Sunday-school, which by 1830 was making its way throughout the country; but it was not a place of perfect ease: children were expected weekly to learn and repeat not less than ten verses of Scripture and were encouraged to prodigious feats of Biblical memory. The Sunday-school book of the time was not the washed-out novel now furnished to good children, but an account of the early piety of some poor little creature, whose reward for goodness it was to be taken away from his parents untimely.

On the frontier the religious exercises were perforce simpler and less frequent, though the camp-meeting, by its intensity, furnished plenteous excitement. It was an era of revivals: great movements of religious fervor swept over states and cities, or, as in the panic year of 1857, over the whole country, arousing and quickening thousands of persons who thenceforward took their part in the work of the churches. In this day of many interests and few enthusiasms it is hard to realize the immense force of religion and religious organizations upon the minds of the people. "Hell and brimstone" preaching was still common. Revivalists like Finney and Nettleton[1] preached the tortures of damned souls until people shrieked and dropped fainting in their pews. Hell was a place very near at hand to the unbeliever, and even the faithful might under some systems of theology "fall from grace" and lose his birthright eternally. The theological schools ran to "systems" which were a combination of philosophy, logic, and St. Paul, accounting for the beginning and end of all things; and men like the Hodges, of Princeton, or Park, of Andover, sent out a school of disciples.

Throughout the country the churches were more than religious organizations: they were ganglia of social life and intellectual influence, strengthened by fifty years of national organization. The Congregational church, the Episcopal church, and the Presbyterian church were the strongest denominations in New England, the middle, and the older southern

[1] Davenport, *Primitive Traits in Religious Revivals*, chap. x.
VOL. XVI.—2

states; the Methodist and Baptist churches took root in the west, where indomitable men like Peter Cartwright went, riding circuit, holding camp-meetings, arousing the impenitent, comforting the seeker for salvation, and thrashing the rowdies who disturbed his meetings.[1] Most of the great churches threw off fragments which formed new sects: such were the Unitarians, seceders from the Congregational church; and several offshoots of the Methodists and Baptists. The Catholic church, maintained up to that time chiefly by descendants of English or French colonial settlers, now began to receive accessions, particularly from the Irish immigrants.

All the churches were touched by a new feeling of responsibility to mankind. Foreign missions, first suggested at Williams College in 1806, were taken up by most of the strong denominations; and in 1812 they began to organize home missions upon the frontiers, both western and southern.[2] The American Bible Society, founded in 1816, carried on a beneficent circulation of the Scriptures, which lasted on a large scale for more than half a century. In all these movements the south, thinly settled and in many places unable to support a paid or educated ministry, profited less than the north, although the devotion to the churches was as strong and active as in the north.

[1] Cartwright, *Autobiography*, 141–143, 231, 311–316.
[2] McMaster, *United States*, IV. 551.

The chief characteristic of the religious life of the time was its sincere effort to make religion effective, to apply the touchstone of Christ's teachings and life to all moral questions, to make individual and community correspond to the principles of Christianity. Hence, in a country where all forms of state aid to religion disappeared, church buildings were multiplied, missionaries were supported, denominational colleges sprang up. To the amiable it was an unspeakable grief that millions of people should be doomed to everlasting perdition because the gospel had not been brought to their ears; and one of the main taproots of abolition was the feeling of horror and responsibility that hundreds of thousands of negro slaves, because outside the fold of accredited believers, should be going down to the pit of endless punishment.[1]

This passionate desire to save the perishing, as well as to raise the standards of the people, led directly to reform by legislation, such as the movement against the recognized excess in the use of intoxicating liquor, begun in 1817, enlarged by the Washington societies in 1830, and later developed into a demand for state statutes forbidding the liquor traffic altogether.[2] In the thirties also sprang up the Woman's Rights movement; at first directed

[1] Cf. Martineau, *Society in America*, II., pt. iv.
[2] Cf. Smith, *Parties and Slavery* (*Am. Nation*, XVIII.), chap. iii.

to the improvement of girls' schools and the placing of a married woman's property in her own hands, it speedily went much further, and in 1848 extended to a demand for woman suffrage.[1]

One of the characteristics of all these reform movements was the feeling that each was "a cause" to which people might well devote their whole lives; and they were organized in national societies, furnished with newspaper organs, and supported by frequent meetings and appeals to the public. Between 1820 and 1840 this uneasy spirit took form in a series of socialistic communities. When the old statutes against strikes and combinations of working-men were being modified, it was an easy transition to the idea that those who worked with their hands might set themselves apart into self-supporting communities. The Shakers, founded half a century earlier, were still organizing vigorous societies which were practically mediæval convents over again. Another communistic society was that of the Rappists, at New Harmony, Indiana; their work was taken over in 1826 by Robert Dale Owen, an enthusiastic Englishman, who made a declaration in favor of free love and saw his community melt away. Later the influence of Fourier was felt in the organization of little communities called phalansteries, especially in western New York and northern Ohio; and various attempts were made

[1] On the reform movements, cf. Martineau, *Society in America*, II., chap. iv.

to found religious socialistic bodies in the far west.[1]

Joseph Smith, of Vermont, in 1827, according to his account, began to receive "revelations," one of which directed him to certain golden plates which through two stones, the Urim and Thummim, he was able to read, and to translate into a book, published in 1830 as the *Book of Mormon*. It was written in Biblical style, an interminable account of the lost tribes of Israel in North America, and included many prophecies apt for the times.[2] First organized at Manchester, Vermont, in April, 1830, with six members, the Mormons moved in 1831 to Kirtland, Ohio, where they took the name of "Latter Day Saints." After attempting to settle in Missouri, Smith gathered in 1840, at Nauvoo, Illinois, a settlement of about fifteen thousand people. He aroused the hostility of the local authorities, and in 1844 was put in jail, and there killed by a mob. This obscure sect, founded on the materialistic basis that God is a material being, "having a body, parts and passions,"[3] supported by a system of tithes, and inspired by timely revelations, had a success and endurance which makes it stand out from all other socialistic communities of the time.

At the other pole of reform through social organi-

---

[1] McCarthy, *Early Social and Religious Experiments in Iowa;* Perkins and Wick, *The Amana Society;* Saxe-Weimar, *Travels*, II., chap. xxi.   [2] Linn, *Mormons*, chap. xi.
[3] Lalor, *Cyclopædia*, II., 910.

zation was Brook Farm, which sprang out of an
idealism traceable in the ruggedest Puritans of the
New England colonies; the force reappeared in the
"transcendental" movement, partly philosophical,
partly religious, and partly social, headed by Ralph
Waldo Emerson.   A band of enthusiastic men and
women gathered in 1841 at Brook Farm, near Boston, among whom as residents or sympathetic
visitors were Charles A. Dana, later editor of the
New York *Sun*, Margaret Fuller, Thomas Wentworth
Higginson, G. W. Curtis, Emerson, and Nathaniel
Hawthorne, who in his *Blithedale Romance* idealized
this community.   After six years' existence a fire
quenched the spirits of the Brook-Farmers, who did
not know how to farm, and the institution ceased
to be; though the influence of those who experienced
it has remained an intellectual and moral force in
New England and throughout the country.[1]

[1] Wendell, *Literary History of America*, 304–310.

CHAPTER II

THE INTELLECTUAL LIFE

(1830–1840)

TO describe in detail all the interesting forms of American social life would be a long task; but the anti-slavery movement made such use of appeals to the understanding that some account of the intellectual conditions of the time is necessary. In 1830, though the Americans were still far from being a literary people, they were a reading people: the remotest communities studied and quoted that fountain of English, the King James version of the Scriptures; and in the larger places there was a book-reading public which, first of all, applied itself to the English classics, especially the eighteenth-century poets and essayists. The English reviews were imported or reprinted and were widely circulated; and as the new school of English authors sprang up—Scott, Dickens, Thackeray, Macaulay, and Tennyson—they found an eager public in the new world. Outside of the towns there was in New England, and those parts of New York, Pennsylvania, and the west which were influenced by New England, an intelligent reading community of farmers, whose daughters taught the district schools, or, going into the mills of the factory towns, founded little literary journals.[1]

These rural communities were much aided by schools and academies planted in their midst, though until near 1800 there was no public provision for teaching girls, and during the first third of the nineteenth century even the New England public schools, outside of a few towns, were miserably housed and poorly taught, while the rich states of New York and Pennsylvania founded no general system of free schools till 1812.

When, in 1837, Horace Mann was appointed at the head of what was virtually a Massachusetts department of education, he exhausted his vocabulary in describing the state public schools, which he said were in session a little more than four months on the average, costing the state less than three dollars annually for every child of school age, paying average wages to women teachers of less than twelve dollars a month, and educating not more than two-thirds of the school-children.[2] His services as secretary of the state board of education did much to remove this stigma and to place the Massachusetts schools in the van. A great step in educating the teacher and giving a professional standing was the

[1] Lucy Larcom, *New England Girlhood*, 209–225; for education and literary life in general, see Hart, *Contemporaries*, III., §§ 151–157.
[2] Horace Mann, *Report*, 1837 (in *Works*, II., 400, 414, 423).

founding of normal schools, soon established throughout the northern states.

Though popular education at public expense was
already taken up in the west and made a principle
in all the American commonwealths north of Mason
and Dixon's line, on the frontier and in the south
the conditions were much worse than in New England. Abraham Lincoln said that when he was a
boy in Illinois a man who knew algebra was thought
to be a wizard; and not a single southern state,
previous to the Civil War, set up a general system
of free public schools. Outside of the cities, which
provided for themselves under state laws, the poor
whites had little opportunity for education. In
1850, of 250,000 adult native whites in Massachusetts, only 1000 were illiterate; out of 500,000 in
Virginia, 75,000 were illiterate, as were, of course,
nine-tenths of the negroes.[1]

This backwardness was not for want of warning,
but rather in defiance of the principles which Jefferson laid down. He desired that Virginia should
establish free local schools everywhere, that the most
promising pupils should be provided with high-school
instruction, and the most successful pupils of the
high schools with college training. Yet a northern
public man with some experience in the south pooh-

[1] A. D. Mayo, *Common Schools in the Southern States*, in U. S.
Bureau of Education, *Reports*, 1900–1901, pp. 357–401; S. B.
Weeks, *Beginning of the Common School System in the South*, in
ibid., 1896–1897, II., 1379–1474; Olmsted, *Back Country*, 330–
337.

poohed at schools because it is "the examples in our daily contemplation at home, and in domestic life, not the discipline of schools, that shape the morals of a people"; and he adds the familiar argument that "the attainment of an education superior to our station or the business for which we are destined is very apt to unfit a man for both."[1]

For secondary education a few northern cities had public high schools, and boys were often fitted for college by the village parson; but the defects in public instruction were in part supplied by excellent endowed academies, charging moderate fees and serving as an intellectual centre for miles around. Many of them received boarding pupils—in some cases, both in the east and west, boys and girls being educated together. The south was very deficient in education of this grade, especially for girls; for though academies were early founded, the constituency of people able to send their children away to school was small, and the schools lacked support.

The college education of the time, though in many ways narrow, was encouraging. The half-dozen pre-Revolutionary colleges in half a century grew to about sixty, of which almost half were in the south. The first provision for a public state university was made by North Carolina in 1791, although it was many years before it became effective; most of the new colleges, north and south, were planted as nurseries of learning and piety by the various re-

[1] Paulding, *Letters from the South* (ed. of 1835), I., 221–223.

ligious denominations. A great impetus was given
to southern colleges by the University of Virginia,
suggested, fostered, and wisely organized by Thomas
Jefferson, who lived to see its buildings opened,
almost under the shadow of his seat at Monticello.
In its spirit and in its work the University of Virginia was in advance of any other American college
of the time; it placed an intellectual stamp on the
whole south, set an example to the country, and became the mother of a lively brood of young colleges.

In the period from 1815 to 1840 a score or more
of young American scholars found their way to
Göttingen or Tübingen or Heidelberg, and imbibed
the German tradition of investigation in search of
ultimate truth. Colleges spread rapidly into the
west, where, in 1826, Western Reserve University
was founded at Hudson, Ohio, as a western Yale;
and in the course of the two decades 1830 to 1850
Michigan and some other of the western states laid
the foundations of a new type of state university.

The number of southern colleges in this period is
striking. In 1830 there were twenty-four; in 1860
they had increased to about seventy, scattered all
through the south, including the Tennessee and
Kentucky mountains. With the exception, however, of the universities of Virginia and North Carolina and the College of South Carolina at Columbia,
none of them had a national reputation, and few
more than a hundred students;[1] and they lacked

[1] *De Bow's Review*, X., 477.

good business management, so that their land grants vanished and their invested funds dwindled. The main reason for the want of prosperity was the small number of students who could be drawn from the community and the competition between too many small colleges. There was complaint also of the dissipation in some colleges.[1] The wealthy planters had a habit of sending their sons abroad,[2] or more commonly north, to be educated. Jefferson himself complained that "Harvard will still prime it over us with her twenty professors,"[3] and objected to sending students to northern institutions where they would unlearn the lessons of their own community. During the decade 1830–1840 about ten per cent. of the students of Harvard and Columbia came from the south; in 1841 twenty per cent. of the Yale students and half of the students of Princeton. Among the southerners thus educated were John C. Calhoun, of Yale, and Barnwell Rhett, of Harvard, both of them examples of the small effect of northern colleges in changing the point of view of southerners.

The sixty-odd colleges, so-called, in the Union in 1830 probably did not include more than four thousand students of real collegiate rank, out of a population of thirteen millions; six times that population

[1] Smedes, *Memorials of a Southern Planter*, 129.
[2] Reprehended in *De Bow's Review*, XXVII., 265; Marshall, *Home Education at the South*.
[3] Jefferson, *Works* (Washington ed.), VII., 202.

now has nearly forty times the number of college students. Except in Latin, Greek, and a few mathematical subjects, the colleges of that time were no further advanced than the best high schools and academies to-day; the students entered at fifteen or sixteen years of age, and lived a life of their own, scandalizing neighbors by horse-play which was not then reported in the metropolitan newspapers. It was an era of remarkable college presidents —Eliphalet Nott, of Union; Mark Hopkins, of Williams; Francis Wayland, of Brown; Thomas Cooper, of South Carolina—vigorous men whose personality left an undying impression upon their students; but the teaching was perfunctory, the range of studies small, and few of the college professors highly trained.

Of professional and technical schools there is little to say at this time. West Point, founded in 1802, was a good school of its kind, but still narrow and unprogressive. Medica schools sprang up in the principal cities where there was clinical material, two of the most prominent as parts of the universities of Pennsylvania and Harvard, but most of them were private institutions carried on for profit by the preceptors. Separate schools for the training of the clergy arose, notably the Congregational Andover Theological Seminary and the Presbyterian Theological School at Princeton.

The truth, painful to an academic person, that a low state of popular education and a high condition

of literature may walk hand-in-hand was made clear
in the decade from 1830 to 1840; for it is the beginning of the golden age of American literature.　Up
to that time the aim of most American writers was
not to please, but to convince.　The favorite kind of
literature was the public speech, for Americans loved
oratory.　Patrick Henry spoke his appeals; Tom
Paine, James Otis, Sam Adams, and John Dickinson
put them within the covers of their pamphlets.
After the Revolution, men like John Randolph and
Josiah Quincy, as a matter of course, approached
their countrymen through their speeches in Congress and out-of-doors.　The year 1830 marks the
climax of American oratory in the Webster-Hayne
debate, in which the great New-Englander's splendid
sentences and lofty principles placed him alongside
Lord Chatham as one of the foremost users of the
English tongue.

Nobody knows how life is breathed into the
nostrils of the writer who can express the spirit of
his countrymen and join in creating a national
literature.　Perhaps the great literary awakening
was due to the different parts of the country coming
together so as to give the poet, the essayist, and the
journalist a national constituency, just when Americans were beginning to feel the exuberant sense of
being a power in the world.　Pulpit eloquence took
on a new form when William Ellery Channing,
Father Taylor the sailors' preacher, and later Henry
Ward Beecher, and their compeers aroused, charmed,

and convinced. By the lyceum system renowned
men were heard from town to town and from village
to village; Edward Everett, with his silver tongue,
earned sixty-eight thousand dollars for the purchase
of Mount Vernon; while John B. Gough made a
reformed drunkard so winning that young men were
almost tempted to experience the process. If a
man had anything that interested the world, his
neighbors were eager to hear his eloquence. Town-
meetings and legislatures were schools of public
speaking, the most successful graduates of which
went to Congress. The enthusiast found his audience
in the convention of his particular cause; the social
reformer and the literary critic had a forum in the
lyceum. Women came forward as writers and even
as platform speakers, among whom Harriet Beecher
Stowe was the only one to achieve a world - wide
literary reputation.

The lyceum and the convention trained people to
listen; the literary leaders taught them to think.
Reward and recognition showed themselves in half
a dozen different fields at once. The first American
to win national reputation for a literary treatment
of American subjects was Washington Irving, who
had the triple gifts of humor, a spirit of investigation,
and a lively historical style. The two founders of
a new school of history were Jared Sparks, almost
the first man to realize the necessity of collecting
scattered and perishing materials for the nation's
history, and George Bancroft, who deliberately set

himself to the mighty task of writing the history of his country up to his own time. In 1834 appeared the first volumes of that immense undertaking, upon which he was engaged for a considerable part of fifty years.[1]

To Bancroft was presently added a group of writers of the same New England origin, and, like him, imbued with the desire of repeating Macaulay's success in bringing history to the comprehension of the average reader and adorning it with graces of style: William H. Prescott began in 1837 to publish his series on the history of Spanish America and of Spain in the colonizing period; later came John Lothrop Motley, who chose for his theme the romantic epoch of the Dutch revolution against Spain. A fourth writer, and the king of American historians, was Francis Parkman; alone of them all he has carried his reputation through three generations, partly from the inextinguishable interest of his topic—the relations of the French and English—but chiefly because of his delightful historical style, his sense of proportion, and his own vigorous and right-minded personality, which has infused his works.

In journalism there was a like notable awakening. In 1830 no daily in America had a circulation of more than two thousand; but a little later several one-cent papers were founded, among which the first success was the New York *Sun;* it became well known through the "moon hoax," an elaborate de-

[1] Hart, in *International Monthly*, II., 306.

ception intended to advertise the newspaper. Then, in 1835, appeared the first issue of the New York *Herald*, which developed a novel system of collecting news of every kind—commercial, legal, and religious —and reported all meetings and occurrences of the day. The *Evening Post*, under the editorship of William Cullen Bryant, appealed to high ideals, but Horace Greeley made the New York *Tribune*, founded in 1841, the first great metropolitan exponent of moral ideas. Quarrelsome, impertinent, and one-sided as these newspapers were, they nevertheless all had editorial pages written with spirit and often with genuine literary force, and they vastly increased the reading public.

The "moon hoax" was but a crude form of the modern short story and responded to a public interest in the novel, which furnished a field for the greatest names in American fiction, especially for Cooper, Poe, and Hawthorne. Cooper began to publish his historical novels in 1821, and issued in all about seventy books. He was the first American to see the element of romance in the Revolution, and still more in the savage; and immediately caused his idealized Indian to be accepted by the world as a true picture. Not a finished writer, he somehow carries the reader along, and unhappy is the boy who has never stayed away from Sunday-school to read *The Last of the Mohicans*. W. G. Simms, of South Carolina, was the only prolific southern novelist. Edgar Allan Poe began his literary career with a little volume of poems in 1827, and for some years he edited the *Southern Literary Messenger* in Richmond.[1] His verses gave him a large reputation, but he lives as one of the world's writers through his tales—eerie, fanciful, ghastly, and a necessary part of every reading man's experience.

Greater than any other of these writers was Nathaniel Hawthorne, whose *Twice - told Tales* came out in 1837, but whose first powerful novel, *The Scarlet Letter*, was issued thirteen years later. Of all American writers, Hawthorne is the most unaccountable, for he revealed neither the Puritan rigor of his ancestors nor the bustling mercantile and seafaring atmosphere of his home town of Salem. A mediævalist in his outlook on life, an Italian in his delicate choice of words, a Frenchman in the finish of his sentences, an Englishman in his traditions and standards, he remains through it all the greatest American imaginative writer.

It is easier to account for the American novel of the thirties than for the American verse. Colonial and Revolutionary poets were vague reflections of English writers, and could not write of Columbus and "Old Put" except in the style of Alexander Pope. Where did William Cullen Bryant find his model when, in the year when Sydney Smith asked, "Who reads an American book?" he burst forth with:

[1] Cf. Miner, *Southern Literary Messenger*, an account of the periodical.

" Whither, midst falling dew,
While glow the heavens with the last steps of day,
Far through their rosy depths dost thou pursue
    Thy solitary way?" [1]

And why, in the six years from 1831 to 1837, should Whittier, Longfellow, and Oliver Wendell Holmes have made their first essays as poets? They not only wrote, they were read; for in that youth of the world people watched for the new volume by the author of "Evangeline " or of the "Deacon's One-Hoss Shay." All the poets appealed to the highest in the hearts of their countrymen, and they all had a hearing; most of them felt a moral responsibility for aiding in the regeneration of the world, and Whittier was the poet of the anti-slavery cause, as Mrs. Stowe was its novelist.

Among these great stars there shone a brighter planet in Ralph Waldo Emerson, philosopher and sage, whose oracles are to be read in his rugged yet fascinating poems and in his gem-studded essays. He shocked conservative New England with a new religious point of view, but he aroused his countrymen with his appeal, "Hitch your wagon to a star"; and he illustrated his own dictum: "In the midst of abuses, in the heart of cities, in the aisles of false churches, alike in one place and in another,—wherever, namely, a just and heroic soul finds itself, there it will do what is next at hand, and by the new quality of character it shall put forth, it shall abrogate

[1] Bryant, *Lines to a Waterfowl.*

that old condition, law, or school in which it stands, before the law of its own mind." [1]

Americans have ever been readier to respond to the sober and severe than to the lighter vein; and no example of the humorist can be found in the eighteenth century except Benjamin Franklin. A new lamp of American literature was lighted when Washington Irving's *Knickerbocker* appeared in 1809; it is still one of the most delightful pieces of good-humored satire that was ever written. In Jackson's administration a popular writer, Major Jack Downing (really Charles A. Davis), was the first to bring out the fun of politics. His professed intimate relations with "Gineral Jackson" amused even that tough old statesman. Then in the forties came the rise of James Russell Lowell in his *Biglow Papers*, the first application of humor to anti-slavery.

[1] Emerson, *New England Reformers.*

CHAPTER III

THE ERA OF TRANSPORTATION
(1830–1850)

UP to 1830 the main economic problem of the
United States had been to develop its natural
riches in the simplest and easiest way; and such was
the abundance of soil, forest, and mineral wealth, that,
in spite of wasteful methods of extraction, the country was getting rich. At the same time it was growing wider, through the rapid taking-up of the northwest and southwest; but these new communities
were cut off from the ready access to the sea enjoyed
by the older states, and found it difficult to reach a
world market with their staples. Up to 1815 the
only route from the interior to the seaboard, or from
one point of the interior to another, was the highway
or the stream. The introduction of steam navigation on a large scale after the War of 1812, and the
building of railroads after 1830, at once reduced the
distance of the producer from his market, and within
twenty years brought Chicago nearer to the seaboard
than Utica had been in earlier times. This remarkable change revealed vast latent potentialities of
wealth, and at the same time opened up competi-

tions which altered business profits and possibilities throughout the country.[1]

The change was the more startling because contrary to the whole experience of mankind. Up to the success of Fulton's steamer in 1807, men, animals, and burdens must use the trail, the wheel road, the natural waterway, or the short stretches of artificial canal then in operation. The United States lacked the Roman tradition of solid roads and bridges, and was behind most of the countries of western Europe in its means of transit; and the distribution of authority between localities, states, and federal government caused confusion and wastefulness of expenditure.

From colonial times the public highways were the care of the local government. Outside the cobblestones of some of the city streets, there was in 1830 hardly a mile of road, built and maintained by local authority, which was good after a heavy rain. The numerous turnpikes and plank roads were constructed by private companies, often subsidized or aided by the local and state governments, and in a few instances by the United States. The federal government reserved its contributions chiefly for the Cumberland Road,[2] an extension of which, from the

<hr />

[1] On the conditions of transportation and travel, see Babcock, *Am. Nationality*, chap. xv.; Turner, *New West*, chaps. xiii., xvii.; MacDonald, *Jacksonian Democracy*, chap. viii. (*Am. Nation*, XIII., XIV., XV.).

[2] Babcock, *Am. Nationality*, 247; Turner, *New West*, 224–228, 287 (*Am. Nation*, XIII., XIV.).

Ohio to the Missouri River, was begun in 1825; during the next thirteen years a continuous stretch was built as far west as Springfield, Ohio. Indiana and Illinois demanded the construction of detached sections of the main route; but Missouri and Illinois quarrelled as to which should benefit by the western terminus, so that no part of the road was ever completed west of Vandalia, Illinois.[1]

When Jackson came into power he found this road under way and signed numerous bills for its construction and repair; but he vetoed bills for other government highways and for aid to turnpike companies, and laid down the principle that the federal government should confine itself to road building in the territories.[2] In 1838 the forces which brought about the Cumberland Road ceased to be effective. The federal government had already begun to turn over the jurisdiction of the road to the states, a process completed in 1856. Long before that time the competition of the railroads so destroyed the usefulness of the road that large parts of it fell out of repair.[3] The final balance - sheet showed that the "two per cent. fund" derived from the sale of public lands in the states of Ohio, Indiana, Illinois, and Missouri was $973,000, as against expenditures of $6,300,000 on the whole road, of

[1] Young, *Cumberland Road*, 28–30.
[2] MacDonald, *Jacksonian Democracy* (*Am. Nation*, XV.), 137–148.
[3] Young, *Cumberland Road*, chap. vii.; Hulbert, *Old National Road*.

which over $1,100,000 was for repairs east of the
Ohio.

The Cumberland Road raised troublesome questions of the respective jurisdictions of the states and
federal government, and a contest between eastern
states which had no wish to lose part of the population, and western communities which desired to make
settlement easy.   Similar rivalries appeared in the
discussions on the improvement of natural waterways which ran from state to state or were otherwise arteries of interstate commerce.   The net-work
of navigable rivers was in the west, but the east had
a system of harbors which needed improvement, and
in 1823 a harbor bill was for the first time made up.[1]
Jackson vetoed several bills appropriating money
for rivers and harbors on the ground that the particular improvements proposed were not national
objects; but he signed in his eight years appropria-
tions for those purposes averaging more than a
million a year, and left it to later presidents to put
a more effective check upon this form of government
expenditure.[2]

Neither roads nor river improvements could solve
the great problem of connecting east and west,
which was a political and economic necessity; and
the prosperity of New York due to the completion
of the Erie Canal in 1825[3] put a powerful pressure

[1] Turner, *New West* (*Am. Nation*, XIV.), 232.
[2] Mason, *Veto Power*, §§ 86–92.
[3] Babcock, *Am. Nationality* (*Am. Nation*, XIII.), 249–251.

upon other states to hold their export trade by
reaching directly west across the mountains. Although canals so far north were subject to freezing
and other interruptions, they were the cheapest
method of freight transportation ever invented, and
about as quick and convenient for travellers as the
stage-coach. With the exception of a few stock
subscriptions, especially for the Chesapeake and
Ohio Canal near Washington, and the eventual construction of canals around the falls of several rivers,
the United States has never spent money for internal
canals; but from 1827 to 1830 it granted lands in aid
of canals to the amount of 1,650,000 acres, and subsequently of about as much more.[1]

These gifts were made to states, intended to aid
them in the tremendous task which they had undertaken of furnishing a net-work of canals, including
four trunk lines across the mountains; and from
1830 to 1840 almost one hundred million dollars went
into this new form of investment. In New England
the few canals were constructed by private corporations, but the face of the country was not adapted
to canal navigation, and they were all eventually
abandoned. Besides paying for the Erie Canal, New
York spent forty million dollars on lines reaching
to Lake Champlain, Lake Ontario, and up into the
central valleys of the state.[2] In order to get the

[1] Hart, *Practical Essays*, 256.
[2] New York Comptroller, *Annual Report*, 1895; Fairlie, in
Quart. Jour. Econ., XIV., 212–239.

eoal out of the mountains of northeastern Pennsylvania several private canals were built to the Hudson and the Delaware, and eventually to tide-water
near New York. A great system, six hundred and
forty miles of canal, was constructed by Pennsylvania at an expense of forty million dollars.

South of Mason and Dixon's line two promising
canal schemes were developed. The states of Maryland and Virginia united in the construction of the
Chesapeake and Ohio Canal, from Washington to
Cumberland, at a cost of eleven million dollars, a
part of which came from stock subscriptions made
by Congress, by the states of Virginia and Maryland,
and the cities of Washington and Georgetown.[1]
From Richmond a canal was projected to run up the
valley of the James and to cross over to the Kanawha,
but it was never finished beyond Buchanan. Farther south the rivers were navigable some distance
up from the coast, and the only improvement of
significance was the Dismal Swamp Canal, from the
estuary of the James to Albemarle Sound, completed
in 1794 and reopened in 1828.

The western region, south of the Ohio River, was
well furnished with navigable streams, especially the
Cumberland, Tennessee, and Alabama rivers; but
the low divide between the Ohio River and the Great
Lakes suggested a system of canals to connect,
through Lake Erie, with the western outlet of the
Erie Canal. Such a net-work was undertaken: Penn-

[1] Turner, *New West* (*Am. Nation*, XIV.), 289–291.

sylvania built a line from Erie to Beaver on the Ohio;
Ohio constructed lines from Cleveland to Portsmouth
on the Ohio; and Indiana, from Toledo through Fort
Wayne to the Ohio River at Evansville. A great
system was planned by Illinois, of which the only
completed stretch was from Chicago to the Illinois
River.

The states in their canal building called for such
enormous sums that the capital was not to be had
in the United States, and for the first time they
discovered that they had credit abroad; but the
crash of 1837 checked the era of canal building.
Many of the enterprises then uncompleted were
never resumed, and of the entire net-work of forty-
four hundred and sixty-eight miles, most of which
was constructed between 1830 and 1840, only twenty - five hundred miles were in service in 1880.
Nevertheless, they more than paid for themselves in
the reduction of the cost of transportation while
they were in operation, and they prepared the public mind for larger schemes of transportation.[1]

The main reason for the disuse of the canals was
not that they failed to give better service than older
methods, but that they were superseded by the railroads. The railroad was nothing less than an economic revolution, for it shrinks distance, defies frosts,
ignores quantities and numbers, and makes next-
door neighbors out of people separated by thousands
of miles. Long used as simple tramways in English

[1] Callender, in *Quart. Jour. Econ.*, XVII., 111-162.

coal-mines, the system was so little known in America that in 1808 the engineer Latrobe was careful to explain that "a railroad consists of two pair of parallel ways, . . . single roads, with occasional passing places, are applicable to some situations"; and he estimated the cost of double track at ten thousand dollars per mile.[1] The early railroad was only a superior kind of plank road, provided with iron strap-rails. All cars were drawn by horses, and no speed greater than five or six miles an hour could be obtained.

The year 1826 saw the beginning of the Liverpool & Manchester, the first important English railroad, and also the construction of several short lines of horse railroad in America, interspersed with inclines over which cars were drawn by stationary engines, to connect the mines with canals leading down the Schuykill and Lehigh valleys and to the Hudson River. The next year, 1827, saw the inception of a railroad from Boston to the Hudson River, and another from Baltimore to the Ohio River, while roads were projected from Albany to Schenectady; from Boston to Providence; from New York up the Hudson; from Philadelphia in various radiating directions; from Charleston to the Savannah River; and from Amboy, on New York Harbor, to Camden, opposite Philadelphia. The success of Stephenson's "Rocket" in 1829 led to experiment, in steam traction; and in 1830 a locomotive

[1] *Am. State Paps., Misc.*, I., 916.

built by Peter Cooper made a successful trial on the
Baltimore & Ohio Road. The system of steam railroads was fairly inaugurated.[1]

Though only twenty-three miles of railroad were
in operation up to 1830, during the next decade
came a period of lively construction. Spur - lines
were built inward from most of the considerable
Atlantic seaports. A line was completed from
Albany westward to Auburn; another from Philadelphia *via* Reading to the coal-fields; a line from
Charleston a hundred and thirty-seven miles northwest to Augusta, then the longest railroad under one
management in the world; a continuous line, except
for numerous ferries and short links of boat travel,
from New York southward to Wilmington, North
Carolina.[2] In 1835 a route was opened through
Pennsylvania of combined railway and canal, with
the Portage Railroad—a system of inclines—over
the mountains, constituting a continuous route from
tide-water to the Ohio at Pittsburg.

The relation of the railroads and their owners to
the public has had a profound influence upon American theories of government and upon the division
of federal and state powers. The original notion
in America was that all highways and navigable
waterways were under public jurisdiction; but the

---

[1] McMaster, *United States*, V., 143 – 145; Reizenstein, *Baltimore & Ohio Railroad;* Johnson, *Am. Railway Transportation*,
16–23; Ringwalt, *Transportation System*, 70–73.

[2] Maps in Coman, *Industrial History*, 206, 234; Johnson, *Am.
Railway Transportation*, 17, 19.

turnpike companies, from their beginnings in 1790, in many cases received by charter the right to exercise the state's sovereign power of eminent domain, so as to secure the necessary continuous strip of land; or they were allowed to occupy public highways and to charge toll for their use. The earlier canals were nearly all built by private companies which had similar authority; and the only public interstate highways were the unimproved roads and watercourses, and the state canals, which were very like high-roads in that anybody could put on his boats and start his horse motive power along the tow-path. At first nobody saw that the railroads were going to be something different from any previous experience; they seemed to be a new kind of turnpike road running across, or even along, public thoroughfares at grade. It was expected that people would put on their own cars and horses, exactly as in the case of the canals. There was little regulation of a thing which almost everybody wanted.

Many of the states were too deeply committed to large outgoes for canals to allow them to think of railroad building; but Michigan set out to construct two public lines across the state, and from 1837 till 1846, when the roads were sold, was a railroad proprietor. Georgia, in 1836, began the construction of a line from Atlanta to Chattanooga, Tennessee, which is still the property of the state, though long since leased; and Pennsylvania owned two short stretches

of road as a part of her through trunk line.   Illinois
built a little section of state road near Springfield;
and Indiana, from 1839 to 1843, owned and operated
about twenty miles of railroad from Madison northward.[1]   North Carolina subscribed a majority of the
stock in what is now the main stem of the Southern
Railway.   These were the only states to own railroads up to 1861; but many states appropriated large
amounts of public money to railroads, sometimes by
subscribing for stock (usually with state membership on the board of directors), sometimes by loans
of money or credit, sometimes by outright gifts.
Massachusetts, in 1836, made the first of a series of
loans of this kind, amounting in all to $6,044,000.
New York, in 1836, voted three million dollars to the
Erie Railroad, which became an absolute gift, and
in the next six years a million and a half to other
roads.   The total state subscriptions previous to
1840 could hardly have been less than ten million
dollars.   Towns, cities, villages, and counties added
stock subscriptions, cash grants, and gifts of right
of way and station ground.   The 2795 miles built
in the decade probably cost seventy or eighty million
dollars, of which all of one-fourth came out of the
public treasuries.   In the panic of 1837 some of the
companies failed, and many of the original stock
subscriptions were entirely sunk.

As soon as the railroads began to operate with
steam-power it became impossible to allow shippers

[1] Smith, *Indiana*, 649.

to put on their own motive power, and this totally transformed the whole business of the railroads and their relation to the state. The people who owned the road-bed must also own the cars and the locomotives, and this was an anomaly in the highway law of A erica. The common law of common carriers was applied to them so far as it would reach, and a body of special statute law also came into being. Nevertheless, till 1850 the railroads were still treated as an improved kind of turnpike: they were built for the most part in short lengths, passengers changing cars every few miles; they were neighborhood affairs, the stock owned by people along the line of the road, who kept an eye upon its management. Their rates were lower than any other kind of land transportation, and the state statutes, after giving them corporate life, meddled little with their rates, management, or operation.

In all sections of the country the railroads were crude enough according to modern standards—small, dark, and dirty stations, badly ballasted lines, light rails, numerous trestle and timber structures, small engines, little power. Lack of safety appliances, weak and fragile cars, heated by cast-iron stoves, and operation without telegraphic supervision, made accidents almost as numerous in proportion to the miles of railroad as they are in the twentieth century. The era of iron bridges had not arrived, and such rivers as the Thames in Connecticut, the Hudson, the Susquehanna, and many smaller streams, broke the continuity of the roads and enhanced the expense of doing business.

In the south, railroad building began as early and was pushed almost as vigorously as in the north, for it was easy to see that the saving of the freight on the cotton coming down to the coast would very soon pay for the railroads. Hence, besides the line from Charleston, roads were early constructed from Savannah to the interior of Georgia, and from Wilmington to Richmond, and some spur-lines leading to the navigable rivers. But the great part of the cotton was grown within reach of navigable streams. With a scanty population and few manufactures the south could not support many railroads, and in 1840 had only six hundred and thirty-six miles out of twenty-eight hundred in the Union.[1] For passenger travel the southern railroads saw less improvement than the northern, but by 1861 continuous lines existed from Washington to Charleston, Savannah, Memphis, Mobile, and New Orleans.

For communication with other parts of the Union the south depended chiefly on steamers. This was the heyday of the Mississippi and Ohio River packets—huge, comfortable, luxurious, and subject to many dangers of fire, collision, sinking, and explosion, so that in 1838 the United States government enacted a law for inspecting and licensing steamcraft. On the Great Lakes the steamer lines became the most convenient means of transportation,

---

[1] *Poor's Manual*, 1869–1870, p. xxvi.

till continuous rail lines reached Chicago in 1853. On the Atlantic coast, steamers were introduced on Long Island Sound in 1816, and coastwise lines made travel easy and delightful between the middle-state and southern ports. The ship *Savannah*, with auxiliary steam-power, crossed the ocean in 1819, but not till 1838 did the *Sirius* and the *Great Western* prove that the Atlantic could be traversed by steam-power alone. In 1840 the Cunard line, from Boston to Liverpool, began the first regular steam sailings. Similar lines were established from New York to Liverpool and Bremen, and from Baltimore to German ports; but till the period of the Civil War most of the ocean freight and the immense immigrant travel were still carried by the fast and graceful American clipper sailing-ships.

Off the main lines of railroad, coast, and rivers, the passenger was dependent, as he had been for two centuries, upon the local highways. All parts of the Union were hampered in their development by the poor wagon-roads, somewhat relieved by the turnpikes of the New England, middle states, and middle western states, including parts of Kentucky; but south of Washington there were very few good roads. The travellers of the time abound in moving tales and remonstrances against both the far western and the southern roads; the latter, however, were in old communities which could afford to make better provision. Several travellers noticed that when a tree fell across the road it was often

allowed to lie indefinitely, passers - by making a
deviation through the brush,[1] and stage travel was
intolerably tedious and interrupted by accidents.
Dickens makes a lively chapter out of his adventures
between Washington and Richmond in 1842.[2]

Foreign travellers in general were not pleasantly
impressed by American hotels, although one distinguished nobleman could not forbear praising an inn
at Utica and its well-spread table, except that "nap-
kins you do not get, and instead, you are obliged
to make use of the table-cloth."[3] In the south,
with its few cities and its small travel, hotels came
in for plenty of frank criticism.   Even the southern
pleasure resorts seemed to the outsider extremely
crude, the hotels dirty, ill-managed, overcrowded,
the guests lodged in crazy cabins, and the table beset
with "quick feeders."[4]

Knowing how little could be found on the road,
the planter removing with his slaves carried provisions with him and camped.[5] But the ordinary
traveller could often find no other shelter than a

---

[1] Saxe-Weimar, *Travels*, II., 23.
[2] Olmsted, *Seaboard Slave States*, 60, 87, 309–314, 320–331,
357–366, 380–382; Murray, *Letters*, 225; Featherstonhaugh, *Excursion*, chap. x.; Quincy, *Figures of the Past*, 188–208; Dickens,
American Notes (ed. of 1842), 3–15; cf. Hart, *Contemporaries*,
III., §§ 165–168.   [3] Saxe-Weimar, *Travels*, I., 65.
[4] Featherstonhaugh, *Excursion*, 22–28; Stuart, *North America*,
II., 83–85; Latrobe, *Rambles*, II., 18; Olmsted, *Seaboard Slave
States*, 74, 305, 309, 332–337, 624, 643.
[5] Smedes, *Memorials of a Southern Planter*, 49, 111; Featherstonhaugh, *Excursion*, 53, 120. 154.

house, and the poor whites had too little for themselves to undertake the business of receiving travellers. Southern hospitality was the boast and the
virtue of a people who had rude plenty and were
glad to see a new face, but it was a virtue which was
intended to be practised upon those who came with
proper letters of introduction or who showed that
they were of the same class as their hosts.[1] In view
of this universal belief in generous hospitality, it
was a shock to some travellers to find that at almost
any house which would entertain them at all a payment was expected, often out of proportion to the
entertainment.[2]

[1] Lyell, *Second Visit*, I., 245; Paulding, *Letters from the South*,
II., 92–97; Bremer, *Homes of the New World*, I., 232; Olmsted,
Seaboard Slave States, 77–79; Hall, *Travels*, 412–415.
[2] Hodgson, *Letters from North America*, I., 266–268; Buckingham, *Slave States*, II., 147–150; Olmsted, *Back Country*, 31, 42–
44, 174–176, 396, 411.

CHAPTER IV

SLAVERY AS AN ECONOMIC SYSTEM

(1607–1860)

THAT slavery should exist in the United States was an anomaly, for the law of England when the colonies were planted recognized neither chattel slavery nor villeinage. Yet forced labor was not unknown in England: the apprentice must serve his seven years, and take such floggings as his master saw fit; the hired servant must carry out his contract for his term of service; the convicts, often including political offenders, were slaves of the state and sometimes sold to private owners over-seas. The colonists claimed these rights over some of their white fellows, and, in addition, had a large class of "redemptioners," who agreed that their services should be sold for a brief term of years to pay their passage-money, and of "indented" or "indentured" servants brought by their masters under legal obligation to serve for a term of years and subject to the same penalties of branding, whipping, and mutilation as negro slaves.[1] These forms of servitude,

---

[1] Butler, in *Am. Hist. Rev.*, II., 12–32; Hart, *Contemporaries* II., § 107; "Diary of John Harrower," in *Am. Hist. Rev.*, VI., 65–107.

however, were limited in duration, and transmitted no claim to the servant's children. The presumption of law was always that a white person was free.

No new community in the midst of virgin soil ever had labor enough to satisfy it, and the English settlers at once began to enslave their Indian neighbors, soothing their consciences with the argument that it was right to make slaves of pagans. Fierce, intractable, unaccustomed to continuous labor, the Indians fled or died in captivity, leaving few of their descendants in bondage. Rather by way of experiment than with any confidence in their usefulness, in 1619 the Virginians began to import African negroes, first from the West Indies; later by a steady direct trade from Africa.[1] For a century the trade was small: in 1700 there were not more than twenty or twenty-five thousand negro slaves in all the colonies, which was perhaps a twelfth of the total population; with little sacrifice or disturbance it was still possible to stop the traffic and to free the inchoate nation from a terrible race and labor problem.

People in these latter days have tried to prove that our ancestors made some effort to check slavery, by calling attention to early prohibitive statutes of Massachusetts and Rhode Island, and to the foundation of Georgia as a free colony; but in Massachu-

---

[1] Andrews, *Colonial Self-Government*, chap. xviii.; Greene, *Provincial America*, chap. xiv. (*Am. Nation*, V., VI.).

setts and Rhode Island these enactments were dead
letters, for slaves were imported, sold, and their
offspring born in slavery; and the Georgians soon
insisted on having slaves like their neighbors. Efforts were, however, made in several of the colonies
to restrict the slave-trade, but rarely from humanitarian objections; the colonial statutes were either
intended to keep out a dangerous class or to secure
some of the profits by laying a tax on the trade.
Whatever the reasons, these acts were systematically disallowed by the British government, and the
trade went on unrestricted down to the Revolution.

On the ordinary principle that the English statute
law, in existence when the colonies were founded,
applied to the colonists, slavery would have had no
legal standing anywhere in the empire; but in all
the colonies local enactments recognized and protected slave property, and criminal statutes established special offences which could be committed
only by slaves,[1] and set up special tribunals for
the summary trial of slaves. These slave codes, of
which many parts lasted till 1865, bear witness to
the ever - present danger of negro insurrection, of
which there are about twenty - five recorded instances previous to the Revolution, the best known
being the so-called New York Slave Plot of 1741,
which resulted in the transportation of eighty negroes, the hanging of eighteen whites and negroes,

[1] Morgan, *Slavery in New York*, in Am. Hist. Assoc., *Papers*,
V., 337-346.

and the judicial burning at the stake of thirteen more. Yet at this day it seems probable that the whole thing was simply one of those panics which sometimes sweeps over a whole community.[1] Another group of colonial statutes related to fugitive slaves and white servants, many of whom made good their escape into other colonies and there founded free families.[2]

The contradiction between the English and the colonial law was brought out in 1772 by the famous case of James Somerset, a negro brought by his master from Boston to England; when that master attempted to take him back to America the negro sued for a writ of *habeas corpus*, which Lord Mansfield allowed on the ground that "the state of slavery is of such a nature that it is incapable of being introduced on any reasons, moral or political. It is so odious that nothing can be suffered to support it but positive law."[3] In every one of the British colonies in America, however, slavery was legal by positive law when the Declaration of Independence was adopted, and continued unless altered by the later state government.

Although slavery thus became the presumptive status of every negro, most of the colonies by law, and all by practice, recognized the existence of free

---

[1] Coffin, *Slave Insurrections*, 7–16; Horsmanden, *Journal of Proceedings;* Greene, *Provincial America (Am. Nation*, VI.), 240.
[2] MacDougall, *Fugitive Slaves*, chap. i.
[3] Hurd, *Freedom and Bondage*, I., 189–191.

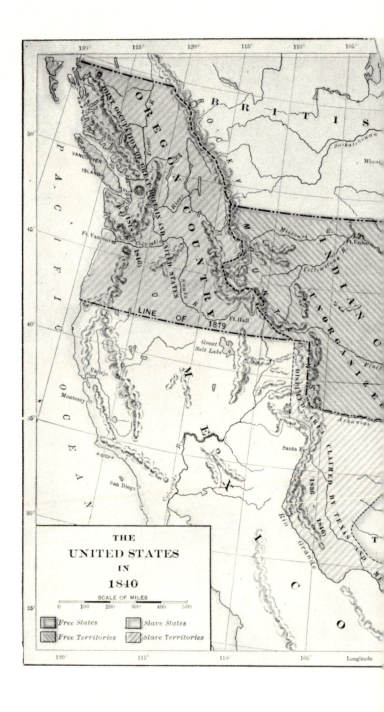

THE
UNITED STATES
IN
1840

SCALE OF MILES

0   100   200   300   400   500

Free States Slave States
Free Territories Slave Territories

negroes, though security had to be given that freed slaves should not become a public charge. The numerous instances of indented servants who, at the expiration of their service, became free members of the community seems to have had a favorable effect upon the status of free negroes, who were allowed property rights, and in all the colonies except Georgia and South Carolina could vote, provided they had the required property or tax qualification.

Though the legal status of slavery was as firmly established as inheritance of property or private ownership of land, objections to it on moral and ethical grounds were always plenty;[1] and during and after the Revolution it lost much of its prestige because it did not seem to pay. In New England, to hold slaves was a mark of dignity rather than of profit; in the middle colonies they never rose to more than a twelfth of the population; and in the south the staple crops of wheat, tobacco, indigo, and rice could not give them all profitable employment. The rise of cotton planting and the effect on the industry of the south and on its attitude towards slavery has already been discussed in this series.[2] Its chief effect was to intensify the feeling that, whatever its ills, slavery was a fixed, unalterable, economic fact—an institution. It was this conviction, rather than the moral objections to slavery,

[1] See chap. xi., below.
[2] Bassett, *Federalist System*, chap. xiii.; Turner, *New West*, chap. iv. (*Am. Nation*, XI., XIV.).

which aroused first the attention and then the antagonism of the north.

The elements of this sectional controversy are simple: the north, from colonial times, both agricultural and commercial, was now becoming also a manufacturing and mining region, while the south still remained almost wholly agricultural. Though by the compromise tariff of 1833[1] the north gave up its contention for permanent protection, the average rate of duties on dutiable articles was still forty per cent., and nearness to the supply gave to the cotton manufacturers of New England and the middle states a great advantage over foreign spinners, so that the cotton factories increased from eight hundred in 1831 to twelve hundred in 1840, and woollen mills increased in like measure. Between 1820 and 1840 most of the considerable water-powers anywhere near tide-water were utilized all the way from Maine to Pennsylvania, as was witnessed by the founding of Lowell and the upbuilding of Nashua, Fall River, Manchester, Paterson, and Cohoes.

The iron industry also underwent a great change. Until 1838 charcoal and coke were the only fuels for smelting; then anthracite coal came into use, and in 1846 bituminous coal, thus opening up immense resources on the upper tributaries of the Ohio. The "pent up Utica" of inventive genius

[1] MacDonald, *Jacksonian Democracy* (*Am. Nation*, XV.), chap. ix.

burst forth, machinery for working iron and wood began to be introduced on a large scale, and sewing machinery followed in the following decade.[1] This lively industrialism, repeated in a thousand heretofore unsuspected sources of profit, was almost confined to the northern states and to some parts of the border slave states: they had capital, they had a financial organization to utilize their greater density of population, and higher average wealth; they had a tariff and a home market; they developed their mineral resources, while the immense coal-fields and valuable iron-ore deposits of the south, previous to the Civil War, were utilized only in Virginia and Tennessee.

The rapid development of the north was not unique: it was what was then going on in England, France, and Germany. The abnormal thing was that a region of great resources and intelligent leaders like the south should have remained for half a century outside the modern economic system, still retaining the provincial conditions of scattered population, little diversified agriculture, and slave labor; while the north had land, ships, mills, forges, mines, rich cities, and a remarkably productive population. Outside of the plantation buildings and moderate accumulations of buildings and stocks of goods in a few cities, the south knew but two forms of wealth, land and slaves. This simple in-

[1] Wright, *Industrial Evolution*, chaps. x., xi.; Coman, *Industrial History*, 226–228.

dustrial system from 1830 to 1860 changed very little, so that a description based on records drawn from any one of the three decades applies fairly to the whole period.

The lands of the south may be classified into four areas, according to their productivity: the rich lowlands of the coasts and the river bottoms; the uplands, including the "black belt," so called from the color of its soil; a more elevated part called barren lands or sand-hills; and the mountains, embracing many fertile valleys and coves. None of these regions were closely settled. From colonial times on, large areas of rich land were constantly being worked out, and, since there was no fertilizer then in use, it must be replaced by breaking new soil on the same plantation or by giving up altogether and moving the slaves to more fertile regions. Tobacco was especially exhausting, and caused fearful destruction of land in Maryland and Virginia. Completely worn-out and abandoned plantations were not uncommon.[1] This system caused the large plantations to grow larger, so that several thousand acres under one hand was not thought remarkable. Some of the planters disliked their poorer white neighbors, and made it a point to buy them out.[2] The untilled or exhausted lands reduced the pro-

[1] Olmsted, *Seaboard Slave States*, 17, 43, 90, 106, 272, 413, 519; Olmsted, *Back Country*, 19; Olmsted, *Texas Journey*, 82; Longstreet, *Georgia Scenes*, 76.
[2] Olmsted, *Seaboard Slave States*, 576; Smedes, *Memorials of a Southern Planter*, 63, 67.

ductive capacity of the soil, so that the census of 1850 showed an average value of land per acre in the south of $5.34 against $28.07 in the middle states.[1]

There was little scientific agriculture in the south, and little knowledge of the relation of soil to crops; and the common rotation of corn and cotton was deleterious.[2] A very general practice was to put in cotton in successive annual crops until the yield would no longer pay for the labor.[3] Southern agriculture, therefore, depended upon controlling more land than could be tilled in a single year; and whenever cotton was high and profits consequently large, the temptation was always to put this gain into more land and more slaves. Since intensive cultivation of any kind was hardly known, the south accepted as normal the disadvantages of a thinly distributed population, and looked southwestward for a region where there was virgin soil for new plantations.

Depending for its exports chiefly on slave labor, the south could raise only such staple crops as could be profitably cultivated by rude labor in large gangs. Tobacco, which had been the wealth of the south in colonial times, was still cultivated, especially in Virginia, Maryland, and Kentucky. The work was

---

[1] *U. S. Census*, 1850, Compendium, 170.
[2] Hammond, *Cotton Industry*, 85–89.
[3] Olmsted, *Seaboard Slave States*, 237; Paulding, *Letters from the South*, I., 81.

less severe and less continuous than on cotton; but the crop ceased to be very profitable, and many of the tobacco plantations ran down.[1]

Rice was cultivated only on islands or the adjacent main-land, which could be irrigated with abundant fresh water, yet be near the sea. The work was hard, the people were plagued with mosquitoes, and, which was the same thing, with deadly malaria, often fatal to both negroes and whites. It was hard to find the necessary combination of tide and river; the building and repairing of the ditches was expensive; and the work was hard and wet, culminating with a watery harvest in the hot September.[2]

Sugar required more capital than any other crop because of the expensive milling; but it was confined to a small area on a few plantations in Louisiana. Of all slave labor the most exhausting was that of the grinding season, when eighteen hours was thought a day's work; yet it was a favorite time for the negroes, because they enjoyed the special privileges of coming together and of eating the cane and drinking the syrup.[3]

The south raised quantities of corn, which was the usual vegetable food of the poor whites, most of whom grew their own food crop. The plantations also raised more or less corn for the food of the

[1] Olmsted, *Seaboard Slave States*, 88–90; Olmsted, *Back Country*, 337.

[2] Burke, *Reminiscences*, 127–129; Kemble, *Georgian Plantation*, 17; Olmsted, *Seaboard Slave States*, 430, 463–475.

[3] Olmsted, *Seaboard Slave States*, 650, 673, 686, 688.

slaves, but immense quantities were imported from the western states, either in the form of shelled corn and corn-meal, or in the products of corn-fed hogs, which supplemented the usual razor-back hams and bacon. The south, up to the Civil War, was not a self-sustaining region; very few large farms or plantations raised the forage for their own work animals, relying upon the importations from the seaboard or down the Mississippi River.[1]

It was idle for northern visitors or southern critics to insist that the plantations ought to cultivate a variety of crops, for the methods of agriculture were stereotyped; slave labor did not adapt itself to diversification, and the steady world-demand for cotton made it the crop which could be most quickly and easily sold. Probably not one-tenth of the white people of the south were dependent for a livelihood on the raising of cotton; but fully three-fourths of the slave labor was applied to that crop, and it became in the minds of southerners and northerners alike the typical southern industry.

One reason for this state of things was that cotton required attention during a considerable part of the year. From the seeding-time in March to the end of picking-time, when frost appears at the beginning of winter, there is always something to do; and thereafter it goes to the gin and thence to the press for baling. Furthermore, it is a crop adaptable to

[1] Olmsted, *Seaboard Slave States*, 378–380.

the labor of girls and women and half-grown men, so that it employs a large proportion of the slave population. It was almost an axiom in slavery times that cotton could not be raised by white labor, partly because to admit the possibility was to lose one of the reasons for slavery; nevertheless, Olmsted found in Texas numerous small cotton-fields, and foresaw a large cultivation by whites.[1]

No wonder cotton seemed important to the south, when the output and the price is reckoned. The simple statement that from 1791 to 1810 the price never fell below sixteen cents a pound, and in 1818 rose as high as thirty-four cents, explains the rapid development of the southwest. From 1821 to 1830 the prices ruled lower, running down as low as eight cents; but the crops, which in the previous decade averaged about eight hundred and fifty thousand bales, from 1831 to 1840 rose to one million three hundred thousand bales. The magnitude of the output did not depress prices, which averaged about twelve cents, and for the year 1835 ran up to over seventeen cents. The immense crop of 1840, at the lowest price for the decade, brought in about one hundred million dollars cash. The greater part of the cotton went over-seas, and it was this steady cotton export, creating a favorable credit balance abroad, which kept before the minds of the southern people the fact that in order to import the manufactures of their own staple, or other goods suit-

[1] Olmsted, *Texas Journey*, 182, 421.

able for their needs, they had to pay a protective duty.[1]

Inasmuch as a large part of this cotton was raised on the larger plantations, where the expense of supervision and maintenance was reduced, the profit in good years was alluring. De Bow figured out some cases where there was seventeen per cent. profit on the capital engaged.[2] These figures, however, are subject to many deductions for waste, wear and tear, and other items. Twenty years later Olmsted found the cotton plantations in the southwest making money furiously. Still, it is a moot question whether the south would not have found a greater profit in other crops, to say nothing of the fact that the cotton crop was the standing excuse for slavery. Good observers believe that, on the whole, cotton cost more than it came to.[3] It is a curious fact that as early as 1826 a German traveller pointed out that in the cotton-seed the south was throwing away enormous resources.[4] Profitable or unprofitable, the cotton fibre was interwoven with the heart of the south, so that Southside Adams was sure that the anti-slavery movement would fail because of the "providence of God, the God of nature, and the God of nations, with respect to that great

[1] Watkins, *Cost of Cotton Production* (U. S. Depart. of Agric., *Miscellaneous Bulletins*, No. 16); Watkins, *Production and Price of Cotton for One Hundred Years* (*ibid.*, No. 9).

[2] De Bow, *Industrial Resources*, I., 161–164; cf. Buckingham, *Slave States*, I., 257.   [3] Olmsted, *Back Country*, 337–341.

[4] Saxe-Weimar, *Travels*, II., 33.

staple of commerce, our cotton." After thus setting the Almighty at work to prepare the cotton-field for the African slave,[1] no wonder the south believed and said that "Cotton is King."

Southern agricultural methods were based on the fixity of crops. The tools used by slaves were heavy and rough, because none others would stand the carelessness of the slave.[2] Edmund Ruffin, of Virginia, for years preached the advantage of using lime and manure in Virginia; and towards the end of the slavery period guano began to come in, under the influence of southern agricultural societies;[3] but improvement of that kind was difficult to bring about in communities which lacked enterprise and spent their capital in buying new slaves.

By the so-called "advance system," most planters mortgaged crop or negroes to keep the plantation going till the annual crop could be harvested.[4] The factors through whose hands the crops must pass usually furnished the capital, but store-keepers also made small advances to neighboring farmers. In any case, interest and profit somehow had to be allowed to the lender, and all the circumstances were such as to encourage extravagance on the planter's part. It was a period of extended credit throughout the country, but nowhere else was so large a part of the annual income spent before it

[1] Adams, *Southside View*, 143.
[2] Olmsted, *Seaboard Slave States*, 397, 481–483.
[3] *Ibid.*, 278, 303.   [4] Hammond, *Cotton Industry*, 107–112.

was received.[1] The "advance system" also served to rivet upon the south its fixity of crops and economic methods, for the planter must raise the crop that would satisfy his obligations; there were few opportunities for capital except agriculture, and the most alluring agriculture was always the cultivation of cotton.

Although the cotton crop was a new factor, the methods and principles of agriculture were much the same as those of colonial times. Maryland and Virginia still grew wheat by slave labor for export, because they lay close to tide-water, with easy shipment to a market. In the interior, away from great waterways, there was little demand for farm products, and flour and provisions of every kind were astonishingly cheap, while household industries supplied a large part of the farming community. New Hampshire and Ohio farmers made their own maple sugar, and the farmers' wives made soap, dipped candles, prepared the winter supply of sausage and mince-meat, and, with their daughters, dyed, wove, and made the family clothing; so, in the south, many of the plantations were almost self-supporting. In some cases the plantation clothing was made wholly by the slaves. The poor whites, who had little for exchange, depended for their few comforts chiefly upon themselves.

The south was not wholly given up to agriculture; it had some small fisheries, and about a sixth of the

[1] Buckingham, *Slave States*, I., 553–556.

tonnage of the United States was registered from the south, but this included the river steamers.[1] Outside of Maryland there was very little ship-building on the southern coast, though the live-oaks and cypresses of the south furnished important materials for northern yards. Tar, pitch, and turpentine were a perennial product of North Carolina and adjacent states.[2] Coal and some other minerals were mined on a small scale in Maryland, Virginia, and Tennessee.

Some manufacturing always went on in the south; a large part of it in small factories of leather goods, clothing, and the like, supplying a local market; and there was an established manufacture of coarse cotton. The censuses of 1840 and 1860 showed less than eight per cent. of the national output of cotton goods in the southern states; the labor being in part poor whites, and in part hands brought down from the north.[3]

The south had good economic training in its banking, though it suffered for a time from the loose conditions of the frontier. The hundred and more southern banks, in 1840, had a capital of one hundred and twenty-six million dollars, and were organ-

---

[1] De Bow, *Industrial Resources*, II., 195.

[2] Olmsted, *Seaboard Slave States*, 338–348, 351–355.

[3] *Ibid.*, 13, 19, 104, 542–548; De Bow, *Industrial Resources*, I., 232–243, II., 107–121, 124–127; Bishop, *American Manufactures*, II., 420, 465; Coman, *Industrial History*, 249–254. Kettell, *Southern Wealth and Northern Progress*, 54, figures out a sixth for the south.

ized with a good system of country branches, furnishing credit not only to the large planter, but to almost any thrifty farmer. After 1850 several of the southern states adopted the "security system," by which the circulation was protected by approved bonds.[1] The state banks of South Carolina and Kentucky were also sound concerns. Here, however, the business training of the south ended; except for the handling of the cotton export, largely in the hands of foreign firms, there was little experience in business.

Although experience proved that the slave-holding south was politically a unit on questions affecting the growth of slavery and the maintenance of the slave-holding power, it was sharply divided into two sections having very different conditions and interests. The so-called border states — Delaware, Maryland, Virginia, Kentucky, and Missouri—were in soil, climate, and productions very like their immediate northern neighbors, considerable areas of which were peopled from the slave-holding states.[2] The great difference was that the number of slaves in the border states was much smaller than in the lower south. In 1830 the figures were: border states, whites, 1,703,948; slaves, 772,303; the remaining southern states, whites, 1,953,660; slaves, 1,231,085. The free negroes were numerous, and slavery was not vital to any one of this populous group of states.

[1] Schwab, in Pol. Sci. Quart., VII., 55.
[2] Turner, New West (Am. Nation, XVI.), chap. v.

Delaware, and still more Maryland, were commercial, and had manufactures. When the crisis of the Civil War came, the line of cleavage left all of them except eastern Virginia still attached to the northern states, with which they had the closest ties of internal commerce. Of the four largest southern cities, three were not dependent on the south for their wealth: Baltimore up to 1830 was built up by the Susquehanna trade, and later by connection with the Ohio River; Louisville and St. Louis were points of distribution for northern products. The crops of the border states were substantially the same as those of their northern neighbors, and their adherence to slavery was not due to its profit, so much as to the social and political prestige of the slaveholder.[1]

[1] See below, chap. xix.

CHAPTER V

THE SLAVE-HOLDER AND HIS NEIGHBOR
(1830–1860)

IN a region like the south, engaged in one main industry, and that the cultivation of a staple crop, with crude labor and appliances, a simple social organization might have been predicted. On the contrary, there was a remarkable complexity of social units, including at least five different strata of the white race. At the top of the social pyramid stood the slave-holder, for in the slave he possessed the one tool which produced a surplus, and he also owned the large areas of land upon which that tool could be employed. This privileged class was small in proportion to the whole population. Out of 12,-500,000 persons in the slave-holding communities in 1860, only about 384,000 persons, or one in thirty-three, was a slave-holder. These figures, often quoted in arguments against slavery, are somewhat deceptive. Since the property of a family was commonly vested in a single person, the true proportion would be about 350,000 white families out of perhaps 1,800.000; leaving out of account the white mountaineers, a fourth to a fifth of the white families in the slave-holding sections had a property interest in slaves. A counter-correction must now be made: about 77,000 owners had only one slave apiece, and 200,000 more owned less than ten slaves each; while only 2300 families owned as many as a hundred slaves. Samuel Hairston, of Virginia, the largest slave-owner of the time, had 1700 slaves and control of 1000 more.[1]

Out of 9,000,000 whites in 1860, certainly not more than 500,000 persons made a substantial profit out of slave-keeping; within that privileged number a body of about ten thousand families was the ruling south in economics, social and political life. The great names in southern public life, such as the Butlers, Barnwells, Hayneses, Brookses, Pinckneys, Rutledges, and Hamptons, of South Carolina; the Lees, Masons, Harrisons, Tylers, and Wises, of Virginia; the Polks, Breckinridges, and Claibornes, of the west, were borne by members of families holding from fifty slaves up. The Drayton mansion, near Charleston, the fine old houses of Athens, Georgia, and such stately abodes as the Johnson-Iredell house at Edenton, still bear witness to a bygone generous life and profuse hospitality which impressed the visitor with the wealth and breeding of the south.[2] Yet, outside of the southern cities and their neighborhood, large houses were few and

---

[1] Chambers, *Am. Slavery and Colour*, 194.
[2] Smedes, *Memorials of a Southern Planter*, 34.

a stately life difficult to maintain.[1] The general tendency was to enlarge the large plantations by putting the profits of cotton, raised by slave labor, into more cotton lands requiring more slave hands; and this process prevented an accumulation of wealth in buildings and estates.

The well-to-do planters travelled widely and went to the cities in winter, and made the Virginia Springs,[2] Newport, and Saratoga, ports of summer entry. Many of the lowland plantations were unhealthy a good part of the year, and their owners formed a small but recognized class of absentee landlords. Even in these cases the owner felt a personal responsibility for the plantation and its inhabitants. Though masters sometimes hired out the whole body of their slaves, corporations very rarely owned slaves, and in the few cases recorded appear to have found the system unprofitable to them.

These great planters, everywhere accepted as the characteristic men of the south, were seconded by a far greater class of small, unprosperous, and unprogressive slave-holders. No writer saw so much of them as Olmsted, who gives us an unpleasant account of their poor houses, unwholesome food, and lack of comfort, thrift, and refinement. They lived

[1] Martineau, *Society in America*, I., 216 et seq.; Page, *The Negro*, 168.
[2] Martineau, *Society in America*, I., 175-193; Featherstonhaugh, *Excursion*, chaps. ii.-v.

in groups of buildings still familiar to travellers in the south, a congeries of house, kitchen, servants' quarters, storehouses of various kinds, and stabling for the animals.[1] It seems unaccountable that, in a country abounding with vegetables and capable of growing many kinds of grain, people who were able to control ten, twenty, or more laborers should have been satisfied with the hog and hominy and discomfort of the frontier. In some cases they were restrained by the feeling expressed by a planter in Florida: "My old woman and I could be much more comfortable if we were not hampered by fifteen negroes, . . . but it would be such a distress and ruin of the poor things if we rid ourselves of them."[2] Such planters lived worse and had fewer opportunities for their children than many a day-laborer in the north; though occasionally you found "a perfectly charming little back woods farm house, good wife, supper and all."[3]

Among the owners of one or more slaves were the professional men. Since white house-servants were almost unknown, it was necessary either to hire from slave-owners or to buy one's own cook or coachman. A slave was not an uncommon present to young people setting up housekeeping; many ministers were slave-holders, and Bishop Polk, of

[1] Olmsted, *Back Country*, 58–61; Olmsted, *Seaboard Slave States*, 329, 384–386, 559–563; Murray, *Letters*, 229.
[2] Murray, *Letters*, 229.
[3] Olmsted, *Seaboard Slave States*, 393.

Louisiana, owned about four hundred and was a notably good master. Clergy, lawyers, physicians, college professors, and the few scientific men were, for the most part, members of slave-holding families, and were completely identified with the great slave-holders in maintaining the institution.

In some parts of the south, notably the border states, existed a class of white farmers, working their own land and accepted as equal members of the community by the neighboring slave-holders; from such a family sprang Henry Clay. Some of them were the descendants of German settlers in the valley of Virginia;[1] a few of them were northerners who had come across the border. Another class of whites who had little relation to slavery was a few laborers, mostly foreigners, found especially in the cities, though several travellers noticed Irish laborers working as deck-hands, or even in ditching operations.[2] In a few cities, notably New Orleans and St. Louis, there was a permanent foreign population furnishing mechanics and small shop-keepers, and a few thousand poor whites were attracted into the cotton-mills.[3]

The general attitude of the south was unfavorable to immigration, either from the north or from foreign countries. The whole state of North Carolina, in 1860, had but 3289 foreign-born residents; and,

[1] See Paulding, *Letters from the South*, I., 91, 107.
[2] Olmsted, *Seaboard Slave States*, 550, 612; Russell, *My Diary North and South*, I., 395. [3] See chap. iv., above.

outside of the border states of Missouri and Maryland, the only two communities having any considerable number of foreign residents were Louisiana, where there were Germans, Irish, and a few
Italians; and Texas, in which there was a vigorous
and successful German colony.[1] In the southwest
was a large population of French descent, and a
still larger body of Mexicans in Texas. Chinese
coolies were repeatedly suggested, but none appear
to have been imported.[2]

Below the slave-holders were the poor whites,
who were subdivided into several elements, of which
the most distinct were the mountain whites and the
lowland whites. [1] At the end of the eighteenth century some thousands of Scotch-Irish settlers established themselves in western Pennsylvania; thence
the more adventurous pushed their way southwestward into the numerous parallel chains of the Ap-
palachian mountain system, reinforced by direct
contingents from western Virginia and North Carolina. As time went on the fertile valleys within the
mountain ranges grew too scant for the population,
and the rising generation was pushed back into the
remoter valleys and coves of the mountains, cut off
from the main currents of travel, living on corn
grown on the hill-sides, and hams and bacon made
from the swine that ran half wild among the settle-

[1] Olmsted, *Texas Journey*, passim.
[2] Adams, *Southside View*, 142; Olmsted, *Seaboard Slave States*,
483.

ments. These people deteriorated, and by 1830
numbered more than a million, scattered through
eastern Kentucky and Tennessee, western Virginia
and the Carolinas, northern Georgia and Alabama.

Among the mountain whites slavery was almost
unknown, and there was more prejudice against the
slave-holder than against the negroes. In Virginia
and South Carolina the state constitution gave them
fewer representatives in proportion to the white
population than was given to the tide-water slave-
holding counties; elsewhere they voted on equal
terms with the lowlanders, but never dreamed of
controlling the state government. Contemporaries
noticed their large families of flaxen-haired children,
their rude and uncompromising manners, the illiter-
acy of people of all ages, the coarse and ill-cooked
food, and the log-houses, rude and dirty without
and bare and comfortless within. A large proportion of the population lived in one-room houses
without a glass window.[1]

However little the mountain whites added to the
wealth of the south, they were remote from the
world's highways and little influenced directly by
slavery. It was otherwise with the lowland whites,
who were chiefly descendants of low, poor, or vi-
cious English colonists. In some states there were
quite distinct groups living in a district by themselves, as the Piney-woods people of Mississippi, the

[1] Buckingham, *Slave States*, II., 153–167, 198–200; Olmsted,
Back Country, 230–232; *Berea Quarterly*, IX., No. 3 and passim.

Pine-landers and Crackers of Georgia, the Clay-eaters of South Carolina, and the Sand-hillers of the Carolinas.[1] Land was everywhere cheap and plenty; it was easy, too, to get the logs from which the few necessary buildings of a homestead could be erected. Like the mountain whites, they had some rugged virtues, such as personal honesty, a spirit of rude hospitality, and devotion to what they thought an ideal; but they lived on just as their fathers and grandfathers had lived, without any accumulation of property, without schools, without reading, without contact with the outer world. Some of them bought negroes, enlarged their plantations, and eventually rose to the class of prosperous slave-holders; the greater part of them were perfectly contented to live at a stand-still. Of the poor whites in 1850, five hundred and fourteen thousand were wholly illiterate. The only one of their own number who tried to arouse them said: "A large portion of our poor white people are wholly neglected, and are suffered to while away an existence in a state but one step in advance of the Indian of the forest."[2]

Olmsted, who had been accustomed to observe white laborers, thought the poor white farmers in every way inferior in intelligence, as in physical condition, to the lowest class of northern white laborers. Nor

[1] Olmsted, *Seaboard Slave States*, 413–416, 514; Kemble, *Georgian Plantation*, 75, 146; Buckingham, *Slave States*, I., 551; Bremer, *Homes of the New World*, I., 365–367; Burke, *Reminiscences*, 23–28; Smedes, *Memorials of a Southern Planter*, 113.

[2] Helper, *Impending Crisis*, 377.

did those of them who had the enterprise to leave
their homes and push southwest into Arkansas and
Texas show much improvement.[1] They had few
chances, for, aside from the intermittent cultivation
of their own farms, there was little occupation for
the poor whites: some digging of ore, turpentine
farming, hunting—these were their principal occu-
pations; for, throughout the south, the poor whites
could very seldom be induced to do field work for
their neighbors on any terms. A southern observer
said that "two bales of cotton a year is as much
as is generally made by people who do not own negroes; they are doing well if they net over fifty dollars a year for their labor, besides supplying themselves with corn."[2]

Except for the rivalries between the mountain
and lowland ends of the states, the poor white seems
hardly to have asked himself whether slavery was
or was not a good thing for him, though occasionally
a man would own that "slavery is a great cuss,
though, I think, the greatest there is in these United
States"; "the majority would be right glad if we
could get rid of the niggers"; and they all agreed that
the negroes, if freed, must be removed from the country.[3] In the thirty years before the Civil War, as the
great plantations enlarged, many of the poor whites

---

[1] Olmsted, *Back Country*, 123, 277, 327, 403, 415, 418; Olmsted,
Texas Journey, 15, 277.

[2] Olmsted, *Back Country*, 328.

[3] *Ibid.*, 203, 239, 259; Olmsted, *Seaboard Slave States*, 572.

thus pushed out simply settled again somewhere in the lowlands. A drift into the newer parts of the country brought a large number of poor whites across the Ohio River into southern Ohio, Indiana, and Illinois, carrying with them a dislike of the negro and a laggard interest in education and progress. In this environment they improved, and there were great potentialities in a strain which could produce an Abraham Lincoln.

One of the perplexing things in human history is that these people, who owned no slaves, who received nothing of the profits of slave labor, and who were put out of the pale of slave-holding society, should have accepted with so little question the leadership of the slave-holders, and should have demanded so little for themselves and their children out of the surplus produced by slavery. Helper's burning appeal to the poor whites for "No co-operation with Slaveholders in Politics—No Fellowship with them in Religion—No Affiliation with them in Society"[1] —met with no response. The planters looked down upon their neighbors;[2] and even the slaves of a master of social distinction were likely to think themselves better than "Po' white trash."

After the decay of the system of white indentured servants, it was a legal principle in every southern state that every white child was born free, remained free, and could not by any possibility become a

[1] Helper, *Impending Crisis*, 156.
[2] Smedes, *Memorials of a Southern Planter*, 67.

slave.   There are, however, some curious instances of white persons detained for a long time on the ground that they were of African blood.   Thus in 1843 a German named Salome Müller brought a successful suit in Louisiana against persons who had kept her in slavery for twenty-five years.[1]   On the other hand, persons outside the white race might legally hold negroes in bondage; the Indians were inveterate slave-holders [2]—indeed, the reception of negro runaways by the Seminoles was the prime cause of the eight-year Seminole War.[3]

Still stranger, a negro, if he acquired freedom either by manumission or by purchasing himself, could hold property, including slaves.   Such a man was then likely to buy his own family, and, unless he went through a formal process of manumission, they thereby legally became his slaves; and there are cases on record where, at the death of such an owner, his children became liable for his debts.   In such instances the legislature commonly came to the rescue.[4]   A more common case was that of free negroes, mostly descendants of the favored children of Frenchmen or Spaniards in Louisiana and Texas, who had inherited property, including slaves.   The anomaly struck one slave, who protested that "One

[1] Jay, *View*, 69–73;   Olmsted, *Back Country*, 90;   Cable, *Strange True Stories of La.*, 145–191.

[2] *Southern Literary Messenger*, XXVIII., 333–335.

[3] Giddings, *Exiles of Florida*, chap. vi.

[4] *Atlantic Monthly*, LVII., 27;   Olmsted, *Seaboard Slave States*, 126;   Brackett, *Negro in Maryland*, 168.

nigger has no business to sarve another; it's bad enough to have to sarve a white man without being paid for it, without having to sarve a black man." Such owners had a bad reputation for cruelty to their own slaves.[1]

Although in 1830 no person could be born into slavery north of Mason and Dixon's line, slavery and the incidents of slavery continued to exist in most of the free states. In Maine, Vermont, New Hampshire, and Massachusetts no permanent slaves appear; in Rhode Island, Connecticut, New York, New Jersey, and Pennsylvania, the census of 1830 shows a total of about twenty-seven hundred slaves; and in 1850 New Jersey still counted two hundred and thirty-six. All the northwestern states except Michigan contained a few slaves in 1840, in part old slaves held previous to 1787, in part persons who had come in previous to 1820 under what were termed indentures with their masters.[2]

[1] Olmsted, *Texas Journey*, 386, 397; Brackett, *Negro in Maryland*, 190.
[2] Wis. Hist. Soc., *Proceedings*, 1892, 82–86; *Iowa Journal of History*, October, 1904, p. 471; Nicolay and Hay, *Lincoln*, I., 141–146.

CHAPTER VI

THE FREE NEGRO

(1830–1860)

NOT so wide was the gulf between Lazarus and Dives as that which yawned between the whites of every class and the negroes; the one, however poor and powerless, was a member of the ruling element of society, with all the potentialities of freemen; the negro belonged to a servile race, and the best that even the free negro could hope was an inferior, imperfect, and unstable status. No legal distinctions were made between the quick negro and the stupid, the coal-black and the mulatto, the son of a planter and the son of a field-hand.

Yet there were many varieties of character, of capacity, and even of race among the negroes. Most of them were descended from the tribes of the west coast of Africa; but members of many inferior tribes reached the coast. On the same plantation could be found Guinea negroes, very black and uncouth; brown or bronze races, almost European in feature; a few individuals of the "copper color" type; and an occasional Arab. None of the African races persisted in America, their language almost en-

tirely disappeared, and except "Buckra" hardly a
word of any African dialect got a permanent lodgment in the language of the masters. The only
visible influence upon the spoken language was a
shortening of vowels and economy of consonants,
which outsiders observed also in the speech of the
white people.[1] So far as speech and traditions of
African life were concerned, they passed away with
the individuals who brought them.

A strong influence to break up the negro race
was its mixture with the whites. Some recent
writers allege that this process did not begin on a
large scale under slavery; the few available statistics, however, perfectly agree with the statements
of all candid observers, to the effect that the mulattoes were from the first very numerous. The certainly incomplete census of 1860 showed five hundred and eighteen thousand mixed bloods, which
was about a seventh of the negro population; and
the births were in about the same proportion.
Under the principle of *partus sequitur ventrem*, which
was universal in North America, every child of a
slave mother was born the slave of her owner, without inquiry as to the father. Of course, many of
the mulattoes were children of mulattoes, but they
all went back to white ancestors. Far too many
were children of overseers, especially on the lonely
plantations of absentee landlords.[2] Others were the

[1] Eggleston, *Transit of Civilization*, 111.
[2] Kemble, *Georgian Plantation*, 140, 162, 199, 208-210.

children of their own masters.[1] An example is the
case of Brazealle, a Mississippi planter, who from
gratitude and affection to a mulatto woman who
had nursed him through a dangerous illness took
her to Ohio, educated her, emancipated her, and
married her, and attempted by will to transfer his
property to their son; but the Mississippi courts
adjudged both mother and child to be slaves of a
distant relative of the testator.[2] Frederick Douglass supposed himself to be the son of his master.[3]
In Louisiana, and, indeed, throughout the south, it
was not unusual for young men to keep negro mistresses, commonly of mixed blood.[4] The quadroon
balls were visited by most travellers, and somewhat
resembled the similar resorts of the Parisian gri-
settes.[5] Some visitors predicted that the "future inhabitants of America will inevitably be mulattoes."[6]

So notorious were these relations that even semi-
official defenders of slavery found it hard to square
them with the prevailing notions as to morality,
and one of them winds up an attempt to explain
the thing away by saying that "a people whose men

[1] Child, *Anti-Slavery Catechism*, 17.

[2] Hinds *vs.* Brazealle, 2 Howard Miss. Reports, 837.

[3] Douglass, *Narrative*, 2; cf. Kemble, *Georgian Plantation*, 227–
229; Stuart, *North America*, II., 64; Rhodes, *United States*, I.,
341–343.

[4] Olmsted, *Seaboard Slave States*, 595–600; cf. Rhodes, *United
States*, I., 339–341.

[5] Featherstonhaugh, *Excursion*, 141; Buckingham, *Slave States*,
I., 358; Saxe-Weimar, *Travels*, II., 61.

[6] Abdy, *Journal*, I., 353; Lyell, *Second Visit*, I., 221.

are proverbially brave, intellectual and hospitable, and whose women are unaffectedly chaste, devoted to domestic life and happy in it, can neither be degraded nor demoralized, whatever their institutions may be." [1]

The result of these relations was a considerable body of slaves who made the color line seem almost imperceptible. The number of such very light slaves may be guessed from the numerous advertisements for negroes with blue eyes, fair skin, or nearly white. When a negro had reached the point where white people were easily deceived into thinking him one of themselves,[2] one of the greatest hardships of slavery became apparent; for not only could a person three-fourths or even thirty-one thirty-seconds white be legally held as a slave, but if set free he was only a free negro.

The disabilities of free negroes were serious, and their effect extended far beyond the boundaries of the slave-holding states. In 1830 there were 137,781 free negroes in the north, the greater number of them in Pennsylvania, New Jersey, and New York. In legal status the free negro had lost ground since the Revolution, as was shown by the limitations upon his suffrage. Besides Georgia and South Carolina, which continued the distinction made in colonial times, between 1792 and 1834 the four border states of Delaware, Maryland, Virginia, and Ken-

[1] Hammond, in *Pro-Slavery Argument*, 120.
[2] Lyell, *Second Visit*, I., 221.

tucky absolutely forbade suffrage to negroes; and every other slave state admitted by Congress came into the Union with a constitution prohibiting negroes from voting. In the remaining slave state, North Carolina, every freeman who paid a public tax was entitled to vote, and it was notorious that negroes could and did take part in elections,[1] till, in 1835, a new constitution excluded them from the suffrage. Such action had a ground in states where the negro vote might conceivably affect slavery; but it was repeated in several northern communities where there was no such excuse. New Jersey in 1807, Connecticut in 1814, and Pennsylvania in 1838 took away the suffrage from negroes; and New York in 1821 required from them an unusually high property qualification.

These exclusions branded the negroes as of a different caste, even in the north, and it was backed up by other unfriendly legislation. Ohio began in 1803 to build up a black code, proceeding to a demand for a bond of five hundred dollars for negroes who might come into the state, and denying to the negro the right of testimony in cases in which a white man was a party, or admission to the public schools. Similar provisions were enacted by Indiana, Illinois, and Iowa when they came into the Union; Illinois even prohibited the coming of negroes into the state on any terms.[2]

[1] Livermore, *Historical Research*, 11.
[2] Hurd, *Law of Freedom and Bondage;* McKinley, *Suffrage in the Colonies;* Hart, in Am. Polit. Sci. Assoc., *Proceedings*, 1905.

The negroes, thus placed upon an inferior political and legal stand-point, were further subject to an unyielding social prejudice. In 1830 the Park Street Church in Boston excluded from its house a colored family which had legal title to a pew;[1] the annual day when the Massachusetts state government was organized was called "nigger 'lection," as being a public occasion when negroes were allowed to appear on Boston Common; when the Boston & Providence Railroad was first opened, a special compartment was set apart for negroes.[2] White men frequently refused to work with negroes on the same jobs.[3] Nevertheless, throughout the north, and especially in cities like Boston, Philadelphia, and Cincinnati, there were many thriving, respectable, and well-educated negroes who keenly felt the humiliation of their condition.

The negro in the north was at least free to move about and engage in such employment as he could find, free to bring up his family without forcible separation. Not so with his brother in the south, to whom manumission brought not freedom, but a half-way status having many of the sorrowful incidents of slavery. In many directions the free negro was steadily losing ground. As late as 1814, General Jackson, by a formal proclamation, promised "to every noble hearted generous freeman of color

[1] May, *Recollections*, 269; Garrisons, *Garrison*, I., 253.
[2] Quincy, *Figures of the Past*, 341.
[3] Abdy, *Journal*, I., 358.

volunteering to serve during the present contest " the same bounty, "monthly pay, and daily rations and clothes furnished to any American soldier." [1] But soon after 1830 he was excluded from the opportunity to serve in the state militia, and in some states from fire companies and similar organizations, though negro musical bands were common.

There seems little doubt that in most of the southern colonies free negroes were considered citizens.[2] But Judge Daggett, of Connecticut, in 1833 held that the free negro was a person and not a citizen.[3] The laws of the United States expressed a doubt on the subject, by recognizing no right of any other than a free white person to acquire citizenship by naturalization. The free negro was clearly not a full citizen in the eyes of the negro codes of the slave-holding states, which in wearisome detail distinguished between whites and free negroes, while frequently placing the free negro with the negro slaves. A few examples will show the character of these codes. In four states free negroes must have official guardians; in eight states they must be registered; in general, the testimony of negroes was not accepted against white men. They were forbidden in some places to sell drugs; in others, to sell wheat and tobacco; in others, to peddle market produce or to own a boat; in several states, from entering the commonwealth from elsewhere;

---

[1] Livermore, *Historical Research*, 210.   [2] *Ibid.*, 19–110.
[3] Jay, *Miscellaneous Writings*, 42–45.

in others a negro, if set free, must forthwith remove from the state.[1]

Well-behaved and industrious free negroes were probably little disturbed, and laws were not too hardly administered against them; but there was a fearful potentiality of punishment. Free negroes were especially forbidden to hold meetings or to teach one another to read and write. They could commonly inherit, hold, and transmit real and personal property, but a free colored man was not allowed to testify against a white man, so that he could neither be witness against an aggressor nor even identify him before the court. In at least one state, by a whimsicality, a free negro was subject to a special poll-tax, the proceeds to be applied to colonization of his race in Africa.[2]

The ground for these discriminations, as stated by the leading literary man of the south in 1837, was that "by emancipation and the pettings of philanthropy the coarse and uneducated negro became lifted into a condition to which his intellect did not entitle him, and to which his manners were unequal; — he became presumptuous, accordingly, and consequently offensive." In contradiction to his own argument, the same writer a few pages further says: "They feel their inferiority to the whites, even when nominally freemen; and sink

[1] Hurd, *Law of Freedom and Bondage*, II., chaps. xvii.–xix.
[2] Simms, in *Pro-Slavery Argument*, 207; Stuart, *North America*, II., 80.

into the condition of serviles, in fact, if not in name."[1]

To be at the same time presumptuous and servile, ambitious and deficient, was an illogical fate. A more frequent charge was that the free negro was a criminal, "the very drones and pests of society."[2] In the northern as well as in the southern states the petty and even aggravated crimes committed by negroes were far above their proportion in the population; and in the south there was the additional feeling that they were a standing incentive to the slave to abjure his allegiance to his master. In many cases, however, the free negroes were the best of the race, set free because of faithfulness and character, reasons which led Roger B. Taney, later chief-justice, to free his own slaves; and he testified years after that he had not been disappointed.[3] In hundreds of cases they were the children of their masters, sometimes petted, indulged, and educated children; in others they belonged to that small but desperately industrious class which bought its own freedom. On the other hand, there were many cases of freemen married to slave women, whose children went to the master of the mother. Whether or not it was the desire of the free negro to support himself and his family respectably, he rarely had the opportunity; dislike and suspicion were against him

[1] Simms, in *Pro-Slavery Argument*, 212, 220.
[2] Dew, in *ibid.*, 422.
[3] Mass. Hist. Soc., *Proceedings*, 1871–1873, p. 447.

everywhere, and the moment he got away from the place where he was known he found himself in danger of kidnapping.

For it must not be forgotten that if a slave could become free, a free negro could also become a slave, and that without fault or neglect on his own part. This reversion to slavery came about in many different methods, all acting steadily and effectively. In the first place, persons who had been set free for years and had no reason to suppose that they were anything else, might be seized upon for defects in the legal process of manumission. There were instances where successful suits were brought for the possession of families who had lived in freedom unmolested for thirty years.[1]

The second method was by kidnapping, which was frequent in the north and south throughout the slavery period. One of the most striking cases, that of Peter Still, was revealed in all its enormity by the return of the stolen person to Philadelphia after more than twenty years' captivity.[2] Of course, a grown man or woman thus kidnapped might find means of communicating with his friends; but Solomon Northup was in bondage twelve years before he could attract the attention of the legal authorities to his undoubted claim to freedom.[3] In

[1] E. g., Rhame *vs.* Ferguson and Dangerfield, in Buckingham, *Slave States*, II., 32; Adams, *Southside View*, 154.

[2] Pickard, *Kidnapped and Ransomed*, 248.

[3] McDougall, *Fugitive Slaves*, § 38; Chambers, *Am. Slavery and Colour*, 192.

the south the offence was a little more dangerous, because it was closely akin to slave stealing, which was one of the most atrocious of all crimes against slave property.

A still more common case was the sale of free negroes for their jail fees, a thing which could hardly be believed but for the accumulation of evidence. In several of the southern states a negro who incurred a fine which he could not pay might be sold as a slave. In Maryland a free negro under certain circumstances might be sold as a perpetual slave, simply for the offence of coming into the state.[1] The practice attracted great attention in the north because of the revelation in 1829 that it was steadily going on in the District of Columbia.[2] The practice of the District authorities was to arrest any colored person who could not give an account of himself, to advertise him, and, if nobody appeared to establish a claim, to sell him in order to reimburse the jailers their fees. In five cases reported the marshal had not only recovered his fees, but about three hundred dollars more. The desperate injustice of condemning a man to slavery because of a failure to prove him a slave was one of the most effective arguments of the abolitionists. The effects of these methods of re-enslavement are hard to calculate; but for some

[1] Case of Ned Davis in Maryland, 1851, Chambers, *Am. Slavery and Colour*, 186–188.

[2] *Debates of Congress*, 20 Cong., 2 Sess., 167, 175–187, 191; *House Reports*, 20 Cong, 2 Sess, No. 60; *Niles' Register*, XXXIV., 191; Tremain, *Slavery in District of Columbia*, 42–49.

cause there was a steady diminution of free negroes in several southern states. Either free negroes could not keep up the natural increase of their race or they were forced back into slavery.

In some instances, freemen for various reasons sought and obtained the status of the slave; and some states authorized any free negro thus to choose him a master who, if he accepted the relation, became responsible for the negro; but upon no point in the history of slavery is there less evidence than of a desire by the free negro for the comforts of a slave home. The whole system of slavery and slave codes was grounded upon the *a priori* belief that every slave desired to be free and every free negro desired to remain free.

In the midst of poverty, degradation, and suspicion, some free negroes came to be persons of consideration in the southern community. Solomon Humphries, a slave who had bought his own freedom, was a well-known business man in Georgia, readily trusted by white merchants.[1] Lundy found at San Antonio a Louisiana negro who had bought the freedom of his family and himself, owned several houses and lots, and his sister was married to a Frenchman.[2] The aggregate property of the two hundred and sixty-two thousand free negroes in the south in 1860 has been estimated at twenty-five million dollars. Some of these people found means

---

[1] Buckingham, *Slave States*, I., 211.
[2] *Life of Benjamin Lundy*, 54.

to make their way into the northern states, hoping for better opportunities, for the more prosperous they were in the south the more striking was their silent argument against slavery. That nearly ten per cent. of the southern negroes should have been free in 1830 was a tribute to the humanity of the southern people, for every one was practically a denial of the principle that slavery was a good thing for the negroes; and every thriving one disproved the argument that if the negro were set free he would starve rather than support himself.

CHAPTER VII

PLANTATION LIFE

(1830–1860)

ONE reason for the outbreak of the abolition movement was increasing knowledge of the conditions of slavery. Improvements in transit, closer commercial relations between north and south, and a spirit of investigation into social conditions made possible an era of travel and observation in the south by foreigners and northerners.[1] The abolitionists at home clipped items from the southern newspapers and listened to the narratives of the fugitive slave. To describe the plantation system, especially its cruel and repulsive side, was their stock in trade; while in the defences of slavery and the replies to the abolitionists the gentler side of slave-holding was held up to view.[2]

The visitor who expected to find a distinct type of slave countenance and person was disappointed. Some had large infusions of white blood and possessed European features; and some pure negroes

---

[1] See list of travellers in chap. xxii., below.
[2] On the general conditions of slavery, Hart, *Contemporaries*, III., §§ 169–173.

had oval faces, slender and supple figures, graceful hands, and small feet.[1] Nevertheless, the majority of the negroes were coarse and unattractive in appearance. Olmsted notes a group of road-making women as "clumsy, awkward, gross, elephantine in all their movements; pouting, grinning, and leering at us; sly, sensual, and shameless in all their expressions and demeanor."[2] Among the negroes, as among other races, there was no fixed standard of capacity or character. Some masters were never weary of telling of the faithfulness and attachment of their slaves; of their care for the children of the family; of their incorruptibility. One champion of slavery enumerates the virtues of slaves: "Fidelity—often proof against all temptation—even death itself—an eminently cheerful and social temper . . . submission to constituted authority."[3] But the general tone towards the negro was one of distrust and aversion. Many masters believed that "the negroes were so addicted to lying and stealing that they were not to be trusted out of sight or hearing."[4] At best they were thought big children, pleased with trifles, and easily forgetful of penalties and pains.

The slaves were rough and brutal among themselves. Friendly observers complained of "the in-

[1] Kemble, *Georgian Plantation*, 42, 85.

[2] Olmsted, *Seaboard Slave States*, 387; cf. Martineau, *Society in America*, I., 212–234.

[3] Harper, in *Pro-Slavery Argument*, 46.

[4] Reported by Buckingham, *Slave States*, II., 87.

solent tyranny of their demeanor toward each other; . . . they are diabolically cruel to animals too, and they seem to me as a rule hardly to know the difference between truth and falsehood." [1]   Their indolence was the despair of every slave-owner, or was overcome by the strictest discipline.   In many small households with few slaves and no patriarchal tradition there was constant friction and flogging; their shiftlessness, waste of their master's property, neglect of his animals, were almost proverbial; and the looseness of the marriage-tie and immorality of even the best of the negroes were subjects of sorrow to those who felt the responsibility for them. [2]

Many of the negroes showed intellectual qualities, especially household slaves; and thousands of slaves learned to read and write.   The art was frowned upon, for "what has the slave of any country to do with heroic virtues, liberal knowledge, or elegant accomplishments?" [3]   Nevertheless, the number of slaves who could read and write was probably not far from one-tenth of the whole. [4]   They were taught by kind-hearted mistresses and children of the family, who liked to give a pleasure and who disregarded the statutes against the practice; once taught, they communicated the art to one another, and secret

[1] Kemble, *Georgian Plantation*, 263.
[2] Harper, in *Pro-Slavery Argument*, 38–41.
[3] *Ibid.*, 36, 46.
[4] Grace E. Burroughs, unpublished manuscript on *Educated Slaves*.

schools for the children of slaves were not unknown.[1]

Some of the letters written by escaped slaves
showed education and superior power of expression.
Yet in this period appeared no such slave prodigies
as Phyllis Wheatley, the slave poet, whose verses
were kindly received by Washington; or Benjamin
Banneker, the astronomer, who was a guest at the
table of President Jefferson. The literary negroes
were nearly all escaped slaves, whose reminiscences
bear the trace of a white man's correcting pen. The
one literary opportunity for the slave on the soil
was the telling of folk-stories, which show a vivid
power of description, an imagination which personi-
fies the ideas of the story-teller, and a rich and
unctuous humor which delights by its sudden turns
of situation. The only art in which the negroes excelled was music. They have an intuitive quick-
ness in picking up simple musical instruments, and
developed, if they did not invent, the banjo; but
their songs were their chief intellectual efforts; the
words, simple, repetitive, sometimes senseless, were
made the vehicle for a plaintive music.[2]

A proportion of the slaves now difficult to ascer-

---

[1] Bremer, *Homes of the New World*, II., 499; Burke, *Reminiscences*, 85; Douglass, *Narrative*, 32-44; Kemble, *Georgian Plantation*, 230, 257; Smedes, *Memorials of a Southern Planter*, 79.

[2] Harris, *Nights with Uncle Remus*, 143-206; Olmsted, *Seaboard Slave States*, 551, 607; Bremer, *Homes of the New World*,
II., 174; Kemble, *Georgian Plantation*, 127, 218; Douglass, *Narrative*, 13-15.

tain was employed in other than household or field tasks. A few were fishermen, employed as cooks or hands on coasting craft;[1] a larger number served as roustabouts on the river steamers, where their picturesque appearance, songs, jollity, and hard work in handling freight and fuel attracted the attention of all travellers.[2] Slaves were freely used in the turpentine industry, which required very little skill, and in the lumbering regions, as wood-choppers and to prepare lumber. Mining employed almost no slaves, the labor of free whites or free negroes was considered more profitable.[3]

In addition to these rough tasks, a fraction of the slaves and free negroes, certainly not one-twentieth of the able-bodied men, were employed in skilled trades, especially building. Nearly all large plantations had a little force of blacksmiths, carpenters, bricklayers, and the like, and such skilled hands were frequently hired out by their masters.[4] Most of the plantation buildings in the south were constructed by slave labor, and many of the town and city buildings. Some slave mechanics could not only build, but draw plans, make contracts, and complete a house, even hiring out their own time and employing men on their own responsibility.[5] This small pro-

---

[1] Olmsted, *Seaboard Slave States*, 351-355.

[2] *Ibid.*, 551-564; Stuart, *North America*, II., 153; Buckingham, *Slave States*, I., 264. [3] Lyell, *Second Visit*, I., 216.

[4] Smedes, *Memorials of a Southern Planter*, 104.

[5] Letter of G. W. Steedman, of St. Louis, to the author; cf. Lyell, *Second Visit*, I., 267.

portion of industrial slaves was not much increased
by slaves working in factories. The few iron fur-
naces in the south employed negro labor, hiring it
at about two hundred dollars a year; and gangs
of slaves could be found in the tobacco factories.[1]
Among the few textile mills was a bagging factory in Lexington, Kentucky, and cotton mills near
Huntsville and at Salada, near Columbia;[2] mills at
Scottsville were profitably carried on by the labor
of slave families owned by the corporation. De Bow,
in 1852, was still hopeful of slave operatives, though
only about one-fortieth of the cotton grown in the
south was manufactured in the south, most of it by
white labor.[3]

Coming back again to the plantation, a sharp
distinction was drawn between two great classes of
slaves — the field slaves and house-servants. The
present tradition in the south is that these house-
servants were universally intelligent, faithful, and
devoted; indeed, there were many warm attachments
between the slaves and the members of the owner's
family,[4] yet people at the time did not find them
either refined or well-kept. On the Butler plantation in Georgia there was neither table nor chair in
the kitchen; the boys slept on the hearth, and the

---

[1] Olmsted, *Texas Journey*, 19; Buckingham, *Slave States*, I.,
43; Pickard, *Kidnapped and Ransomed*, 43–45; Bremer, *Homes
of the New World*, II., 509.

[2] *Hunt's Merchants' Magazine*, XXXVIII., 509; XXXIX., 755.

[3] De Bow, *Industrial Resources*, II., 112.

[4] Smedes, *Memorials of a Southern Planter*, passim.

women on rough board bedsteads strewn with a little tree-moss. Rooms for household servants were almost nowhere provided; either they slept in separate buildings or stretched themselves on the floor or the passages, or even in the rooms of the family.[1]

One reason for the glamour cast over household slaves was that the best of the race was drawn into that service. The highest position to which a slave could aspire was to be butler or cook in the great house, where food was plenty, company enjoyable, and perquisites many.[2] The black mammy, who perhaps had brought up a whole family of white children —for white nurses were almost unknown—is still cherished in the minds of many southern people; but when she was young she was not always a person whose moral character influenced for good the children for whom she cared; and the maids too often had special temptations and dangers in the presence of the master and the master's sons.

The characteristic life of the negro was as a plantation laborer; he raised the greater part of the surplus product of the south and was the basis of most wealth; but he was a very unsatisfactory laborer. That a thrifty farmer like Olmsted should be scandalized at the inefficiency of the negro is not remarkable;[3] but he made the same impression on his

[1] Kemble, *Georgian Plantation*, 23, 66.
[2] Smedes, *Memorials of a Southern Planter*, 82–84.
[3] Olmsted, *Back Country*, 432; Olmsted, *Seaboard Slave States*, 10, 44–47, 99, 105, 480–483.

master, who freely acknowledged that slave labor could never be so cheap as free labor.[1]   Owner after owner complained to visitors of his slaves.   "In working niggers we must always calculate that they will not labor at all except to avoid punishment; . . . it always seems on the plantation as if they took pains to break all the tools and spoil all the cattle that they possibly can."[2]

On some plantations slaves worked from sunrise to sundown, about the hours of northern laborers then, and in addition had to cook their own meals. In many parts of the south there was task work. The task which was an average for a gang could be performed by some members of it so quickly that they got through as early as three, or even one o'clock; but it was almost impossible to increase the average result by any reward or punishment. On all plantations the women worked alongside the men, even to the extent of driving a plough. Too little attention was paid to the peculiar needs of working-women near childbirth, and lifelong injuries from overstrain among them were not uncommon. Nevertheless, the testimony of witnesses is that, in general, the day's work of a slave was considerably less than that of hired workmen in the north.[3]

The ordinary food of the slave was corn-bread and

---

[1] Harper, in *Pro-Slavery Argument*, 26.
[2] Conversation in Olmsted, *Seaboard Slave States*, 105.
[3] Olmsted, *Seaboard Slave States*, 334; Olmsted, *Back Country*, 49, 80, 81.

bacon, with sweet-potatoes and some other vegetables; a peck of meal and three pounds of bacon a
week, with a little sugar and wheat-flour, was
thought a suitable ration for a hand; but many
slaves had a little time for cultivating their own
garden-patches, kept chickens, and sometimes pigs,
with an occasional opossum or even a bear from their
nocturnal hunting. The ordinary rations seem to
have been sufficient for keeping up health. The
conditions of life were easy in the south, and none
but an extraordinarily stupid or cruel master would
keep his slaves down to a point where they could not
do full work; and the household servants and their
families, who swarmed in and out of the kitchen,
never suffered. The delightful southern cooking in
such households, the inimitable fried chicken, the
delicious beaten biscuit, the unrealizable methods of
cooking fowls, turkeys, and game, did not extend
among the poor planters or the poor whites, who
for the most part lived in an atmosphere of grease
and frying, with corresponding ill effects upon their
digestion.

The clothing of slaves was of every variety, from
the smart mulatto lady's-maid, who wore the still
fresh dress that had been her young mistress's, down
to the pickaninny of three, five, or eight years of
age, who went as nature made him. Most plantations issued coarse clothing at stated intervals. The
shoes and some clothing on large plantations were
made up by slaves set apart for that purpose, and

house slaves often took pride in being smartly dressed in clothing fitted to them by professional tail-
ors.[1]

The cost of maintenance of field slaves was a question much discussed, and estimates by planters varied from fifteen dollars a year, for food and clothing,
up to fifty dollars;[2] to which should be added medical attendance, which might be five dollars a head,
and overseer's wages, an average of ten dollars
a head. If, therefore, the annual product of the
plantation averaged seventy-five to one hundred
dollars per head of all the slaves, there was something to pay for wear and tear, interest, tools, etc.,
and a profit; but leaving out the old, the sick, the
children too young to work, and the women necessary for household and other services, not more than
one-third of the slaves on a plantation could ordi-
narily be put into the field.

The ideal plantation had a "great house," or
family mansion, with its avenue of live-oaks sweep-
ing up to the front doors, and at a little distance
the negro quarters. Here are two accounts written
within six years of each other: "Each cabin was a
framed building, the walls boarded and whitewashed
on the outside, lathed and plastered within, the roof
shingled; . . . divided into two family tenements,

---

[1] Olmsted, *Seaboard Slave States*, II., 27, 112, 686–694; Adams,
Southside View, 29–32; Kemble, *Georgian Plantation*, 52, 179;
Burke, *Reminiscences*, 113.
[2] De Bow, *Industrial Resources*, I., 150.

each twenty - one by twenty - one; each tenement divided into three rooms. . . . Besides these rooms, each tenement had a cockloft, entered by steps from the household room. Each tenement is occupied, on an average, by five persons." [1] "No attempt at any drainage or any convenience existed near them. . . . Heaps of oyster shells, broken crockery, old shoes, rags, and feathers were found near each hut. The huts were all alike windowless, and the apertures, intended to be glazed some fine day, were generally filled up with a deal board. The roofs were shingle and the white-wash which had once given the settlement an air of cleanliness, was now only to be traced by patches." [2]

Slavery made real family life almost impossible, except on the smaller plantations, where one or more families of slaves were often the sole valuable asset of the owners, and they grew up alongside their masters. On the larger plantations the house slaves could bring up their own families, but marriage was subject to many difficulties. Many planters disliked to have their slaves married to slaves of their neighbors. On their own plantations owners exercised a kind of *pater potestas* over the alliances of their slaves, occasionally uniting them in such simple marriage services as, "Do you make Joe build a fire for Phillis and see that Phillis cooks for Joe and

[1] Olmsted, *Seaboard Slave States*, 422.
[2] Russell, *Diary North and South*, I., 212; cf. Olmsted, *Seaboard Slave States*, 44, 111, 421, 629, 659, 692, 698.

washes his clothes." [1]   The negroes preferred a marriage ceremony, and sometimes were united in form
at the great house.   "I had a weddin'—a big weddin'—for Marlow's kitchen.   Your pa gib me a head
weddin'—kilt a mutton—a round o' beef—tukkeys
—cakes, one on t'other—trifle.   I had all the chany
off de sideboard, cups and saucers, de table, de white
table-cloth.   I had on your pa's wife's weddin'
gloves an' slippers an' veil.   De slippers was too
small, but I put my toes in.   Miss Mary had a mighty
neat foot.   Marster brought out a milk-pail o' toddy
and more in bottles.   De gentlemans an' marster
stand up on de tables.   He didn't rush 'mongst de
black folks, you know.   I had a tearin'-down weddin, to be sho'.   Nobody else didn't hab sich a
weddin." [2]

In the nature of things, slave marriages were
unstable.   The negroes themselves did not feel a
strong sense of obligation to their spouses, and frequently deserted one another.   However, so long as
there were little children, somebody must take care
of them, though, inasmuch as the little negro was
welcomed chiefly as adding to the wealth of his
master, the ordinary beautiful relations of child and
parent were difficult.   On some plantations there
was a nursery for the babies while their mothers
were in the field.   As the old slave woman expressed
it, "You feel when your child is born you can't have

[1] Pickard, *Kidnapped and Ransomed*, 153.
[2] Aunt Harriet, in Smedes, *Memorials of a Southern Planter*, 55.

the bringing of it up." [1] As children grew up they were employed for light tasks about the house and the place, and often were made petted playthings and riotous companions for their young masters, unless, indeed, their yellow tinge suggested to some member of the household that they were "a little more than kin and less than kind." [2]

One of the strong arguments for slavery was that it abolished the poor-house and provided for the infirm and the aged. Absolute abandonment of a slave by a master who had the means to provide for him was next to impossible, because he would thereby become a public charge; and the slave codes commonly provided penalties for such cases. Sometimes old slaves were protected characters; [3] but there were many instances of sick and old slaves who had but a pittance for their support. [4]

On many plantations the negroes were allowed privileges, such as the right to keep bees, or to sell small articles that had been made; and occasional holidays, especially at Christmas-time, when work was sometimes suspended for several days. [5] The right to keep truck-patches and to cultivate them was highly appreciated by the negroes. Money gifts to slaves were not uncommon, especially at Christmas, when tobacco, clothing, and molasses were

---

[1] Adams, *Southside View*, 84; cf. Page, *The Negro*, 174.
[2] "Southern Woman," in N. Y. *Independent*, March 17, 1904, p. 586.   [3] Adams, *Southside View*, 47.
[4] Parsons, *Inside View of Slavery*, 154; Elliot, *Sinfulness of Slavery*, I., 212.   [5] Adams, *Southside View*, 35.

often liberally dealt out, sometimes to the value of
ten dollars for each slave.[1]   Some slaves earned considerable sums by working for themselves on Sunday.   The negro also had his recreations, picnics,
and barbecues, visiting from plantation to plantation; in the cities going to shows, racing horses, and
fighting.[2]

"Yes, honey," said a reminiscent slave, "dat he
did gib us Fourth o' July,—a plenty o' holiday,—a
beef kilt, a mutton, hogs, salt and pepper, an' ebery-
thing.   He hab a gre't trench dug, an' a whole load
o' wood put in it, an' burned down to coals.   Den
dey put wooden spits across, an' dey had spoons an'
basted de meat, an' he did not miss givin' us whiskey to drink,—a plenty of it, too.   An' we 'vite all
de culled people aroun', an' dey come, an' we had
fine times.   Our people was so good, and dey had
so much.   Dyar warn't no sich people no whyar.
Marster mus'n't be named de same day as udder
people." [3]

The slaves greatly enjoyed religious meetings.
Some churches had special galleries set apart for
negro attendance, and there were also many separate negro churches, like the rural white churches,
small and rough buildings, standing at cross-roads

[1] Olmsted, *Back Country*, 51; cf. Olmsted, *Seaboard Slave
States*, 439–443, 484, 682, 695.
[2] Olmsted, *Seaboard Slave States*, 63, 75, 101–103, 394, 439,
630; Burke, *Reminiscences*, 92; Smedes, *Memorials of a Southern
Planter*, 161–164.
[3] Smedes, *Memorials of a Southern Planter*, 58.

far away from settlements. Like their poor white neighbors, any one who had a gift of exhorting and praying, thereby became a minister; and in both city and country churches there was an immense amount of the shouting which was equally enjoyed by many white congregations.

Such religious services, though sometimes imbued with a genuine religious spirit and an incitement to the better life, were more often an appeal to the emotional nature. In the camp - meetings, which were held on the same model as those of the whites, and sometimes in the same place, though in separate amphitheatres, the negro had his highest enjoyment. An eye-witness says: "In the camp of the blacks is heard a great tumult and a loud cry. Men roar and bawl out; women screech like pigs about to be killed; many, having fallen into convulsions, leap and strike around them, so that they are obliged to be held down. It looks here and there like a regular fight; some of the calmer participants laugh. Many a cry of anguish may be heard, but you distinguish no words excepting 'Oh, I am a sinner!' and 'Jesus! Jesus!'" [1]

In a Christian community believing that all men had souls to save, it would have been monstrous to deny the opportunity of salvation to the African. Some plantations had little churches of their own; masters permitted prayer-meetings in the houses of negroes; elsewhere services were held at the great

[1] Bremer, *Homes of the New World*, I., 309.

houses by the owners, although many people thought it dangerous.[1] Wherever attempts were made at formal religious instruction to slaves the question at once arose of their being encouraged to learn to read the Bible, though it must be presumed to be in accord with slavery. The safest way seemed to be to give the African "acquaintance with the word of God . . . through oral instruction."[2]

One side of the Christian religion was made sufficiently familiar to most negroes—namely, injunctions to servants to obey their masters and to be satisfied in the station to which the Lord had appointed them; yet many thousands found comfort and hope in the belief that a life of labor and privation was to be followed by a glorious eternity in heaven, although even here there was a doubt as to whether it would be the same heaven as that of the white people.

The question of a future life came home to the negro because he was so much more subject than his white brother to death; among the diseases most fatal to negroes were congestion of the lungs, yaws (a contagious filth disease), "negro consumption," and colic. Some medical authorities diagnosed also "hebetude of mind," a general breaking-down of the will and nervous force which overseers commonly supposed to be simple insolence and punished accordingly. The negroes were liable

---

[1] Kemble, *Georgian Plantation*, 267.
[2] Adams, *Southside View*, 57.

to intermittent fever, probably of a malarial character, and other forms of mysterious fevers. The
greatest loss of life was among children, who had
poor food and often most ignorant care.[1] Epilepsy
was infrequent, and the census of 1840 showed
only 1407 insane slaves, although there were doubtless many who were really *non compos*, but were
retained on the plantation. Good plantations always had a contract doctor by the year to attend any cases that occurred; but the overseer
was frequently the judge as to the nature of
the disease, the remedy, and the moment when
the work was to be resumed. Large estates had
hospitals and separate lying-in hospitals, the character of which depended upon the humanity and
intelligence of the owner.[2]

The death-rate of the negroes was then, as it has
continued to be, much larger than that of the
whites.[3] Registration statistics in slavery times are
incomplete except in Charleston. The very unsatisfactory figures of 1850 showed a white and free-ne-
gro death-rate of 13.6, and a slave-rate of 16.4 in
the thousand. That the negroes continued to increase at about the same ratio as the whites was
due to their phenomenal birth-rate.

[1] De Bow, *Industrial Resources*, II., 292–303, 315–329; Kemble,
Georgian Plantation, 39, 90.
[2] Olmsted, *Back Country*, 77; Kemble, *Georgian Plantation*,
30–35, 121, 214–216.
[3] Eighth U. S. Census, 1860, *Population*, Introduction, p. xlv.

CHAPTER VIII

CONTROL OF THE SLAVES

(1830–1860)

SLAVE labor always depends upon physical force abundant enough, swift enough, and thorough enough to compel obedience and to break down insubordination; and the slave system was backed up by a large body of statutory law and a private system for punishing offences. The slave codes included much of the law applicable to the free negro,[1] with special provisions applicable only to bondmen.[2] In selecting out of the mass of legislation some of the most characteristic provisions, it should be remembered that the slave codes were always more severe in the communities having the largest number of slaves—that is, in the lower south.

In part, the slave codes were intended for the protection of the slave against ill-usage. Several states had laws against Sunday work, others against undue tasks, others provided for a minimum ration, or for a mid-day rest. All the slave-holding states made the malicious and unnecessary killing of a

---

[1] See above, chap. vi.
[2] Hurd, *Law of Freedom and Bondage*, I., §§ 216–230.

slave a capital offence, but the master was allowed to
exercise authority sufficient to protect his life and enforce his commands; and the Tennessee laws of 1836
specifically provided that "any slave dying under
moderate correction" could not be held to be murdered.[1] Statutes also forbade the maiming or branding of a slave by the master. On the other hand,
the slave codes recognized the master as sole owner
of such property as a slave might nominally possess.
Whether taken as real-estate, which in several states
the negro was legally held to be for purposes of
mortgage and inheritance, or as a chattel, the law
upheld the master in such leases or sale of the slave
as seemed to him desirable; and a slave was liable
to forced sale in payment of the master's debts.
The spirit of the law was throughout to emphasize
the power, authority, and right of the master.

Slaves were subject to a body of statutory law
against assembling. In Delaware, six men slaves
meeting together, not belonging to one master,
might be whipped for that offence. To keep a gun
was punishable, in Virginia, with thirty-nine lashes;
to be on horseback without the written permit of a
master meant twenty - five lashes; fishing with a
seine in certain waters, thirty-nine lashes.[2] Furthermore, for some offences, such as arson, the punishment of the slave was more severe than of a white
or a free negro. One of the unforgivable crimes
was the killing of a white man by a slave; and

[1] Stroud, *Slave Laws*, 61.   [2] *Ibid.*, 162, 166, 167.

though the courts sometimes humanely stepped in to save the negro who had taken life simply to defend his own life, public sentiment usually demanded the death of the assailant.[1]

The ever-present fear of insurrections caused most of the southern states to make special provisions against the movement of the negroes, especially at night; hence some of the cities had curfew laws, and throughout the south there was stringent legislation against negroes being away from their own plantation without written permission from the master or his representative.[2]   To make these laws effective, there was a system of patrols, "the patter rollers," with whom Uncle Remus threatened little boys.   The vigilance exercised in a town is described by a contemporary: "Last night a slave passing the jail was ordered by Esq. Wilson to stop.   'Where are you going?'   'My master sent me after the doctor.'   'It is a d—d lie,' said Wilson, 'pull off your shirt.'   'I can't do that,' said the slave and took hold of Wilson.   The guards came to his help and held the slave while Wilson gave him twenty lashes.   'Now go home,' said he.   'I shan't; I shall go after the doctor,' replied the slave, and ran, Wilson pursuing him.'"[3]

The patrol was really a kind of police-militia made up of men of the neighborhood, who rode the high-

[1] Hurd, *Law of Freedom and Bondage*, II., chaps. xvii.–xix.; Stroud, *Slave Laws*, 169–188.

[2] Adams, *Southside View*, 24; Burke, *Reminiscences*, 17; Olmsted, *Seaboard Slave States*, 558, 592; Northup, *Twelve Years a Slave*, 157.   [3] Thompson, *Prison Life*, 60.

ways in bands, received a small payment for each night of service, and freely stopped all negroes whom they found on the roads, whipping those whom they recognized as out without leave, and detaining unknown negroes as probable runaways. Imprisonment was no penalty for a slave, who could not be kept employed and who must be fed; and therefore the minor delinquencies of laziness and neglect were usually visited by the whip of the master or mistress or overseer. More serious offences, such as theft, small personal injuries to other negroes, and the like, though punishable by the courts, were commonly taken care of in the same way; and aggravated offences of insubordination, or of running away, were treated with greater severity of the same kind. Mild-tempered mistresses and even masters often sent household slaves to the calaboose, which was the local jail, with instructions that they should be whipped by the jailer for a small fee. Thus De Bow could truthfully say: "On our estates we dispense with the whole machinery of public police and public courts of justice. Thus we try, decide, and execute the sentences in thousands of cases, which in other countries would go into the courts." [1] For man, woman, and child, the only ultimate sanction for a command was force, and the community did not feel kindly towards masters who spoiled their slaves by leaving them uncorrected.[2]

[1] De Bow, *Industrial Resources*, II., 249.
[2] Olmsted, *Seaboard Slave States*, 194, 195.

The spirit and extent of slave punishments depended upon a combination of two conceptions: the negro was treated as a child who must be thumped into obedience; at the same time he was looked upon as an adult, capable of understanding responsibility and of wilfully defying his master. No cold-blooded reason could fairly apportion punishment under such contradictions. If a task was set, not to complete it must be, according to the temper of the overseer, either a child's shirking or a man's insubordination; if a negro was reproved, his explanation might be only a silly subterfuge or a desperate defiance; an attempt to run away, in order to avoid a thrashing, was either a piece of boyish folly or a wilful aggravation of the original offence; and to put out the hand to ward off a blow might be an involuntary act or the unpardonable sin of resistance to a white man.[1]

The most common instrument of punishment was the cowhide or the black - snake whip of leather, which could be used freely in the fields; but the cowskin, if used with determination, was likely to cut into the skin and leave indelible scars; hence there were advocates of the rival strap or paddle. For a thoroughgoing whipping, the slave was usually triced up, often hung by the thumbs, with his or her toes just touching the ground, or made help-

[1] Douglass, *Narrative*, 78; Kemble, *Georgian Plantation*, 289; Olmsted, *Seaboard Slave States*, 438, 484; Olmsted, *Back Country*, 82.

less by a stick tied under the knees, or he was "staked out." [1] "A mere whipping" or "a good thrashing" or "a dose" were euphemisms for the torture of the lash. Yet flogging was in this period the normal punishment in the navy and merchant marine, had barely disappeared from the army, was still legal towards apprentices, and in some communities towards wives, and was a common punishment throughout the south for the less serious crimes of whites. To most slaves the sight of the lash was too familiar to make it a disgrace. If slavery was allowed at all, perhaps whipping was as mild a means of enforcing it as could be devised.

To whip big, lusty men, whose hides had been tanned by a dozen floggings, was one thing; but people brought up with a sense of the dignity of the human body thought frightful "the brutal inhumanity of allowing a man to strip and lash a woman, the mother of ten children, to exact from her toil which was to maintain in luxury two idle young men, the owners of the plantation." [2] Somehow the sight of a girl found skulking in a ditch, upon whom the overseer most indecently bestowed fifty or sixty blows, "well laid on as a boatswain would thrash a skulking sailor or as some people break a balking horse," turned the stomach of Olmsted; and we can hear her, as he did, writhing, grovelling, and screaming—"Oh, don't, sir! oh, please stop, master! please

[1] Pickard, *Kidnapped and Ransomed*, 35, 39.
[2] Kemble, *Georgian Plantation*, 125.

sir! please, sir! oh, that's enough, master! oh Lord! oh master, master! oh, God, master, do stop! oh God, master! oh God, master!" [1]

Even such brutal floggings belong to the milder side of slave discipline. For crimes committed either by free negroes or by slaves there was the machinery of the law. The general impression was that the free negroes, though guilty of many small offences, seldom committed serious crimes; [2] and they were tried by the usual tribunals even in such serious matters as insurrection. Slaves guilty of assaults and murders also usually went to the regular courts. The master was always interested in defending his own slave from an unjust accusation or unlicensed punishment, and it does not appear that courts were unduly prejudiced against the slave; but the universal rule that no testimony of negroes, slaves or free, could be received against a white man made justice difficult in cases involving both whites and negroes.

A great number of crimes not capital when committed by whites were punishable by death if committed by a slave, including arson, rape, conspiracy to rebel, striking a master or any member of the master's family, resisting legal arrest or punishment, and burglary. [3] The difficulty was that an execution destroyed a valuable piece of property,

[1] Olmsted, *Back Country*, 83–88.
[2] Adams, *Southside View*, 41.
[3] Stroud, *Slave Laws*, 170–184.

for which the master of the slave must be paid by government; and in many cases the real penalty was that the negro was sold into some other county or state. As late as 1808 slaves were burned alive by order of a court in Charleston; and for supposed complicity in setting a fire in Augusta, in 1830, a slave woman was executed and quartered.[1]

In several states summary tribunals were provided by law to take cognizance of slave offences. For example, in South Carolina there was a justice and freeholders court of three members, which was judge, prosecuting attorney, and jury in one. Such courts, in South Carolina, could even inflict the punishment of death, and in 1832 "sentenced and caused the execution of thirty-five slaves on a charge of insurrection."[2] That the system was not satisfactory was shown by a protest of the governor of South Carolina, in 1853, who held up the decision of such courts as "rarely in conformity with justice and humanity."[3]

Beyond these regular and special courts was a system of dealing with both slaves and free negroes by lynch law, commonly for murder of whites or for violent crimes against white women; for such crimes were considered a kind of rebellion of the inferior race against the superior, the serpent biting the heel; among thirty recorded cases of the burning

[1] Stuart, *North America*, II., 82; Olmsted, *Seaboard Slave States*, 499.   [2] Jay, *Miscellaneous Writings*, 133.
[3] Olmsted, *Seaboard Slave States*, 499.

of a negro by a mob, between 1825 and 1860, the most conspicuous was that of McIntosh in 1835: a mulatto, who, for killing an officer of the law who was trying to arrest him, was taken out of jail by a mob in St. Louis, tied to a tree and burned to death. Judge Lawless, the county magistrate, charged the grand jury that if this lynching "was the act . . . of the many—of the multitude, in the ordinary sense of these words, . . . of congregated thousands, seized upon and impelled by . . . frenzy, . . . then I say, act not at all in the matter; the case then transcends your jurisdiction—it is beyond the reach of human law." [1]

As the years went by, the number of such lynchings increased, although in the decade between 1850 and 1860, of forty - six recorded negro murders of owners or overseers, twenty were legally executed and twenty-six were lynched, of whom nine were burned at the stake; for rape, five negroes were legally executed and twelve were lynched, of whom four were burned, although many other cases of rape received a lighter punishment. [2]

Another series of legal offences could be committed by white people with reference to slaves. Consorting with negroes, free or slave, was a serious offence strictly prohibited; trading with slaves was also forbidden, for a constant complaint of planters

[1] Lovejoys, *Lovejoy*, 168–178; Cutler, *Lynch Law*, 108; criticised in Lincoln, *Works*, I., 10.

[2] Cutler, *Lynch Law*, 126 – 128; data prepared for the author by G. T. Stephenson, of Pendleton, North Carolina.

was that their supplies and crops disappeared and were turned into luxuries or whiskey by exchange with low-down white men in the neighborhood.[1] Another crime was the heinous one of slave-stealing, akin in malevolence to horse-stealing on the frontier. Inasmuch as the slave could tell where he came from, it was hard to carry it out successfully without the collusion of the negroes, who were sometimes persuaded to run away by a promise to take them to Canada, and sometimes entered into a conspiracy by which they were sold, ran away, and returned to the confederate, who sold them again.[2] Helping a slave to escape was also slave-stealing, as the few abolitionists found who were detected in the act.[3]

One offence totally unknown to the law of the northern states, was the teaching of negroes, and especially of slaves, to read; in North Carolina it was a misdemeanor to sell or give a slave any book or pamphlet. That the laws were no dead-letter was shown when Mrs. Anne Douglass, a South Carolina woman living in Norfolk, Virginia, set up a little school for teaching colored children. In 1853 she was arrested, convicted, and imprisoned for thirty days for breaking a law, of the existence of which she had no knowledge.[4]

Wherever there was as many as twenty slaves it

---

[1] Olmsted, *Seaboard Slave States*, 349, 634.
[2] Marryat, *Diary in America* (Am. ed.), 127; 2d series, 89–92.
[3] See chap. xx., below.
[4] Chambers, *Am. Slavery and Colour*, 190; Massie, *America*, 88.

was common to employ an overseer, and on large plantations there must, under the law, be several white men. Many of the cruelties and excesses of slavery came from this almost universal system of delegating authority, even when the master was on the plantation. The calling of the overseer was disreputable, and was almost never sought by members of the large slave-holding families; hence the immediate care of the slaves fell upon members of the poor white class, rough, uneducated, and brutal. The main purpose of the overseer was to "make his crop," and where the land-owner was absent the whole or the greater part of the year, his judgment of the overseer depended upon the surplus available for his own support. The overseer was paid an annual salary, up to about one thousand dollars a year, and sometimes had a share of the profits. He had little or nothing to do with the household slaves, but otherwise occupied the combined responsibility of a farm manager, the warden of a jail, and the elder brother in a rude and tumultuous family.

To get good overseers was hard. A man on a plantation described them as "passionate, careless, inhuman, generally intemperate, and totally unfit for the duties of the position." [1] He was in general opposed to improvement in the processes of agriculture; his system of management was severe, and his moral influence upon the negroes unwholesome.

[1] Olmsted, *Back Country*, 44, 51–64; Olmsted, *Seaboard Slave States*, 485–487; Chesnutt, *Conjure Woman*.

He set few of those examples of refinement and
Christianity which the house servants often enjoyed,
and was a standing refutation of the theory that
slavery tended to raise the negro through his contact with superior white people.

On a few plantations there was a negro foreman,
who was practically the manager of the estate.[1]
Such men must be carefully distinguished from the
so-called "slave-drivers," who were simply gang-
bosses relieved from physical labor, armed with a
whip, and set among the slaves to see that their
tasks were performed.[2] The drivers had to justify
their being by urging their fellows to work, and were
liked by neither side.

How far slavery, as a system, was inhuman and
barbarous is difficult to decide. Charges of cruelty
were fiercely pressed by the abolitionists, who threw
out a drag-net for every case that came to their
knowledge; and they proved beyond question that
there were many awful instances of barbarity which
public opinion did not check. Take the case of
Madame Lalaurie, of New Orleans, in 1834, who
forced a little slave girl with a whip to the roof of
her house, where, in despair and terror, the child
fell off and was killed; and chained her cook to the
wall, till the woman, in utter despair, set fire to the

---

[1] Pickard, *Kidnapped and Ransomed*, 155; Olmsted, *Seaboard
Slave States*, 426.

[2] Olmsted, *Seaboard Slave States*, 205–208, 436–438; Olmsted,
Back Country, 48.

house, and the fire-company discovered the miserable story. The woman had to flee for her life from the city, to which she never returned, but she had for years been known to be a cruel mistress.[1]

On the other hand, the defenders of slavery pointed out that the slaves were protected by the master's self - interest; "who but a drivelling fanatic," asks one, "has thought of the necessity of protecting domestic animals from the cruelty of their owners?"; and another pointed to the unpopularity of the harsh and brutal slave-owner. Nevertheless, people perfectly well known to be habitually cruel to their slaves were not excluded from good society.[2] What the abolitionists complained of was not cruelty in itself, but a system in which cruelty was held to be an indispensable element.

The worst excesses came from that disregard of a man's interest in his own property which is roused in any owner of a balky horse and which was immensely aggravated by the fact that the negro could speak, reason, and remember. Those travellers most disposed to see the bright side of slavery record instances of masters who killed their own slaves or who lost them by abuse and neglect.[3]

[1] Cable, *Strange True Stories of La.*, 200–219; Bremer, *Homes of the New World*, II., 244.

[2] Harper and Simms, in *Pro-Slavery Argument*, 31, 228; cf. Smedes, *Memorials of a Southern Planter*, 105; Bremer, *Homes of the New World*, II., 511.

[3] Hodgson, *Letters*, 186–189; Burke, *Reminiscences*, 169–174; Olmsted, *Seaboard Slave States*, 569–571.

They also saw cases where white men were prosecuted for the murder or ill-usage of their own slaves or of other negroes,[1] but such checks acted slowly and irregularly.

The control of the slaves by any severity necessary to preserve slavery was deeply inwrought into the whole fabric of southern law and society. Its worst features began in colonial times, when like harsh and brutal treatment was accorded to white servants and to negro slaves. The ferocious legal punishments of slaves were not unlike those of the English common law. White convicts were habitually governed by the lash as the slaves were To the minds of the southern people, therefore, slavery did not present a case of a deliberate building-up of a cruel régime; it was rather a continuance of a state of things not exactly comfortable, but without which slavery could not exist; barbarities, fierce and sanguinary punishments, lynchings, did not seem abnormal to the slave-holders; and if slavery itself was allowable in a Christian and enlightened community, any method necessary to keep it up was justified. The indictment of slavery was that it was a deliberate refusal to go along with the rest of the world in the enjoyment of a more humane spirit than that of the eighteenth century.

[1] Adams, *Southside View*, 37–40; Child, *Oasis*, 242–250.

CHAPTER IX

THE SLAVE-MARKET

(1830–1860)

WITH very small exceptions the negro slave was absolutely subject to sale at such times, to such persons, and on such terms as pleased his master. The ownership was as absolute as that of a horse or a watch. Although prosperous masters commonly did not sell slaves, the threat of being "sent down the river" for bad conduct was often realized; and able-bodied slaves who began to lose their vigor and vitality were sometimes sold because no longer profitable as work-hands; or at the death of a master, especially if the estate went to several heirs, among whom the proceeds had to be divided. There was always an undercurrent of feeling that to part with one's slaves was ignoble; hence the most frequent reason for selling was simply that the master was obliged to realize, either to pay for something that he wanted to buy, or because he was in debt.

Was it true, as charged by the abolitionists, that slaves were bred in the border states for no other purpose than to sell them? Probably the truth was expressed by the Mississippian who said: "A man might not raise a nigger with a well-considered plan to sell him eighteen years after he was born; he might never sell a nigger, but for all that, it was the readiness with which he could command a thousand dollars for every likely boy he had, if he should ever need it, that made him stay here and be bothered with taking care of a gang of niggers who barely earned enough to enable his family to live decently." [1]   The fact that some thousands of negroes every year left the border states for the south seemed to show that there was a profit in keeping them alive; but recent investigations seem to establish that the greater number of these negroes were taken in a body by the men who owned them to settle in other states, and there was no undue proportion of young negroes in the border states such as would have been evident if there had been a definite system of selling the adults. [2]

In many cases slaves passed simply from vendor to purchaser like fancy stock, but the usual way was to attract buyers by advertisements. Within two weeks there appeared in the columns of sixty-four southern newspapers advertisements for the sale of forty - one hundred negroes, besides thirty lots to be sold at auction, as, for example: "PRIVATE

[1] Olmsted, *Back Country*, 284.
[2] Collins, *Domestic Slave-Trade*, 38, 61; Olmsted, *Seaboard Slave States*, 55–59, 278–283; Rhodes, *United States*, I., 317; Saxe-Weimar, *Travels*, II., 63; Smedes, *Memorials of a Southern Planter*, 47–54.

SALES. Excellent Cook. Will be sold at private sale, a Woman, about 22 years of age, an excellent cook, (meat and pastry) Plain Washer, etc. She is sound and healthy and can make herself generally useful." [1]

The greater part of the traffic was in the hands of dealers and auctioneers, who acted as middlemen. The common method was for a firm to have a buying-house, with headquarters in the border states, as at Washington or Norfolk; they rode through the country with cash in their pockets, as cattle-buyers rode farther north, and picked up likely negroes wherever they could; the slaves were then brought together in barracoons, or private slave jails, and there kept until a sufficient number had accumulated for a sale or shipment. The slave-traders had no social reward for this useful service; a traveller in a steamer noticed "that the planters on board . . . shunned all intercourse with this dealer, as if they regarded his business as scarcely respectable." [2]

However despised, the business was profitable. The private sales involved no public exhibition of the merchandise, and in many cases showed some regard to the preference of the slaves. The public sales brought out the worst side of the whole system. The north was shocked by such grouping of human and brute merchandise as: "SHERIFF'S SALE. I will

---

[1] *Key to Uncle Tom's Cabin*, 142; *Charleston Mercury*, July 6, 1857.

[2] Lyell, *Second Visit*, I., 232; cf. Adams, *Southside View*, 77.

sell at Fairfield Court House, 2 Negroes, 2 Horses and 1 Jennet, 1 pair of Cart Wheels, 1 Bedstead, 1 Riding Saddle. Sheriff's Office, Nov. 19, 1852."[1] Nowhere was the repulsiveness of slavery so apparent as in the slave auction-rooms maintained in most southern cities. One spectator saw a woman put upon the block, obviously very ill, who owned to a bad cough and pain in her side, to which the auctioneer replied: "Never mind what she says, gentlemen, I told you she was a shammer. Her health is good enough. Damn her humbug. Give her a touch or two of the cow-hide, and I'll warrant she will do your work. Speak, gentlemen, before I knock her down."[2] Another was shocked at the free - and - easy treatment of women: "There were some very pretty light mulattoes. A gentleman took one of the prettiest of them by the chin, and opened her mouth to see the state of her gums and teeth, with no more ceremony than if she had been a horse."[3] Another was struck by the offer of "a woman still young, and three children, all for $850." Another was startled to see a negro baby sold on the block without its mother, but was preternaturally reassured when told by a slave-holding friend that "nothing of the kind ever took place before to our knowledge."[4]

[1] *Key to Uncle Tom's Cabin*, 134.
[2] Hamilton, *Men and Manners in America*, 317.
[3] Bremer, *Homes of the New World*, II., 204.
[4] Chambers, *Things as they Are in America*, 280; Adams, *Southside View*, 68.

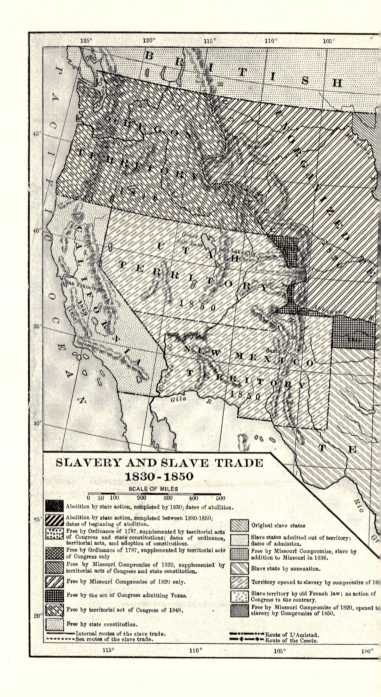

SLAVERY AND SLAVE TRADE
1830-1850

SCALE OF MILES

0   50 100   200   300   400   500

Abolition by state action, completed by 1830; dates of abolition.

Abolition by state action, completed between 1830-1850; dates of beginning of abolition.

Free by Ordinance of 1787, supplemented by territorial acts of Congress and state constitutions; dates of ordinance, territorial acts, and adoption of constitutions.

Free by Ordinance of 1787, supplemented by territorial acts of Congress only.

Free by Missouri Compromise of 1820, supplemented by territorial acts of Congress and state constitution.

Free by Missouri Compromise of 1820 only.

Free by the act of Congress admitting Texas.

Free by territorial act of Congress of 1848.

Free by state constitution.

Internal routes of the slave trade.
Sea routes of the slave trade.

Original slave states

Slave states admitted out of territory; dates of admission.

Free by Missouri Compromise, slave by addition to Missouri in 1836.

Slave state by annexation.

Territory opened to slavery by compromise of 18

Slave territory by old French law; no action of Congress to the contrary.

Free by Missouri Compromise of 1820, opened to slavery by Compromise of 1850.

Route of L'Amistad.
Route of the Creole.

The hateful thing about both public and private sales was the transfer from a kind and indulgent to an unknown and perhaps cruel master. A slave might be, and sometimes was, transferred for a gambling debt, or from mere caprice; or one might see a negro leading a little group of his fellows tied with a rope; or very light and handsome girls were sold to supply the worst of businesses.[1] There were cases of the sale of slave preachers, and a story is current that one such was bought by his own congregation.[2]

Where an estate of slaves was divided among humane people, the slaves were separated into lots equivalent in value to the shares of the various heirs.[3] In other cases, branches of the family that had the money bought in as many as possible of the negroes to prevent separation; but the annals of the time contain thousands of instances of the heartless breaking-up of families. "Sixteen children I've had, first and last," said Charity Bowery; ". . . from the time my first baby was born, I always set my heart upon buying freedom for some of my children, . . . but Mistress Kinnon wouldn't let me have my children. One after another—one after another—she sold 'em away from me. Oh, how *many* times

[1] Thompson, *Prison Life*, 352; Kemble, *Georgian Plantation*, 259; Olmsted, *Seaboard Slave States*, 30; Bremer, *Homes of the New World*, I., 373.

[2] Related to the author by Mr. C. S. McGehee, of Atlanta; cf. Olmsted, *Seaboard Slave States*, 567.

[3] Pickard, *Kidnapped and Ransomed*, 200.

that woman's broke my heart!" [1]   It was no sufficient answer to point out that slave families were
not the only ones broken up, and that such accidents must not be remembered against ten thousand
acts of kindness. [2]   Still more contrary to the ordinary instincts of humanity was the occasional sale
of a master's children. [3]   Some masters abandoned
them without a thought; but whatever efforts a
humane father might make to secure his own offspring from the abyss, those very persons might be
singled out for the animosity of other children of a
more honorable origin.   The breaking-up of families
was a denial of the principle upon which the community of white persons was founded, and it was
practically an acknowledgment that the slave parent had no right even to his own flesh and blood.
Slave-holders and ex-slave-holders have condemned
the practice as an unpardonable mistake. [4]

The price of slaves varied from locality to locality
and from decade to decade.   In 1798, just after
cotton became profitable, $200 was a good price for
a field-hand. [5]   In 1822 the average value, as they
ran, was supposed to be about $300.   In 1830, $600
was a good price.   In 1840, prime cotton hands were
worth $1000 or more; and in 1859, at Savannah,

[1] Hart, *Source Book*, 256; other examples in Stuart, *North
America*, II., 56; Thompson, *Prison Life*, 367; Burke, *Reminiscences*, 160–162; Botume, *First Days among Contrabands*, 164.

[2] Adams, *Southside View*, 79, 80.

[3] Buckingham, *Slave States*, I., 248; II., 213.

[4] Wise, *End of an Era*, 87.   [5] Kettell, *Southern Wealth*, 130.

prime women sold at $1100 to $1200; men as high
as $1300. An eye-witness records the sale of two
negro girls, one with a child in her arms, for $3565.[1]

No such figures could possibly have been obtained
in the border slave states had it not been for the
opportunity of selling to other communities; and
there was a brisk movement of slaves from north to
south. This lively interstate trade bristled with
points for the anti-slavery agitators. The traffic was
under a sort of ban, especially as the external slave-
trade was generally thought unnatural. Though
the carrying of slaves by sea from the ports of
Maryland and Virginia to South Atlantic and Gulf
ports involved no shocking cruelties, the preliminary
collection of slaves and their lodgment in the barracoons profoundly affected northern sentiment. In
the year 1829, 452 slaves were deposited in the federal prison in Washington, to keep there safe until
they could be shipped; and in 1834 a thousand slaves
were being shipped from Washington every year.
This demand for slaves to be sold south was a set-
back for the colonization scheme, since in the border states the money value of slaves was too high
to make manumission popular.[2]

The overland trade aroused much unfavorable
comment: coffles of slaves were not infrequently
seen crossing the country from northeast to southwest, "the men chained together in pairs, and the

---

[1] Chambers, *Am. Slavery and Colour*, 207.
[2] Dew, in *Pro-Slavery Argument*, 359–362.

women carrying the children in bundles, in their march to the South."[1] Others travelled by steamers on the rivers, especially the Ohio, Tennessee, and Mississippi. Louisiana and Mississippi were among the best markets for slaves in this period, and were also on the road to Texas, where many slaves were carried after 1845.

On general principles the federal government had power to regulate the interstate slave - trade, like any other interstate commerce; but such action was violently opposed by the south. The only legal restrictions, therefore, were found in state acts prohibiting importation of slaves for a short term of years, or the importation of slaves of bad character, or convicts. Just how many slaves were transferred from one state to another by this process is hard to estimate; the negroes in Mississippi increased from 32,814 in 1820 to 146,820 in 1840, the greater part of whom must have come from outside. The 300,000 negroes who were in Virginia in 1790 must have had almost a million and a half descendants in 1850, of whom only 470,000 were left in Virginia. In the decade from 1850 to 1860 something like 200,000 left the border states for the lower south.[2]

Closely akin to purchase and sale was the hiring-out of slaves, which was a transfer of their services

---

[1] Buckingham, *Slave States*, II., 553; cf. Featherstonhaugh, *Excursion*, 46; Sutcliffe, *Travels* (ed. of 1807), II., 187; Olmsted, *Texas Journey*, 88; Lincoln, *Works*, I., 52.

[2] Collins, *Domestic Slave-Trade*, 66.

for a limited time.   Some small slave-owners made
it a business to hire out all their slaves, both men
and women, at rates varying from one hundred to
two hundred dollars a year and board, according
to the kind of work and skill of the slave.   Occasionally contractors and corporations advertised for
slaves to be hired out to them.   It seems, on the
whole, to have been a milder form of servitude.
Slaves hiring their own time found the conditions
different; for their object was always to earn something more than the sum agreed upon with the
master, and this was a confession that no pressure
could secure from the slave all the labor that he was
capable of.[1]

A frequent purpose of a slave's hiring out his own
time was to accumulate enough to buy his freedom;
and good-natured masters often put a moderate
price upon their chattel for this purpose, or gave to
the negro opportunities of extra earnings, in sympathy with his aim.   To buy one's self was a task
sometimes lasting eight or ten years.[2]   It was subject to such accidents as the death or forgetfulness
of the owner; and a case is recorded where a slave
three times saved money enough for his own freedom, and each time was sold regardless of the agreement.[3]   As soon as a man was free, he was likely to

[1] Buckingham, *Slave States*, I., 136; Pickard, *Kidnapped and
Ransomed*, 209; Hodgson, *Letters from North America*, I., 111;
Olmsted, *Seaboard Slave States*, 103; Smedes, *Memorials of a
Southern Planter*, 104.   [2] Thompson, *Prison Life*, 333.
    [3] Pickard, *Kidnapped and Ransomed*, 47; Goodell, *Slave Code*, 247.

buy his wife and children; and cases are on record where a whole family was thus acquired by the labor and saving of the head.[1]

In anti-slavery days a favorite charity was for the friends of a fugitive slave to furnish money for his purchase, though some abolitionists had conscientious scruples at purchasing a slave to set him free.[2]   Peter Still, a kidnapped freeman who escaped from slavery, actually raised five thousand dollars for the purchase of his wife and three children by going from town to town telling the story of his experience in slavery.[3]

Most slaves who became free did so by manumission at the hands of their masters, and were the progenitors of the later free negroes. The process of manumission was always restricted; usually the owner must give a preliminary bond to protect the community against the future support of the slave, and manumission must follow legal forms; in more than one - half of the slave - holding states emancipated slaves must remove from the state. No master could relieve himself from debt or contract obligations by freeing slaves, who might be then subject to attachment by his creditors.[4]

In spite of these restrictions, manumissions took

[1] Bremer, *Homes of the New World*, I., 363; Thompson, *Prison Life*, 275; Child, *Life of Isaac T. Hopper*, 176-179.
[2] Garrisons, *Garrison*, III., 210; cf. Olmsted, *Seaboard Slave States*, 15.
[3] Pickard, *Kidnapped and Ransomed*, 313-319, 336.
[4] Hurd, *Law of Freedom and Bondage*, chaps. xvii.-xix.

place in all the slave states, and were frequent in some. The censuses of 1850 and 1860 attempted to collect statistics on this subject, and the certainly incomplete figures show that in 1850 1467 slaves were manumitted, being one to every 2181 slaves; in 1860, 3018 were manumitted, or one out of every 1309. In a few cases negroes were set free by the states in which they lived, as a reward for public services.[1] Slaves were occasionally set free by masters for some special service or in fulfilment of a promise; and one of the most touching incidents in the history of slavery is that of the slave-trading speculator who bought Charity Bowery, and then said to her: "You've been very good to me and fixed me up many a nice little mess when I've been poorly; and now you shall have your freedom for it and I'll give you your youngest child." [2]   In all cases it was common to make an attested statement of the circumstances, a copy of which was retained by the freeman as his "free papers," a precious possession which, unfortunately, could not always protect him. Among the slave-holders who set free all their slaves in their lifetime was John Jay.[3] Among those who occasionally rewarded deserving cases was Henry Clay.

A more common method of manumission was by will, for among the slave-holders many distinguished and high-minded men, for various reasons, could not

[1] Livermore, *Historical Research*, 195–197.
[2] Hart, *Source Book*, 257.   [3] Roberts, *New York*, II., 483.

bring themselves to set their slaves free in their own
lifetime, but at their death set free the whole body;
this number included George Washington,[1] Thomas
Jefferson, Chancellor Wythe, and Horatio Gates.
John Randolph in his will said: "I give and be-
queath to all my slaves their freedom, heartily
regretting that I have ever been the owner of one";[2]
This will was finally confirmed, and three hundred
persons were thus set free and colonized in Ohio.[3]
Another very interesting case was that of John
McDonogh, a citizen of New Orleans, who left a
large fortune for educational purposes, and, during
his life, made elaborate provisions for the training
of his slaves, so that they could take care of themselves, and for their transportation to Liberia.[4]

It was a prevailing belief in the south that most
negroes preferred slavery to freedom;[5] the real
sentiments of the blacks were not easy to reach upon
this subject, though a few indications are afforded
by slaves who became confidential with visitors.
"Why, you see, master," said one of them, ". . . if
I was free, I'd have all my time to myself, . . . I
would not get poor, I would get rich; for you see,
master, then I'd work all de time for myself."[6]   As
another slave said: "In the time of the war [of 1812]

---

[1] Washington, *Writings* (Sparks's ed.), I., 569.
[2] Garland, *Randolph*, II., 150.
[3] *Life of Benjamin Lundy*, 273.
[4] Allan, *John McDonogh*, 44–52, 75.
[5] Smedes, *Memorials of a Southern Planter*, 175.
[6] Olmsted, *Seaboard Slave States*, 683.

all were for liberty. Every ball that was shot was for liberty; and I am for liberty too." [1] Some of Randolph's slaves returned to Virginia and asked to be restored to slavery, perhaps on the principle of the Georgia slave who, when asked if he would like to be free, replied: "Free, missis! what for me wish to be free? Oh no, missis, me no wish to be free, if massa only let we keep pig." [2]

Undoubtedly there were cases of negroes who preferred shelter and support to responsibility; but the whole trend and tenor of the slave codes rested upon the well-grounded belief that the normal frame of mind of the negro was a desire for freedom; and this belief is supported by the countless instances of fugitives who had no better reason to give for running away than that obstinate desire to be free which the white people counted among their chief claims to the admiration of mankind.

[1] Thompson, *Prison Life*, 297.
[2] Kemble, *Georgian Plantation*, 48.

CHAPTER X

THE DEFENCE OF SLAVERY

(1830–1860)

FROM the foregoing description of slavery it is plain that generalizations are difficult: in some places and under some masters it was cruel and debasing; in other communities and under different personalities it was a patriarchal system, in which master and slave felt themselves members of one family. There was an opportunity for the south itself to discriminate by making the milder slavery the legally approved and almost universal type. Down to 1830 such a spirit was abroad in the south;[1] churches, the missionary societies, and individuals urged moderate treatment. Then a different spirit manifested itself: the denunciation of slavery slacked; the efforts at amelioration hesitated, and eventually ceased: the former excuses and pleas for slavery changed to justification, then to positive praise of slavery, then to a state of mind in which the admission that any part of its "Peculiar Institu-

[1] See chap. xi., below.

tion " ought to be reformed was regarded as disloyal to the south.[1]

The defenders of slavery were many, and made up for their lack of literary prestige by the liveliness of their feeling. Some foreign visitors, especially Sir Charles Lyell, condoned slavery; and some northern ministers were enthusiastic champions, especially the Reverend Nehemiah Adams, of Boston, on the basis of a brief visit to Savannah. Within the south the cudgels were taken up for slavery by leaders of every kind. ' The southern clergymen almost without exception defended the system. There was hardly a college president or professor who would not enter the lists in behalf of slavery, and Chancellor Harper, of the College of South Carolina, was one of a group of contributors, including Simms, the literary man, Dew, a college professor, and Hammond, a public man, who joined in a semi - official defence of slavery entitled *The Pro - Slavery Argument*. State governors, like Mc-Duffie, of South Carolina, joined in the conflict, and legislatures adopted long, defensive reports.

In the discussion the south had a technical advantage in that not a single southern public man of large reputation and influence failed to stand by slavery; while from the northern ranks some, like Webster, stifled their natural objections; others, like Cass, "Northern men with Southern principles,"

[1] Examples of defence of slavery, in Hart, *Contemporaries*, IV., §§ 25–27.

ranged themselves alongside their southern brothers in an open defence of slavery.

The first argument in favor of slavery was that it was an institution traceable to the very roots and origins of society, "a principal cause of civilization. Perhaps . . . the sole cause." Aristotle recognized and approved slavery; the Romans had slavery, and it was the cause of their prosperity.[1] The Jews had slavery under a system closely resembling that of the south. Hagar was a slave, "and the angel of the Lord said unto her, Return to thy mistress, and submit thyself under her hands." Against the objection that the mediæval Catholic church was resolute against slavery was set the authority of some of the church fathers.[3] Had not England admitted villeinage? Did not the philosopher Locke permit slavery in his model Constitution for the Carolinas?[4] That Greece and Rome had perished in spite of their system of slavery; that England had for centuries disavowed both chattel and villein servitude; that by 1830 all Europe, except Russia, had rid itself of serfdom, took away the force of this argument of precedent, which is put forth chiefly by learned and casuistical writers.

[1] Harper, in *Pro-Slavery Argument*, 3, 69–72.

[2] *Genesis*, xvi., 9; *Exodus*, xxi., 20, 21; Hopkins, *View of Slavery*, 74–98; Bledsoe, *Liberty and Slavery*, chap. iii.

[3] Hopkins, *View of Slavery*, 99–119, 269–275.

[4] *Ibid.*, 262–264, 276–283; Dew, in *Pro-Slavery Argument*, 312–316.

The argument of the authority of the Scriptures was living, vital, and very effectual; for the Reformation habit of referring all cases of moral conduct to the Bible was almost universal in the United States. The advocates and the opponents of total abstinence, of woman's rights, of imprisonment for debt, of instrumental music in churches, of theatres, dipped into that great sea and fished out "proof-texts" which were triumphantly held to be conclusive. It was undeniable that both the Old and the New Testament mentioned, legislated on, and did not expressly condemn slavery; that though the word "slave" appears in but two places in the King James version, the word "servant" frequently refers to slaves. The Tenth Commandment forbids the coveting of "his man-servant, nor his maid-servant." The Jews were allowed to buy "bondmen and bondmaids. Moreover, of the children of the strangers that do sojourn among you, of them shall ye buy." "If his master have given him a wife, and she have borne him sons or daughters; the wife and her children shall be her master's" "If a man smite his servant, or his maid, with a rod, and he die under his hand; he shall be surely punished. Notwithstanding, if he continue a day or two, he shall not be punished: for he is his money." In these and some similar passages were found Scriptural sanction for the purchase, sale, and extreme punishment of slaves, and even for

¹ *Exodus*, xx., 17, xxi., 4, 20, 21; *Leviticus*, xxv., 44, 45.

the separation of families, in the United States of America.[1]

Another Scriptural argument, a thousand times repeated, goes back to the unseemly behavior of Ham, youngest son of Noah and father of Canaan; when the old patriarch "drank of the wine, and was drunken." And he said, "Cursed be Canaan; a servant of servants shall he be unto his brethren. And he said, Blessed be the Lord God of Shem; and Canaan shall be his servant."[2] If Shem was the ancestor of the Anglo-Saxons, if Canaan was the ancestor of the Africans, was it not a Q. E. D. that African slavery was not only allowed, but divinely ordained and commanded? In a generation ignorant of any theory of the Aryan race, and still little troubled by the damnation of unregenerate infants, such a curse upon unborn generations for a technical fault of a remote ancestor seemed not unreasonable

The New Testament also contained passages highly encouraging to the slave-holders, such as, "Let every man abide in the same calling wherein he was called." Servants, be obedient to them that are your masters according to the flesh, with fear and trembling, in singleness of your heart, as unto Christ." "Let as many servants as are under the yoke count their own masters worthy of all honor." And most comfortable of all was St. Paul's appeal

---

[1] Brief summaries of these arguments in Hopkins, *View of Slavery*, 7–18; Hammond, in *Pro-Slavery Argument*, 105–108, 155–159.   [2] *Genesis*, ix., 18–26.

to Philemon to receive Onesimus (asserted to be a fugitive slave), who had "departed for a season, . . . not now as a servant, but above a servant, a brother beloved, specially to me." [1]

That both Old and New Testaments recognized the existence of slavery when they were written, and nowhere instituted direct commands against it, was absolutely irrefutable; but the anti-slavery people quoted Scripture against Scripture. They argued that the references to slavery in the Old Testament were precisely like those to polygamy; and if slavery was justified because of Hagar's children, concubinage was equally justified. There were also passages in the Old Testament bidding the master to set his bondsman free after seven years, and against man-stealing. Were not the Jews themselves, after four hundred years of slavery in Egypt, conducted into freedom by a divinely appointed leader? As for Onesimus, Paul speaks of him as a "brother" and a "beloved brother"—not a useful comparison for a slave-owner.

The most telling counter-argument was always the general spirit of Christ and the apostles. How could slavery be made to fit with the injunction, "Go ye into all the world, and preach the gospel to every creature"; with the appeal to "be kindly affectioned one to another with brotherly love; in honor preferring one another." [2] If Abraham was a

---

[1] 1 *Corinthians*, vii., 20; *Ephesians*, vi., 5; 1 *Timothy*, vi., 1; *Philemon*, 10-16.   [2] *Mark*, xvi., 15; *Romans*, xii., 10.

slave-holder, Christ was not; and His message was
to the poorest and lowliest of His time. The very
fact that the Christian people of the south in general
admitted that the slaves had souls to be saved or
lost, that they were admitted to baptism, to church
membership, even in the white churches, made it
difficult to set the negro apart as subject to the
curses and the admonitions of the Bible, but not
entitled to its promises, its comforts, or its principles of equality in the sight of God, that "no re-
specter of persons."

Another group of arguments was based upon the
character of the negro, and led to inconsistencies
not easy to reconcile. "By what right is it," asked
Chancellor Harper, "that man exercises dominion
over the beasts of the field? . . . The savage can
only be tamed by being enslaved or by having
slaves"; and he proceeds to demonstrate that the
African negro is, at best, an inferior variety of the
human race.[1] This inferiority was at great length
argued on physical grounds: the negro brain is
lighter in proportion to his weight; his skin has an
extra quantity of pigment; he has a long head,
unusual proportions, woolly hair; his features are
brutal; his vocal organs incapable of pronouncing
white folks' language; he has an animal odor—such
are the arguments repeated by writer after writer.[2]

The negro's intellectual inferiority was equally

[1] Harper, in *Pro-Slavery Argument*, 13–16.
[2] Van Evrie, *Negroes and Negro Slavery*, passim.

set up against him, though few southern writers
went to the extent of saying "none has given evidence of an approach to even mediocrity of intellectual excellence."[1]   That ignorant slaves were
inferior to educated masters was self-evident; the
materials were not at hand for so complete a judgment as to whether they were in all cases inferior
to ignorant white people; and it was difficult to
maintain that no person having negro blood was
capable of intellectual effort.   The difficulty with
the argument of mental inferiority, as also with
most of the Scriptural arguments, was that they
applied equally to inferior white races or to inferior
members of the Anglo-Saxon race.

The literature of the subject is full of descriptions
of the favorable effect of slavery upon the negro:
slavery brought him out of savagery into the
elevating influences of civilization, from heathen-
dom into the light of salvation; it gave him care
and medical advice in illness, and saved him from
the mysterious diseases of the jungle.[2]   The negroes
"are undergoing the very best education which it is
possible to give. . . . They are in the course of being
taught habits of regular and patient industry";[3]
slavery brought him into intimate personal relations with the white people, and even into warm
friendships and affections with the master's family.

[1] Harper, in *Pro-Slavery Argument*, 56–60.
[2] Pollard, *Black Diamonds*, 81–84.
[3] Harper, in *Pro-Slavery Argument*, 95.

"When I was a boy," says Pollard, "I esteemed Tom to be the best friend I had in the world. . . . I had a great boyish fondness for him, gave him coppers, stole biscuits for him from the table, bought him a primer and taught him to read." [1]

On good plantations there was indeed little suffering and much enjoyment. The owner was often a patriarch whose counsel and sympathy were freely sought by the slaves, to settle their disputes and to reconcile quarrels. To see the master come back was one of the great pleasures in distant and neglected plantations. [2] The slaves were free from the responsibility of choosing their career or insuring their own support. They had to be fed and clothed when northern laborers were thrown out of work by hard times, and they were cared for in sickness and in old age. So much did this happy state of things please the slave-holders that sometimes they wished it might be extended to the white people. "If some superior power should impose on the laborious poor of some other country—this as their unalterable condition—you shall be saved from the torturing anxiety concerning your own future support and that of your children." [3]

[1] Pollard, *Black Diamonds*, 75; cf. Murray, *Letters*, 211; Olmsted, *Seaboard Slave States*, 656–659; Olmsted, *Back Country*, 181; Child, *Freedmen's Book*, 114; Smedes, *Memorials of a Southern Planter*, 76; Bledsoe, *Liberty and Slavery*, 292–300.

[2] Adams, *Southside View*, 15–19; Simms, in *Pro-Slavery Argument*, 219.

[3] Harper and Simms, in *Pro-Slavery Argument*, 26, 49, 226; Adams, *Southside View*, 61.

If the ordinary slave was expected to be happy, much more the fortunate negroes who were placed in positions of responsibility—the butler, the family cook, the old nurse, beloved and kissed by generations of white children—people who had the profoundest pride in "our family." These were the negroes seen handsomely dressed on the streets of the cities, engaging in subscription assemblies, or even holding a little property recognized by the master as their own.[1] A few such specially trusted slaves were actually managers of the master's estates, though a white overseer was always present.[2]

With regard to the argument of the good of the negro, two questions must be asked: were the negroes really happy? and how far was happiness an evidence that slavery was a good thing for them? Upon the first point the evidence is overwhelming that many slaves were as well fed and housed as the poor whites of the neighborhood, and were unconscious of serious injustice.[3] Even when torn from their kindred and sold to the dreaded "down river," the negroes quickly recovered their cheerfulness. When the advocates of slavery insisted that their slaves were better off than agricultural laborers and factory operatives in England or even

---

[1] Page, The Negro, 173–181; Olmsted, Seaboard Slave States, 554.

[2] Coffin, Reminiscences, 161; Olmsted, Seaboard Slave States, 425–429, 553–555, 623; Kemble, Georgian Plantation, 43–45.

[3] Paulding, Letters from the South, 96–98; Murray, Letters, 263–266; Pollard, Black Diamonds, 41–46.

in the northern states, they could be contradicted. It was a time of misery and degradation in the factory population of England, and parliamentary inquiries revealed horrors which led to immediate reforms of the worst abuses; these evils served as a text for the south, but the reforms were not imitated.[1]

The condition of the slave, in comparison with the free labor of the north, may be gauged by two lines of evidence: they were certainly no better off than the poor whites of that day, who were, and still are, far inferior in comfort to what the memory of man knows to have been the ordinary conditions of working-men in the north at that time. This indirect argument is confirmed by the testimony of Olmsted, a farmer, an employer of labor, and an economist, who asserts that hired laborers in the north could not be induced to remain a day in the conditions of the slaves on the best plantations. If the slaves were all happy and contented, it was a fair question why they desired to be free. It was, after all, an odd kind of happiness which no free negro sought, and against which white men would have fought to their last breath.

Perhaps a more candid argument was the good of the white man. Slavery caused a larger production than could be had by any other form of labor; slavery was favorable to the increase of wealth,

---

[1] Hammond, in *Pro-Slavery Argument*, 135–138; Fitzhugh, *Cannibals All*.

partly by emphasizing the sacredness of vested property,[1] partly because slaves, unlike white laborers, were wealth, exchangeable from hand to hand, and partly because slavery favored the accumulation of capital in a few intelligent hands.[2] That other countries and other states were prosperous without slavery, and had greater accumulations, was neither understood nor recognized by the south. Certainly the profits of slavery, down to 1860, built up very few fortunes, even measured in slaves; and neighboring parts of states of equal fertility, such as Kentucky and Ohio, or Maryland and Pennsylvania, showed a superiority of northern wealth of every sort, which is hard to account for on any other theory than a better type of labor. Whatever the advantages of slavery to the white race, they were not shared by the poor whites, who had no part in the annual produce of slavery, and for whose education and improvement nothing was spent out of that surplus; while they were exposed to the wide-spread contempt for labor with the hands, and to the degradation brought about by the nearness of a subject and immoral race.

The south was not a mercenary community, and was probably more affected by the argument of social well-being than by the argument of profit.

---

[1] Olmsted, *Seaboard Slave States*, 620–624; *De Bow's Review*, XXI., 455; Dew, in *Pro-Slavery Argument*, 385–390.

[2] Hammond, in *Pro-Slavery Argument*, 121–123, 163; Harper, in *ibid.*, 83–85; Bledsoe, *Liberty and Slavery*, chap. i.

It was generally believed in the south that slavery was necessary to relieve the whites from the danger of labor in a hot climate, and still more from the degradation of manual labor of any kind. Slavery also, by its discipline and the out-door habits of the whites, fostered a military spirit and thus provided for the maintenance of order and for future defence. Hints were not wanting that the masterful race might even organize a negro army officered by white men which would be a protection against exterior enemies.[1]

Slavery was also supposed to be favorable to the manners and breeding of the white race, and it was a notable fact that southerners who visited England were commonly received on better terms than northern gentlemen,[2] while in the midst of all that was noxious in slavery there bloomed the lovely and hardy flower of southern womanhood. The seduction of white women was almost unknown in a society where black women were so easily accessible; and the whole force of society was brought to bear to protect white girls from the dark and earthly sides of life. On the plantations the mistresses were often springs of bounty, kindness, and genuine affection for the slaves.

The evil effects of slavery on young men even southern writers could not deny, for from child-

---

[1] Harper and Hammond, in *Pro-Slavery Argument*, 67, 73, 79, 111; Olmsted, *Back Country*, 386.
[2] Kemble, *Georgian Plantation*, 305.

hood upward they were exposed to the basest temptations to temper and to morals.[1] A state of things in which a boy expected and received the unquestionable obedience of every slave on the plantation was not favorable to self - control or moderation. The south abounded in brawls and homicides.[2] The poor whites were often quarrelsome and murderous, and even in the highest circles affrays and duels were frequent. That slavery was the sole reason why so many of the negroes, both male and female, were unchaste was a criticism that could not be sustained; but that slavery magnified the evil influences on the blacks and whites was so self-evident that a witness above cavil says: "We may and do acknowledge our guilt in the south, but not as slaveholders." [3]

Another line of argument was that slavery was absolutely necessary for the safety of the whites. The fear of insurrection has been discussed elsewhere.[4] One of the most frequent arguments in favor of slavery was the example of the fitful and disturbed republic of Haiti, which was accepted as proof positive that the negroes, if set free, would never permit their masters to live, and that they could not maintain a civilized community of their

[1] Rhodes, *United States*, I., 343; admitted by Harper, in *Pro-Slavery Argument*, 61.

[2] Buckingham, *Slave States*, I., 557.

[3] Simms, in *Pro-Slavery Argument*, 228-230; cf. Martineau's chapter on "Morals of Slavery," in *Society in America*, I., 106-136. [4] See above, chaps. iii., viii.

own.[1] Yet this argument was thought compatible
with the theory that slavery was a necessary condition of a genuine republican government—for the
masters. Thus Hammond, after paying his re-
spects to the "nowhere accredited dogma of Mr.
Jefferson that 'all men are born equal,'" argues
that in the south the slave-holders "are both educated and independent in their circumstances,
while those who unfortunately are not so [that is,
the poor whites], being still elevated far above the
mass, are higher toned and more deeply interested in preserving a stable and well-ordered government."[2]

The time even came when slavery was defended,
not as a system that might, by an effort, be explained or justified, and still less as an institution
that must remain simply because it was ineradicable,
though that argument was sometimes heard.[3] John
C. Calhoun said, in his seat in the Senate, February
6, 1837: "But let me not be understood as admitting
even by implication that the existing relations between the two races in the slave-holding states is an
evil;—far otherwise, I hold it to be a good, as it has
thus far proved to be to both."[4] This was the
theory eventually settled upon by practically the

[1] Hopkins, *View of Slavery*, 249–252.
[2] Hammond, in *Pro-Slavery Argument*, 110, 111.
[3] *Richmond Enquirer* and *Richmond Examiner*, quoted in
Olmsted, *Seaboard Slave States*, 298–300.
[4] Calhoun, *Works*, II., 630.

entire reasoning south.[1] From this position the corollary naturally followed that so good a system ought to be extended into the northern states to replace the dangerous and destructive principle of political equality and universal suffrage. For example, in 1858, Senator Hammond said of the Mississippi Valley: "We own the most of that valley; . . . those who have settled above us, are now opposed to us, another generation will tell a different tale. They are ours by every law of nature. Slavery will go over every foot of this valley."[2] Another corollary was that if slavery were endangered through the union of free and slave-holding states, the union must give way. "Come what may," wrote Hammond, in 1845, "we are firmly resolved that our system of domestic slavery shall stand."[3]

---

[1] Harper, in *Pro-Slavery Argument*, 17–24; Goodell, *Slavery and Anti-Slavery*, 83; Seabury, *American Slavery*, chap. xviii.; the author has under his hand between fifty and a hundred citations to the same effect.

[2] *Cong. Globe.*, 35 Cong., 1 Sess., 961.

[3] Hammond, in *Pro-Slavery Argument*, 169.

CHAPTER XI

THE ANTI-SLAVERY MOVEMENT

(1624–1840)

MOST of the arguments in favor of slavery can be traced to the eighteenth century; and two centuries before the anti-slavery movement of 1831 protests had been heard against slavery in America. Half a century later the subject was taken up by Richard Baxter, an English devotional author, who, in his *Christian Directory*, in 1678, declared that "to go as pirates and catch up poor negroes or people of another land that never forfeited life or liberty and to make them slaves and sell them is one of the worst kinds of thievery in the world." [1] As slavery spread through the colonies, these objections became more and more animated both from northern and southern men, especially the Quakers, who began to make "slave keeping" a reason for disfellowship; their anti-slavery apostle, John Woolman, made it his life-work to go about the country and to argue against slavery, because contrary to Christianity and because "liberty was the natural right of all men equally." [2]

[1] Locke, *Anti-Slavery*, 16.   [2] Hart, *Contemporaries*, II., 305.

A second line of argument was intensified by the American Revolution and its political results. In the first draught of the Declaration of Independence the slave-trade was styled a "cruel war against human nature itself, violating its most sacred rights of life and liberty." [1] When the pressure came for raising troops for the Revolution, negroes were freely enlisted, receiving their freedom, and then that of their families. The Revolution was also based on a lofty assertion of the natural rights of man, phrased in such terms as that of the Virginia Declaration of Rights, that "all men are by nature free and independent." To be sure, negro slaves were not in the minds of those who penned these splendid generalizations; but it became difficult to explain why nature should take account only of white men, especially when many negroes were actually enjoying the political equality described by those documents.

The Revolution gave a leverage for the movement against slavery by bestowing on the states authority over slavery denied while they were colonies. April 14, 1775, the first anti-slavery society was formed in Philadelphia, and at once began to memorialize the legislature of Pennsylvania to set the slaves free. Meanwhile two states in the Union uprooted slavery —Vermont, in 1777, and Massachusetts, in 1780— both by constitutional provisions, a method initiated by New Hampshire in 1783.[2] The Pennsylvania leg-

[1] Jefferson, *Works* (Washington ed.), I., 23.
[2] Bassett, *Federalist System* (*Am. Nation*, XI.), chap. xii.

islature passed a gradual emancipation act in 1780, an example followed by Rhode Island and Connecticut in 1784, and in 1799 and 1804 by New York and New Jersey.

This movement, which several southern states seemed likely to follow, had an unexpected effect upon the Union. As early as July, 1776, Congress discovered that northern and southern members were at odds over slavery: one side persisting that the negroes should not be considered as members of the state more than cattle; to which a northern member replied that in that case they ought not to be included in the basis of representation under the proposed confederation.

With regard to the western territory, Congress three times faced the issue of prohibiting or permitting slavery. The passage of Jefferson's Ordinance of 1784 for gradual emancipation in the western territories was lost for lack of a single vote; Rufus King's Ordinance of 1785, which included a clause for the return of fugitives, did not come to a vote; in the Northwest Ordinance of 1787, Congress, with the approval of every member except one New-Yorker, made it a matter of fundamental compact with the people of the northwest that "neither slavery nor involuntary servitude shall be permitted except for the punishment of crime whereof the party shall have been duly convicted." [1]

[1] McLaughlin, *Confederation and Constitution* (*Am. Nation*, X.) chaps. vii., viii.

By this ordinance, which practically extended westward the status of freedom resulting from state enactments in the east, the Union was practically divided into two belts, a northern free area and a southern slave-holding region. Inasmuch as the expectation was that the southern territories would share the fortunes of the southeastern states, the eleven years between the first rising of the slavery question in Congress and the Northwest Ordinance marks the separation of the newly created union into two well-defined and sharply contrasted sections.

The rivalry and jealousy between those two sections was clearly revealed in the work of the federal convention of 1787. It led to the "federal ratio" for the House of Representatives, which was a sectional compromise on the slave-trade. South Carolina threatened to break up the whole plan, and the convention was obliged to postpone that power for twenty years. The existence of free states made necessary a clause for the delivery of "fugitives from service or labor" who might escape from one state into another. In addition, Congress received power over the territories, over the seat of government, and over interstate commerce; and a provision for giving to citizens of one state "all privileges and immunities of citizens in the several states" included some negroes. On the whole, the convention dealt wisely with the slavery question in not committing the new federal government to a policy upon what seemed a declining institution.

In the organization of the government no seriously contested questions arose out of slavery. The
Northwest Ordinance was, without opposition, re-
enacted in 1789; and the next year the territory
south of the Ohio River (Tennessee) was organized
with the purposeful omission of any restriction on
slavery; for the District of Columbia an act of
Congress of 1801 simply re-enacted the existing
Maryland statutes in the part north of the Potomac, and the Virginia statutes in the part across the
river, thus making a slave code without mentioning slavery.[1] In 1793 Congress accepted federal responsibility for the capture of fugitives by passing
a fugitive-slave act,[2] and a strong public sentiment,
shared by the border slave states, led to a succession of minor statutes regulating the trade. Congress
re-enacted the Ordinance of 1787 for the successive
territories—Indiana, Illinois, Michigan, and Wisconsin—carved out of the Northwest Territory, and resisted the repeated efforts, between 1796 and 1811,
to repeal that ordinance for the Indiana Territory,
which then extended to the Mississippi; so that
both Indiana and Illinois were admitted into the
Union on anti-slavery constitutions. In the Missouri Compromise of 1820, Congress reiterated its
right to prohibit slavery in any territory at its
discretion.

The distinct anti-slavery spirit of Congress was a

[1] Tremain, *Slavery in the District of Columbia*, 11–14.
[2] Bassett, *Federalist System* (*Am. Nation*, XI.), 187–189.

reflex of a powerful movement which showed itself in pamphlets, public addresses, organized societies, anti-slavery journals, and a few acts of state legislatures, and was encouraged by the contemporary fight against the British slave-trade. It was discouraged by the first instance of an emancipated colony in America. The island of Haiti was the seat of a sugar industry employing about six hundred thousand slaves and busying eight hundred vessels. A civil war between the whites and the free negroes led to a slave insurrection in 1791. The English invaded the island in 1793, and the French authorities, to whom the Spanish end of the island was ceded in 1795, declared the slaves free.[1] Haiti was for a time blotted out of political life, and emerged in 1801 with a negro government. Hundreds of refugees reached the United States, and specific point was given to their warnings, in 1800, by an insurrection planned by a negro named Gabriel, in Henrico County, Virginia.

"It is evident," said a contemporary, "that the French principles of liberty and equality have been effused into the minds of the negroes."[2] Before the insurrection could be consummated, Gabriel was betrayed, arrested, duly tried, and convicted, and, four days afterwards, executed. The outbreak increased both the American and English objections to the slave-trade; and twenty-three days after the

---

[1] Jay, *Miscellaneous Writings*, 171-178.
[2] Higginson, *Travellers and Outlaws*, 197.

United States act of 1807, Parliament, led by Clarkson and Wilberforce, absolutely prohibited the slave-trade either by English subjects or to English colonies; the two statutes seemed to strike hands for the destruction of the traffic and for the assertion of the principle that it was iniquitous to buy and sell Africans. Congress enacted in 1819 that slaves taken in transit should be returned in freedom to Africa; and in 1820 declared the slave-trade to be piracy, which made the trader liable to the penalty of death.

This work accomplished, the hostility to slavery became a distinct propaganda, which took on three different forms: an attempt through churches and other existing means to arouse public sentiment; an organized emancipation agitation directed by a national society; and colonization. Unlike later abolition, this whole movement was carried on by people who lived in or adjoining the slave-holding states, who worked upon their own legislatures and were able to reach the slave - holders with their literature. Thus James G. Birney set himself with success to securing acts of the Alabama legislature for the more humane treatment of slaves, and William Swaim freely published anti-slavery articles in North Carolina.[1]

By far the most interesting figure in this movement is Benjamin Lundy, born a New Jersey Quaker, but later a resident of several slave states. In 1815

[1] Weeks, *Southern Quakers and Slavery*, 240.

he began to organize anti-slavery societies, some of them in southern states; in 1821 he founded an abolition paper, *The Genius of Universal Emancipation*. He was sure that the open discussion of slavery would bring about its downfall, and he made many long journeys through the southern states to gather experience and to preach his doctrines. In 1828 a journeyman printer, named William Lloyd Garrison, fell in with Lundy in Boston, and said of him afterwards: "His heart is of a gigantic size. Every inch of him is alive with power. . . . Within a few months he has travelled about twenty-four hundred miles, of which upwards of sixteen hundred were performed *on foot!* during which time he has held nearly fifty public meetings." [1]

Several other anti-slavery papers appeared between 1815 and 1829, especially *The Philanthropist*, published in St. Clairsville, Ohio, and *The Freeman's Journal*, published by a negro in New York City; and there is a literature of formal books attacking slavery, most of them by members of slave-holding families. Thus John Rankin preached and wrote against slavery in Kentucky, and then settled in Ohio, where he published a volume of *Letters on Slavery*, which became a sort of text-book for abolitionists. Another group was made up of middle-states men, who argued against slavery on general principles — among them William Rawle, a renowned constitutional lawyer, and Isaac T. Hop-

[1] Garrisons, *Garrison*, I., 92.

per, for fifty seven years a public opponent of slavery.

Upon such moral questions the best way of concentrating public opinion was through the state and national assemblies of the great churches. In 1812 the Methodist General Conference voted that no slave-holder could continue as a local elder. The Presbyterian General Assembly in 1815 urged that the slaves be educated, as a step towards emancipation, and in 1818 unanimously resolved that slavery was "a gross violation of the most precious and moral rights of human nature, as utterly inconsistent with the law of God . . . and as totally irreconcilable with the spirit and principles of the gospel of Christ."[1] Some of the Baptist churches withdrew from their loose general organization because of a lack of testimony against slavery; and a few separate congregations refused to admit to Christian brotherhood any holder of slaves. The Quakers were, as always, the most constant and resolute opponents of slavery.

The anti-slavery agitators were among the first to discover the usefulness of organized societies, encouraging each other, spreading information and arguments from community to community, and combining in a national convention. The Pennsylvania Society continued unbroken existence from 1775. By 1808 societies had appeared in New Jersey, Kentucky, and New York; in Delaware, in

[1] *Niles' Register*, XVI., Supl., p. 153.

1809; in Tennessee, in 1814; in Ohio and North Carolina, in 1816; in Maryland, in 1817; in Virginia, in 1823. The total number of local societies under the labors of Lundy and others increased towards 1830 to upward of one hundred, representing every state in the Union except only New England, the extreme southern states, and Indiana. Such societies held meetings, issued addresses, memorialized legislatures, protected negroes, and sustained anti-slavery publications.

The strongest anti-slavery force was the organization first called the "American Convention of Delegates from Abolition Societies," but after 1818 "The American Convention for Promoting the Abolition of Slavery and Improving the Condition of the African Race." [1] From 1794 to 1806 the convention met annually; then every three years till 1815; thereafter, at least as often as once in two years. The local societies were all free to send delegates, but after 1809 none came from beyond North Carolina and Tennessee. The middle states furnished about half the delegates; the other half came from the six southern states lying nearest to the border.

The convention was an active and forth-putting body: it heard reports on the condition of the reform; its minutes were published and distributed; it bought, encouraged, and sent out anti-slavery

[1] For details with regard to this and the local societies I am indebted to an unpublished monograph by Alice Dana Adams, *Anti-Slavery, 1808–1831—a Study of a Neglected Period.*

publications and its own resolutions; it addressed petitions to state legislatures and to Congress. No phase of slavery was left out of its discussions. The convention urged the education of slaves and their training to take care of themselves, so that they might safely be set free. It tried to create public sentiment against slavery in the District of Columbia, and memorialized Congress to abolish it there and also in the territory of Florida. It kept the discussion alive and did something to arouse the public conscience of the south; but the meetings grew less vigorous, till in the last convention of 1829 only seven societies were represented, and of those only two were from the south.

This decay of the American Convention was due to the rise of cotton culture, which made slavery profitable, and to the counter - movement of the American Colonization Society. The idea of carrying the negroes out of the country can be traced back to Jefferson's *Notes on Virginia*, in 1784. In 1816 was formed "The American Society for the Colonization of the Free People of Color of the United States," under the presidency of Judge Bushrod Washington, subsequently of Henry Clay. It founded an organ called *The African Repository*, and raised money to send out agents to Africa, in 1818, to select a site for a colony. Great impetus was given to the movement in 1819 when Congress passed an act providing that negroes captured while being illegally imported into the United States should be returned to Africa, and appropriating one hundred thousand dollars, which was intended to be used by the new society.

A new reason for the movement was furnished in 1822, at Charleston, by Denmark Vesey, a free negro, who made an elaborate plot to rise, massacre the white population, seize the shipping in the harbor, and, if hard pressed, to sail away to the West Indies. One of the negroes gave evidence, Vesey was seized, duly tried, and, with thirty-four others, was hanged. The desperate plan was so nearly successful that it left an ineradicable distrust of the free negroes and a desire to get them out of the country.[1]

Backed up by the approving resolutions of several state legislatures, north and south, by a small appropriation from Virginia, and a much larger one from Maryland—which went, however, to a separate state society—supported by many state auxiliary societies, and with the national government in the background, the Colonization Society proceeded to plant its colony. In 1820 eighty-six negroes were sent to Africa, and in 1822 a settlement was made on the west coast to which the name of Liberia was later given. These powerful influences, however, were not sufficient to overcome distance, malaria, savage neighbors, and a tropical climate. In the ten years from 1820 to 1830, with an expenditure of one hundred thousand dollars, the society was

[1] *Niles' Register*, XXII., 320; Higginson, *Travellers and Outlaws*, 215–275.

able to transfer only 1162 people, all but two hundred from the coast border states; of these the greater part died within a few years after landing.[1]

Till 1830 there seems to have been no notion that slavery was a subject which must not be discussed in Congress, and a variety of national and international questions brought it up. Contrary to a clause in the peace of Ghent of 1814, the retiring British carried away several hundred slaves, in behalf of whose owners the federal government at once demanded compensation, and eventually the British government paid twelve hundred thousand dollars. Having prohibited the slave-trade to their own colonies, it became the interest of the British government to stop it to other American colonies, and treaties were made with Denmark, Holland, Spain, and Portugal to that effect. By the treaty of 1814 the United States agreed to "use their best endeavors" to bring about a general abolition of the detested trade, a promise which slumbered for some years; but in 1824 John Quincy Adams negotiated a treaty giving to British cruisers the right, which was absolutely necessary if the trade were to be stamped out, to search American vessels engaged in the trade. The Senate threw over the treaty on a technicality, and it was eighteen years before the two parties again came together on the question.[2]

After 1825 the southern leaders in Congress began

[1] Am. Colonization Soc., *Fiftieth Annual Report*, 64, 65; McPherson, *Liberia*, passim.   [2] See below, chap. xix.

to grow more nervous. In 1826 they objected to sending delegates to the Panama Congress because the negro republic of Haiti was to be invited, and the meeting might lead to an insurrection in Cuba; for the freeing of slaves so near our coast was thought likely to be a dangerous object-lesson for the southern slaves. The abolitionists opened up a good point of attack against slavery in the District of Columbia, where the three municipalities of Washington, Georgetown, and Alexandria made a series of local ordinances for the discipline of the negroes, and the law of the District permitted negroes who could not give an account of themselves to be sold for their jail-fees. About 1828, Miner, of Pennsylvania, made himself the leader in the movement, introducing petitions and bills for gradual emancipation in the District, which the legislature of Pennsylvania instructed its senators to vote for; and a petition from the District was presented with a thousand signatures. The number of slaves in the District in 1830 was only 6060, and slavery might easily have been extinguished; but the south was awake to the moral effect of such action, and Congress ignored the movement.

When Jackson became president, in 1829, anti-slavery seemed, after fifty years of effort, to have spent its force. The voice of the churches was no longer heard in protest; the abolitionist societies were dying out; there was hardly an abolitionist militant in the field; the Colonization Society absorbed most of the public interest in the subject, and it was doing nothing to help either the free negro or the slave; in Congress there was only one anti-slavery man, and his efforts were without avail. It was a gloomy time for the little band of people who believed that slavery was poisonous to the south, hurtful to the north, and dangerous to the Union.

The arguments against slavery during this period were substantially the same as those used by the later abolitionists, and turned mainly on natural right, Christianity, humanity, the bad effects on the southern whites, and the injury to the whole Union. The argument of natural right was in accord with the text of all the slave-state constitutions and of the principles of government in the south.   If there were any "inalienable" rights, property in man was impossible; to exclude negroes from the principles of the Declaration of Independence they must be looked on as something else than men;[1] and, there-fore, pro-slavery writers sometimes abjured the Declaration of Independence as false and unthink-able.[2]   Human rights were expanding both in con-tent and extent: Anglo-Saxons were being relieved from the arbitrary control of employers and jailers, and the alien was admitted to both the old and the new privileges.   To hold that men could be excluded from the beneficent principles of free government

[1] Channing, *Works*, II., 17–50.
[2] Hopkins, *View of Slavery*, 19–29.

because they were inferior to other men was a doctrine which struck at the basis of free government in America.

The anti-slavery argument from Christianity appealed to the principles of Christianity. Who was to shut the negro out from the Golden Rule, from the glorious message of the gospel, from the building-up of his own character through the grace of God? It was hard to escape from the dilemma that if the negro was a hopeless pagan, incapable of civilization and of the Christian virtues, his presence was an unspeakable curse to the community; and if he was a man who could respond to the divine truths, who made the white man his keeper? [1]

Africa might perhaps be held responsible for the low morals of the slave; but it was a fair argument that slavery denied both Christianity and civilization when it broke up families. To say that negroes "are themselves both perverse and comparatively indifferent about this matter, . . . the negroes forming those connections, knowing the chances of their premature dissolution," was to admit the damaging charge that slave life paralyzed the natural family instincts even of the savage.[2]

The cruelty of slavery was also an unfailing argument; from the southern newspapers themselves, from every-day advertisements, from the reports of

[1] Cheever, *Guilt of Slavery*, passim.
[2] Channing, *Works*, I., 41, II., 69–72; Hammond, in *Pro-Slavery Argument*, 132.

travellers, incidents could be gleaned which sickened and appalled the reader. The rejoinder that cruelties occurred constantly in northern institutions, such as jails, poor - houses, and orphan - asylums, was not conclusive; in the northern states public sentiment was watchful, and nobody felt that the whipping of defenceless people was necessary for the preservation of society.

Anti-slavery people took exceptions to the restrictions, legal and practical, on the intellectual improvement of the negro, and to the cynical defences of those restrictions.[1]

The anti-slavery argument covered not only the slaves, but the white men. It criticised the imperiousness of the master, the demoralizing effect of the relations of the sexes, the setting-up of the great slave-holding families as the head of social and political life, the effect on the poor whites of the degradation of labor. In the national government the influence of the great slave-holders was paramount during the whole period from 1815 to 1860. Of the five northern presidents—John Quincy Adams, Van Buren, Fillmore, Pierce, and Buchanan— not one stood against the pro-slavery men while in office. No recognized abolitionist and few out-and-out anti-slavery men, after 1840, were appointed to a foreign mission or a consulate, or a collectorate or important postmastership, or to the federal bench. In Congress, the southerners, by their abilities, their

[1] See Harper, in *Pro-Slavery Argument*, 51.

long terms of service, their habit of standing together, and their success in holding a part of the
northern men, almost always had their will.

The most telling argument against slavery in the
long-run was that it did not pay. Inasmuch as it
did pay some people, as the wealth of the south increased from decade to decade, it was hard to make
anybody believe that slavery was really a drain on
the community.[1] The census of 1850, the accumulated materials in journals like *Niles' Register* and
De Bow's Review, and the criticisms of Olmsted
brought out the fact that the south was gaining
wealth slowly, and that in value of land, value of
crops, value of buildings, miles of railroad, and
extent of shipping, and also in schools, journals,
and other evidences of intellectual growth, had
fallen behind the rest of the Union. The anti-
slavery people were sure that the only reason was
that the north had free labor and the south had
slave labor. The experience of the last forty years
has shown that slavery was not a complete explanation. The negro could not be made as efficient as
the intelligent, well-rewarded, and productive labor
of the north simply by setting him free. The south
was equally mistaken in insisting that slavery was
the only thing that made the negro efficient; it was
clinging to a cast-iron and rigid system which America had outgrown.

[1] Buckingham, *Slave States*, I., 201–204, 399–404.

CHAPTER XII

GARRISONIAN ABOLITION

(1830–1845)

WHY did the anti-slavery movement, which had been going on steadily for half a century, apparently die down in 1829 and then suddenly blaze up with renewed fierceness? One reason was that the western world was growing tired of human bondage: the last vestige of serfdom was disappearing in central Europe, and the same spirit extended to the European colonies in America. The influence of the Latin-American revolutions was against slavery. Bolivar emancipated his own slaves, and in 1821 secured a general emancipation in New Granada,[1] which was followed by all the Latin-American powers except Brazil. The influence spread to the West Indies, where slavery had long since ceased to exist in Haiti; and in 1848 it was abolished in the French islands by the home government. Spain was soon the only power that retained slavery in the West Indian islands.

For a powerful movement was working against

[1] Jay, *Miscellaneous Writings*, 169; *Genius of Universal Emancipation*, VII., 12.

slavery in Jamaica and the other British West Indies. The prohibition of the British slave-trade in 1807 was made effective by a large and active British navy. Then, in 1823, was formed a "Society for the Mitigation and Gradual Abolition of Slavery throughout the British Dominions," in which appeared as leaders Buxton, Clarkson, and Wilberforce. They urged with unrelenting vigor two principles destructive of slavery: one that colonial slavery was contrary to the spirit of the British Constitution; and the other that the remedy was immediate emancipation.[1] Under the stimulus of a parliamentary agitation, fed by petitions and public meetings, and by an anti-slavery journal, Parliament passed an emancipation act in 1833, by which colonial slavery was to be gradually extinguished in seven years, with a compensation of twenty million pounds to the owners. The two predictions, that the negro would sit down and die rather than turn his hand to earning his living, and that the blacks and the whites would be drawn into a war of mutual extermination, were both set at naught. For a time the freedmen took a holiday, and the sugar plantations of Jamaica never recovered their importance; but the negroes finally settled down as peaceful small proprietors.[2] This experi-

---

[1] Hopkins, *View of Slavery*, 258; Goodell, *Slavery and Anti-Slavery*, 353–356.

[2] Child, *Letters from New York*, 2d series, 101–103; Channing, *Works*, VI., 9–41; Cochin, *Results of Emancipation*.

ment, so near our shores, so contrary to the arguments and pleas of our slave-holders, could not but affect public sentiment in the United States.

The rise of abolition was coincident with a change in the attitude of the public mind towards the weak and the helpless, which was shown in reforms in the treatment of paupers, convicts, and the insane, and in the beginnings of public provision for the training of the blind, deaf and dumb, imbeciles, and other defective persons. This sense of public responsibility was as much needed in the south as at the north; but, partly because of a sparse agricultural population, partly because of an unconquerable frontier rudeness, the south was much less affected by these reforms than the northern communities; and the presence of an inferior and servile race which had to be kept under, worked against the humanitarian spirit.

Slavery was also unfavorably affected by the sudden opening-up of new fields of economic activity. The development of manufactures, the growth of large cities, the exchange of products far and wide, called for a kind of labor which was unsuited to slavery, and for a kind of laborer who instinctively felt that the slave was a competitor. On its side, the south, which in the nullification contest reacted into a type of state rights which had been decried in that section since Jefferson came to power in 1801, also reacted from an open discussion of slavery to an intense hostility towards anti-slavery within its own limits or anywhere else.

In 1830 there was little conscious anti-slavery feeling in either section. The few agitators, of whom Benjamin Lundy was the chief, were in despair at the apathy of the north. Even the seizure of two fugitive slaves in Boston in 1830, one of them a woman, raised not a ripple of excitement in New England. The people who felt an interest in the subject went, with few exceptions, no further than anti-slavery—that is, they believed that slavery was wrong and dangerous, and wished to see a period put to its extension and to its ill effects upon society. Such men, on the northern side, were Benjamin Franklin, John Adams, and Taylor and Talmadge in their attempts to prevent slavery from going into Missouri.[1] Such men were eager to be rid of slavery in their own community, and deprecated it wherever it existed, not so much out of sympathy with the oppressed negro, as from the belief that slavery was an injury to their own neighbors and constituents, and that the influence of the slave power in national affairs was harmful. Most of the northern anti-slavery people disclaimed any intention of interfering with slavery in the southern states, but they instinctively disliked any project for enlarging the boundaries of slave-holding territory: their principle was that slavery and the slave-holding power should remain where they were.

Very different in their outlook were the abolitionists, a term already made familiar by such agitators

---

[1] Turner, *New West* (*Am. Nation*, XIV.), chap. x.

as Rankin and Lundy. Their objection was not only to slavery in the abstract, but to concrete slavery, as they saw it in their own communities or in neighboring parts of the country. Every abolitionist was an anti-slavery man, but he went far beyond the ordinary anti-slavery standards: he was heart and soul opposed to slavery as it existed; he was bent on persuading or coercing the master to give up his authority; he had in mind, not a distant political and sectional influence, but the blows of the overseer and the tears of the slave. He wished to get rid of slavery speedily, root and branch, cost what it might, suffer who must, for the salvation of the souls of the masters, for the preservation of the Union, for the rights of man, for the love of Christ. The true abolitionist ignored all difficulties and scoffed at the idea that there could be vested right in the person of man and woman. His ears were deaf to appeals to the authority of ancient custom, of state laws, of the guarantees of the federal Constitution. The abolitionist's creed was, give up your unblessed property, forsake your evil habits, change your laws, alter the Constitution.

Anti-slavery was a negative force, an attempt to wall in an obnoxious system of labor so that it might die of itself; abolition was a positive force, founded on moral considerations, stoutly denying that slavery could be a good thing for anybody, and perfectly willing to see the social and economic system of the south disrupted. As time went on, the anti-slavery and abolition movements in the north came closer together and sometimes joined forces, partly through the appearance of political abolitionists like Salmon P. Chase and Charles Sumner, who built up a little anti-slavery party and secured the support of thousands of men who were never conscious abolitionists; and partly by the warming-up of the anti-slavery people, as the contest grew fiercer, to a belief that abolition might, after all, be the only way to stop the advance of slavery. Yet two such conspicuous champions of anti-slavery as John Quincy Adams and Abraham Lincoln always said that they were not abolitionists. In the heat of the fray southern leaders and speakers got into the habit of calling everybody "abolitionist" who was in any degree opposed to slavery; but the distinction was clear enough, all the way down to the Civil War.[1]

Abolition, in its extreme form, could not exist in the south, because, after 1830, public sentiment would not permit such aggressive attacks on the property and character of the leaders of the community; but in several parts of the border states anti-slavery men continued to live and even to agitate, and for some years feeble efforts at a gradual emancipation were permitted. To the last, in private conversation, slave-holders and free farmers occasionally admitted that slavery was a bad

[1] On abolition in general, see Hart, *Contemporaries*, §§ 172–178.

thing for the south,[1] and as late as 1850, in the University of Virginia, a student criticised slavery in a public address.[2]

In North Carolina, where a strong Quaker influence against negro slavery never quite expired, in 1832, Judge William Gaston, in an address at the State University, called upon the students to aid in the "extirpation" of slavery, because "it stifles industry and represses enterprise .*. . and poisons morals at the fountain-head."[3] Daniel R. Goodloe, in 1841, published an *Inquiry*, which was one of the first searching economic arguments against slavery;[4] and as late as 1857, Hinton R. Helper, of that state, published an appeal to the poor whites.[5]

In Virginia the anti-slavery feeling was intensified by the Nat Turner Insurrection of 1831, which led the *Richmond Enquirer* to say: "Something must be done, and it is the part of no honest man to deny it —of no free press to affect to conceal it." When the legislature next met, in a debate of many days the strongest opinions were expressed against slavery, especially by members from the mountain counties, though a lowland member said: "Slavery in Vir-

[1] Olmsted, *Seaboard Slave States*, 675; Olmsted, *Back Country*, 177–186, 270–272.

[2] Bremer, *Homes of the New World*, II., 188–193, 529–531; Kemble, *Georgian Plantation*, 77.

[3] Gaston, *Address delivered before the Dialectic and Philanthropic Societies*.

[4] Weeks, in Southern Hist. Assoc., *Publications*, II., No. 2, 115–130.

[5] See Chadwick, *Causes of the Civil War* (*Am. Nation*, XIX.).

ginia is an evil, and a transcendent evil—a mildew
which blights in its course every region which it has
touched from the creation of the world." And another member from a slave-holding county charged
that "slavery has interfered with our means of enjoying life, liberty, property, happiness, and safety."[1]

A curious delusion, oft-repeated with regard to
this debate, is that a bill to abolish slavery in Virginia failed in the general assembly by only one
vote, and that vote the casting vote of the speaker.[2]
It is true that four different times within four years
the representatives of Virginia carefully discussed
certain phases of slavery in that state. The first
was the constitutional convention of 1829–1830, in
which no proposition was made looking to emancipation; the burning question was whether the lowland slave-holding counties should continue in the
enjoyment of a larger representation in proportion to
the whites than the people of the mountain counties.
The lowlanders triumphed on a tie vote, the presid-
ing officer of the convention casting his vote on their
side.[3] In the legislative session of 1830–1831 a
proposition for the more rigorous restriction of free
negroes was voted down by 58 to 59, but subsequently passed.[4] In the next session, after the Nat

[1] Goodloe, *Southern Platform*, 42–54.
[2] Page, *The Negro*, 235.
[3] *Proceedings and Debates of the Virginia State Convention of 1829–1830*, passim.
[4] *Journals of the House of Delegates*, 1829, pp. 30, 74, 139, 156, 157, 176, 187; *Journals of the Senate*, 129, 130, 135.

Turner insurrection, came the debate from which extracts are quoted above; petitions were presented, respectfully received, and referred, asking for an emancipation act, but a test vote on the proposition to submit to a popular vote the question of whether such an act should be passed was defeated, January 25, 1832, by 58 to 73, and the only vote on a negro question was on a bill for removing free negroes from the state.[1] In not one of these four sessions was emancipation squarely faced, though there were several narrow votes on other questions of slavery, the nearest approach to action being a proposition, voted down by a considerable majority, to take the sense of the people on a side question.

Two out-and-out Kentucky abolitionists stood to their guns to the end. John G. Fee, who founded a little college at Berea for the education of the neighboring mountain whites, and Cassius M. Clay, of Kentucky, a cousin of Henry Clay, who in 1833 set his own slaves free and remained throughout a long life a persistent opponent of slavery. His two avowed principles were: "I proudly aver myself the eternal enemy of slavery, and Kentucky must be free." He even published, at Lexington, an anti-slavery paper, *The True American*, and remained

[1] *Journals of the House of Delegates*, 1831–1832, pp. 15, 29, 93, 95, 99, 109, 110; *Senate Journal*, 110, 112, 134, 136, 137, 157, 158; *Journal of the House of Delegates*, 1832–1833, pp. 168, 222, 227; *Senate Journal*, 168–170.

an impassioned ally of the northern abolitionists.
Some people in the thirties still expected that Kentucky would emancipate its slaves, and even formed
a new Kentucky Anti-Slavery Society as an auxiliary
of the general anti-slavery society.[2]

By far the most effective southern abolitionists
were those who shook the dust from off their feet
and left the south because they could not bear to
live in the midst of slavery. Angelina and Sarah
Grimké, members of a Huguenot family in Charleston, became so convinced of the iniquity of slavery
that they came north, published appeals to the
women of the south, and were among the earliest
women speakers at abolition meetings.[3] James G.
Birney, an Alabama planter, came north to learn the
meaning of the anti-slavery movement, connected
himself with a colonization society, and then, about
1834, became an abolitionist and moved to the
north.[4] Another group of eager young southern
abolitionists included James A. Thome, who became a minister in a Cleveland church, and Asa
Mahan, who became president of Oberlin College.

Nearly all these men joined themselves to an
abolition movement which they found in full action

[1] Garrisons, *Garrison*, III., 379–382; Olmsted, *Texas Journey*,
12; Bremer, *Homes of the New World*, II., 106–108; Von Holst,
United States, III., 118–127.

[2] Stuart, *North America*, II., 184; Jay, *Miscellaneous Writings*,
167.

[3] C. H. Birney, *Sarah and Angelina Grimké;* May, *Recollections*, 232–236.   [4] W. Birney, *James G. Birney*, passim.

in the north, the originator of which was undoubtedly Benjamin Lundy, who continued his agitation
after 1830 to his death in 1838.[1] To him must always be ascribed the credit of being the first abolitionist journalist and the first link in a chain of
impulse to which nearly all the other abolitionists
traced their beginnings. From his first meeting with
Garrison, in 1828, he had a disciple greater than his
master, and himself to become an apostle.

That William Lloyd Garrison, young, friendless,
without especial literary or forensic training, should
have made himself one of the most widely known
men of his time, should have established a celebrated newspaper, and should have been the reputed
head of a moral movement which convulsed the
whole country, is a high tribute to his abilities and
character. Returning northward from Baltimore
in 1830, he conceived the idea of founding a newspaper of his own, and the first number of the
Liberator appeared January 1, 1831, in Boston, the
very paper on which it was printed bought on credit,
and the type set by his own hand. This first number included a brief "address to the public," in which
are the key-notes of Garrison's later career: "I shall
strenuously contend for the immediate enfranchise-
ment of our slave population—I will be as harsh as
truth and as uncompromising as justice on this subject — I do not wish to think, or speak, or write
with moderation—I am in earnest—I will not equiv-

[1] See above, chap. xi.

ocate—I will not retreat a single inch, and I *will be heard!*" Then followed a copy of a petition for the abolition of slavery in the District of Columbia; a cutting from a Washington paper criticising the slave-trade in the capital; an account of his own trial in Baltimore; a report of the meeting of the Manumission Society; extracts from correspondents; brief items and clippings from southern newspapers, and several verses.   It was a microcosm of the whole abolition agitation.[1]

The newspaper thus obscurely founded soon found friends, who from time to time provided the modest sums necessary to keep it afloat; and it was at once sent into the citadel of the enemy, for in September, 1831, angry inquiries came from the south to the mayor of Boston, who replied that he could find nobody who had seen the paper, and that it was supported by the free colored people.   It was really chiefly supported by its editor's unconquerable spirit. Garrison was a natural journalist, in that he had a keen eye for lively and interesting news, and the influence of the paper was extended through quotations made from it by other newspapers; he excelled in the editorial combats which were the habit of the journalism of that time, and he had a genius for infuriating his antagonists.   No banderillero ever more skilfully planted his darts in the flank of an enraged bull.   The immediate circulation of the *Liberator* was never large; it rose to about fourteen

[1] Garrisons, *Garrison*, I., 224–226.

hundred in 1837, and was given up in 1865, when its work was accomplished. It was always a losing concern, and a journalist who, in the conduct of a political or party newspaper, could have rivalled and excelled Bennett, Dana, and Greeley, drew the barest subsistence from his paper.

Garrison was not only a remarkable writer, he was an effective speaker, and for the same reason in both cases; he put his whole strength and vitality into his addresses, violently and often unfairly attacking foes and even friends, but hammering his principles home. This influence was greatly extended by occasional journeys, though not until 1842 did he tour New York State. He says of one of his meetings on this trip: "The whole town is in a ferment, every tongue is in motion, if an earthquake had occurred, it would not have excited more consternation." [1]

Towards the slave-holders Garrison was pitiless; his own mind had no room for excuses or palliation or half-way convictions; he made no fine distinctions between the slave-holder who treated his slaves as balky beasts of burden, and the conscientious man who recognized his responsibility to his slave household but did not see a duty of emancipating them. Upon those who met Garrison he made a variety of impressions. "One sees in his beautiful countenance, and clear eagle eye, that resolute spirit which makes the martyr." [2] And Theodore Parker said of

[1] Garrisons, *Garrison*, III., 170.
[2] Bremer, *Homes of the New World*, I., 123.

him: "I am to thank you for what your character has taught me—it has been a continual Gospel of Strength. I value Integrity above all human virtues. I never knew yours fail,—no, nor even falter." [1] Miss Martineau said: "His speech is deliberate like a Quaker's but gentle as a woman's." [2] On the other hand, Hezekiah Niles called him a "man who is doing all possible injury to the cause of emancipation." [3] Another styled him the "Whip master general and supreme judge of all abolitionists, as though he wore the triple crown and wielded an irresponsible sceptre." [4] As for the south, the *National Intelligencer* said of the agitation of the *Liberator:* "The crime is as great as that of poisoning the waters of life to a whole community." [5]

Just a year after the founding of the *Liberator*, Garrison organized a New England Anti-Slavery Society; it was an obvious step to proceed thence to a federation like those of the churches and other philanthropic societies. Local societies sent delegates to the meetings of the state society; then, in December, 1833,[6] the American Anti-Slavery Society was founded in Philadelphia to concentrate the agitation of the whole country. This anti-slavery convention, called while Garrison was out of the country, and presided over by Beriah Green, of New

---

[1] Garrisons, *Garrison*, III., 481.   [2] *Ibid.*, II., 70.
[3] *Niles' Register*, XLI., 145.   [4] Garrisons, *Garrison*, II., 271.
[5] *Ibid.*, I., 238.
[6] *Ibid.*, 392–414; May, *Recollections*, 79–97; *Old South Leaflets*, No. 81.

York, formed a simple constitution and put forth a declaration of principles, including the statement that "slavery is contrary to the principles of that natural justice, of our republican form of government and of the Christian religion; an organization ought to be formed by appeals to consciences, hearts and interests of the people to awaken a public sentiment throughout the nation." [1]

From this time on the local societies rapidly increased throughout the east. In 1835 there were 200; in 1836, more than 500; in 1840, about 2000 auxiliary societies, with between 150,000 and 200,000 members. The income of the society rose from $1000, in 1834, to $47,000 in 1840. The whole organization was on the high-tide of prosperity. All these societies had periodical meetings, local, state, and national, and paid agitators, arousing interest and organizing societies.

A figure like Garrison, who sprang into the centre of the arena, forced the fighting, and gave and took the hardest kind of blows, at once attracted allies and supporters, and he found himself at the head of a cohort. One of his warm friends and coadjutors was John Greenleaf Whittier, a New England Quaker, who in 1833 came into the agitation and helped to organize the American Anti-Slavery Society. Whittier always had a liking for political organization, in which he showed remarkable aptitude, and during the three years 1835 to 1837

[1] MacDonald, *Select Documents*, 304.

he was a member of the Massachusetts legislature, and had such weight in the Essex district that he compelled Caleb Cushing to make pledges to him as the only means of securing an election to Congress.[1] For a time he edited an anti-slavery paper in Philadelphia, and was author of various anti-slavery documents; but his chief service was as the poet of the anti-slavery cause. "The Farewell of a Virginia Slave Mother" is perhaps the best known:

> " Gone, gone,—sold and gone,
>   To the rice-swamp dank and lone,
>   From Virginia's hills and waters;
>   Woe is me, my stolen daughters!"

No less than eighty of his poems appeared in the *National Era* alone. Less aggressive, although an out-and-out abolitionist, Longfellow also gave his aid to the cause by his verses, especially the *Poems on Slavery* (1842).

The man who most resembled Garrison in the fierceness and mercilessness of his attacks was Wendell Phillips, who, in December, 1837, then a young law student, at a meeting held to protest against the recent murder of Lovejoy at Alton, Illinois,[2] sprang into the forefront of the anti-slavery speakers. Possessed of a wonderfully easy and beautiful diction, animated on occasion to the

---

[1] Pickard, *Whittier*, I., 172–186, confirmed by a personal statement of Whittier to the author of this book.
[2] See chap. xvii., below.

highest flights of oratory, and never held back by adhesion to plain and common-sense facts, Phillips, "the silver-tongued orator," was a force in the anti-slavery meetings, and throughout the contest was called upon to electrify and arouse. If he had little or no power of logical reasoning, he did appeal to the great principles of human liberty; and he sealed his adherence to the unpopular cause of the weak and the oppressed by parting company with his own intimate friends.[1]

Later to enter the lists and throw an established literary reputation into an unpopular cause, was James Russell Lowell. Earlier in life Lowell took the conventional view of abolition, but when, in 1845, he went to Philadelphia to write for *The Pennsylvania Freeman*, his first anti-slavery utterance was called out by the capture of some fugitive slaves. Presently he found himself an abolitionist and an editor of the *National Anti-Slavery Standard;* and there followed, in 1846, the unrelenting satire to which he gave the name of *The Biglow Papers*, in which he fused a fierce hatred of slavery with vigorous anti-slavery arguments against extension of southern territory. "Leaving the sin of it to God," said he, "I believe and still believe that slavery is the Achilles heel of our polity; that it is a temporary and false supremacy of the white races, sure to destroy that supremacy at last, because an enslaved people always prove

[1] Higginson, *Contemporaries*, 258–268.

themselves of more enduring fibre than their en-
slavers." [1]

These were the leaders, but with them were associated a host of other men who gave their lives to
the cause, some of whom made more impression
upon contemporaries than upon posterity; Charles
C. Burleigh, for example, celebrated for his apt
answers to questions and his objections to razor
and shears; John G. Palfrey, of Massachusetts, who
inherited fifty slaves, worth about nine thousand
dollars, brought them to Massachusetts and set
them free; [2] Dr. Charles Follen, exiled from Germany for what would now be called a Nihilist conspiracy, and the one professor of Harvard College
who unswervingly gave himself up to anti-slavery; [3]
Theodore Parker, the trenchant Boston minister
and protector of fugitives. The cause was cheered
and strengthened by the adhesion of several members of the old Boston families, especially Edmund
Quincy, who, like Phillips, was roused by the attempt to justify the assassination of Lovejoy. Even
Charles Francis Adams, son of the ex-president,
wrote at the time: "I wish I could be an entire
abolitionist, but it is impossible; my mind will not
come down to the point." [4]

[1] Scudder, *Lowell*, I., 257.   [2] May, *Recollections*, 397.
[3] *Ibid.*, 249-258.   [4] Adams, *C. F. Adams*, 36.

CHAPTER XIII

NON-GARRISONIAN ABOLITION

(1831–1860)

THE forces which brought abolition to the front
were older than Garrison, and would have made
themselves felt if he had never lived. In New England and outside arose anti-slavery men like Adams,
who never acted with him, and plenty of abolitionists who never accepted allegiance to him; while
many of his earlier followers cast off his leadership
and pursued ends of which he disapproved. Three
groups of non-Garrisonian abolitionists may be distinguished—the New England, the middle state, and
the western.

In New England one of the great moral forces
was Dr. William Ellery Channing, Unitarian minister in Boston and Newport. His sympathy was
naturally with the movement, but he disliked Garrison's severity of tone and method, and was un-
moved by a personal appeal from Garrison in
January, 1834.[1] The great authority of his pen was
more successfully sought by others, and in December, 1835, he published a volume setting forth the

[1] Garrisons, *Garrison*, I., 464.

terrible evils of slavery, but suggesting other remedies than immediate emancipation.   During the remaining four years of his life Channing continued
his argument, quite outside the Garrison movement, and his books furnished an arsenal of material against slavery.

The middle states group was strong in New York
City and among the Quakers of Pennsylvania,[1] and
the aged Gallatin, throughout his life an opponent
of slavery, in 1844 squarely placed himself as an
anti-slavery man.[2]   William Jay, son of the chief-
justice, early joined the movement and wrote effective criticisms of slavery, based on historical data.
Horace Greeley, editor of the *Tribune*, contented
himself, during the earlier struggle, with anti-slavery
ground.[3]   Rev. Samuel J. May, of Syracuse, was a
sort of New York Garrison, though less caustic and
aggressive.

In the middle states group were several wealthy
and generous friends of the cause.   The brothers
Arthur and Lewis Tappan, merchants of New York,
for years active colonizationists, in 1833 came over
to the abolitionist column, and helped to found a
New York society.   They supported with timely
gifts several struggling newspapers, issued tracts,
and attempted to form a colored college.[4]   Of similar
character was Gerrit Smith, of Peterboro, New York,

[1] Child, *Hopper*, passim.   [2] Adams, *Gallatin*, 671.
[3] Parton, *Greeley*, 250.
[4] Bowen, *A. and L. Tappan;* L. Tappan, *Life of A. Tappan.*

the son of a New York slave-holder and the owner
of about seven hundred and fifty thousand acres of
land.   At first a colonizationist, in 1835 he became
an abolitionist, and in course of years gave to the
national and New York societies at least fifty thousand dollars in cash, besides presenting forty acres
of land to each of three thousand colored men.   His
money gifts were the smaller part of his interest in
the cause: his house was a caravansary for abolitionists and a refuge for fugitives; he was one of the
earliest political abolitionists in the country, and
aided in the formation of the Liberty party in 1839.[1]

The third group of abolitionists grew up with little care or knowledge of Garrison.   Slavery was a
familiar issue in the west, while New England was
still inactive, but a new public excitement on the
subject was aroused by the debate in Lane Theological Seminary in Cincinnati in 1832.   The president, Dr. Lyman Beecher, was an eastern man, whose
daughter Harriet made some observations during
her residence which were later incorporated into
Uncle Tom's Cabin.   The students were partly
drawn from the northern and partly from the
southern states, including the sons of slave-holders.
At the suggestion of Arthur Tappan, one of the
founders of the seminary, the students took up
colonization and abolition, and eighteen consecutive
nights were spent in hot discussion.   Theodore F.

---

[1] May, *Recollections*, 167–170, 321–329; Goodell, *Slavery and
Anti-Slavery*, 405, 463; Frothingham, *Gerrit Smith*.

Weld, a student from the east, a disciple of Garrison, much affected the minds of his fellows; and a majority of the students became abolitionists and began to practise their principles by setting up Sunday and day schools for colored children.

The trustees were aroused, and voted that there must be no further public discussions, in which Dr. Beecher concurred, whereupon four-fifths of the students withdrew (May, 1833), and fifty-four joined in a public statement that they could not give up their right to inquire into slavery. For some months they set up some sort of institution of their own, listening to lectures by Dr. Gamaliel Bailey. Asa Mahan, then a minister in Cincinnati, resigned from the board of trustees, and, with Rev. John Morgan, who had been a professor in the seminary, piloted the students to Oberlin.[1]

This secession was practically the beginning of organized abolition in Ohio, and it resulted in the creation of an abolition centre in the west. Philo P. Stewart, manufacturer of an excellent cooking-stove in Albany, and the Rev. John J. Shipherd, a minister in Ohio, in 1833 conceived the idea of a Puritan commonwealth on the frontier. Securing a tract of land at some distance from any other village, they named it Oberlin, for a benevolent pastor in the Vosges Mountains, and in December, 1833, opened

---

[1] Lyman Beecher, *Autobiography*, II., chap. xxxiv.; Stanton, *Random Recollections*, 43–48; Birney, *Birney*, 135–137; *Statement of Reasons for Withdrawal from Lane Seminary* (pamphlet).

a school in which fifteen of the forty-four students were girls. The education of boys and girls together, even in boarding-schools, was not unfamiliar in New England and the west; but when, two months later, the new institution secured a charter as the "Oberlin Collegiate Institute," including among its objects "the elevation of female character, by bringing within the reach of the misjudged and neglected sex all the instructoral privileges which have hitherto unreasonably distinguished the leading sex from theirs," [1] it was evident that here was a new idea; for the first time in the history of the country the opportunity of a thorough college education was given to women; and in due time some of them received from this college the first degrees of A.B. conferred on women in this country.

Now arose the question of joint education of whites and blacks. In December, 1834, Mr. Shipherd insisted that students must be admitted "irrespective of color." For a time the trustees hung back; but when informed that unless negroes were admitted they could not obtain Professor Morgan from Lane Seminary, nor Mahan, the gifted southerner, to be their president, nor Finney, a noted theologian and revivalist, nor ten thousand dollars that was waiting for them, the trustees, February 9, 1835, voted: "That the education of the people of color is a matter of great interest and should be encouraged and sustained in this institution."

[1] Fairchild, *Oberlin*, 41.

Thereupon the three desired professors appeared, together with thirty Lane students. Weld visited Oberlin, and, by his powerful abolition arguments, revolutionized the sentiment of the place. The students formed anti - slavery societies, began to hold meetings in the neighborhood, and in a few years formed a focus of active anti-slavery sentiment. In the first year only one of the 277 students was colored, but others gathered, and eventually about one-fifth of the population of the place was negro, and it became a great station on the Underground Railroad.[1]

Some of the pre-existing Ohio anti-slavery societies, in April, 1835, joined in forming a state society, in which the leaders were Samuel Crothers, John Rankin, and others from the slave states, Elizur Wright, a professor in the Congregational Western Reserve College, and a group of the Lane Seminary seceders. Within a year a hundred and twenty societies had been formed, with more than ten thousand members. The next year the movement was strengthened by the coming of James G. Birney, who had been driven out of Kentucky because he was trying to print an anti-slavery paper, and he set up the *Philanthropist*, which was soon accepted by the Ohio society and became its organ. A few months later the office of his paper in Cincinnati was sacked by a mob and Birney's life was endangered. The movement was now under full

[1] Fairchild, *Oberlin*, 55–77, 111–115.

headway. Although Theodore F. Weld introduced the leaven, it was 1847 before Garrison saw the western slope of the Alleghanies. Then he travelled with Frederick Douglass, held conventions and open-air meetings throughout the Western Reserve, and visited Oberlin, where he found himself opposed in debate by President Mahan; but he was never recognized as the head or leader of the western abolitionists.[1]

The movement soon made itself felt in others of the northwestern states. Indiana had only a small proportion of eastern settlers and was slow in taking up abolition. Illinois began to form local societies in 1835, which were strongest in the northern counties. In Michigan the movement began in 1834, and there may have been thirty societies in 1840 as against several hundred in Ohio.[2] In Illinois there was a young member of the legislature, named Abraham Lincoln, who, on March 3, 1837, joined with one Dan Stone in a formal written protest setting forth that "They believe that the institution of slavery is founded on both injustice and bad policy, but that the promulgation of abolition doctrines tends rather to increase than abate its evils."[3]

The reason for the unequal development of the three areas of abolition is to be found in part in the difference of conditions. In New England abolition

---

[1] Garrisons, *Garrison*, III., 203.
[2] Smith, *Liberty and Free Soil Parties*, 13.
[3] Nicolay and Hay, *Lincoln*, I., 140.

dealt with an extraneous motive: slavery had all but disappeared, and few of those engaged in the movement had any personal experience of it. It was not till negroes began to appear on the New England platforms and to be hunted through the streets of New England cities that slavery seemed a personal thing. The middle states had about three thousand slaves in 1830, and they were much more familiar than the New England states with the coming of fugitives and free negroes, and were subject to various sorts of border difficulties; slavery was therefore to them a more practical evil. In the west the relation was still closer and more pertinent, for though the slaves were but a few hundred, almost the whole length of the Ohio River was a slave-holding frontier. Thousands of northwestern people visited Virginia, Kentucky, or Missouri, and the presence of many anti-slavery "come-outers" from the slave-holding states gave a vividness to the movement which it nowhere else possessed. Cincinnati, deeply interested in southern trade and much visited by southerners, was also a centre of anti-slavery discussion, and the home of James G. Birney, the best-known southern critic of slavery; of Gamaliel Bailey, the most vigorous western anti-slavery editor; and of Salmon P. Chase, the most striking political abolitionist in the west.

A New Hampshire man by birth, educated in Washington, and settled in Ohio in 1830, Chase easily took on the characteristics of that bustling community. He was aroused to anti-slavery by the attempt to silence and to mob Birney in 1836; and in 1841 he threw himself into the movement, attended and addressed anti-slavery meetings, and helped to organize an abolition party.[1]

One reason for the force which abolition early acquired in Ohio was the fallow field waiting for it in the Western Reserve. This region, settled by Connecticut people between 1790 and 1820, was still a little New England, its churches, schools, and local government closely modelled on those of Connecticut. Western Reserve College, planted at Hudson, near Cleveland, in 1826, was a western Yale; though at first inclined to hold back in abolition, it became, like its neighbor Oberlin, a seminary of anti-slavery sentiment. In the Western Reserve, abolition societies, meetings, and agitators flourished; and from it, in 1838, was chosen Joshua R. Giddings, the first western abolitionist member of the House of Representatives; eleven years later, through the deciding vote of a member of the legislature from a district which included Oberlin, Salmon P. Chase was elected senator from Ohio.[2]

All three sections had their part in the great abolition struggle; all three groups contributed forces necessary for the struggle. New England raised up orators, poets, and satirists—the spokesmen of the rights of man and the obligations of

[1] Hart, *Chase*, chap. iii.
[2] Hart, "Anti-Slavery in Ohio," in his *Chase*, chap. iii.

society. The middle states furnished a considerable part of the sinews of war; kept up the journals, east and west; founded schools and aided colleges; and made a point of resistance to the commercial influences of New York and Philadelphia. The western abolitionists organized the Underground Railroad, which helped to make slavery unprofitable; drew in the aid of southerners themselves; and, above all, devised and set in motion a political abolition party.[1]

That Garrison made no effort to build up a following in the middle and western states was partly due to a series of conflicts within the eastern abolitionists, which led, after five or six years of strife, to a weakening split. The main grounds of difference between the Garrisonians and other abolitionists were five — personal disagreements, the status of women, the Bible, non-resistance, and politics.

The abolitionists were not all lambs, and not all reasonable; and Garrison was unsparing of his friends as well as of his enemies. He had what his biographers call "an unyielding purpose to expose and refute the errors, fallacies, and misrepresentations of every proselyte to the cause, or every ally, however great his name or desirable his accession." [2] Especially towards Channing he felt all the bitterness of a radical against a liberal, and he characterized Channing's extremely strong and effective at-

---

[1] Smith, *Parties and Slavery* (*Am. Nation*, XVIII.), chap. xii.
[2] Garrisons, *Garrison*, II., 90.

tack on slavery as "moral plagiarisms from the writings of the abolitionists."

Up to this time, except among the Methodists and Quakers, women were not expected to take part in any sort of public meetings, and St. Paul was quoted against them: "But I suffer not a woman to teach, nor to usurp authority over the man, but to be in silence."[1] Nevertheless, when the convention of 1833 was held at Philadelphia, Lucretia Mott and other women took part in the proceedings unrebuked. Thereafter women joined freely in the abolition movement; to whom, as Dr. Channing said, "above all others slavery should seem an intolerable evil because its chief victims are women."[2] A separate women's society was formed in Boston. In many places women entered the local societies as members, officers, and even speakers. The Grimké sisters lent force to the movement by their personal testimony to the iniquities of slavery. Lydia Maria Child, an author of much repute, took up the cudgels in a book—*An Appeal in Favor of that Class of Americans called Africans*—which cost her her market in the south. Many other women gave their pens and their voices; and some foreign women, by their criticism of slavery as they saw it —especially Fanny Kemble and Frederika Bremer —much inflamed public opinion. In 1837 an effort was made to stay this tide by a pastoral letter to the churches, issued by the Massachusetts Associa-

[1] *1 Timothy*, ii., 12. [2] Channing, *Works*, II., 66.

tion of Congregational Ministers, based on the principle that the "perplexed and agitating subjects which are now common amongst us . . . should not be forced upon any church as matters for debate at the hazard of alienation and division"; and that it portended changes which "threatened the female character with widespread and permanent injury— the vine usurps the role of the elm."[1] With his accustomed wrath, Garrison repelled the charges of disrupting the churches and unsexing women; but when, in 1838, the Massachusetts Anti-Slavery Society formally accepted women as members, a separate Massachusetts Abolition Society was formed, with Elizur Wright as secretary, stating as "ground of separation from the old that the latter upheld a change in the sphere of woman's action."[2]

A serious charge was that Garrison was drifting into infidelity. Always a man of strong religious feeling, and beginning as a very orthodox church member, observant of the forms of prayer and churchgoing, Garrison at one time adhered to perfection— that is, the doctrine of personal holiness; later in life he inclined to spiritualism. In 1836 he protested against attempting to enforce the observance of the Sabbath "as a positive tyranny which ought to be resisted by all the Lord's freemen."[3] Among the principles thus taken up and urged by Garrison

[1] May, *Recollections*, 237–244; Garrisons, *Garrison*, II., 133.
[2] Garrisons, *Garrison*, II., 305–307.
[3] *Ibid.*, 112; III., 375–377.

was that of peace, and the only way to assure it was
for all men to practise non-resistance, an idea in our
day revived by Tolstoï. Then Garrison's principle
grew till it embraced non-participation in any government which permitted the use of force to re-
strain the slave. In 1837, in his tribute to the
murdered Lovejoy, he lodged a solemn protest
because Lovejoy and his friends had armed themselves; and in 1838 he called together a peace convention in Boston, which voted that "we cannot
acknowledge allegiance to any human government;
neither can we oppose any such government by a
resort to physical force. Our country is the world,
our countrymen are all mankind. We love the land
of our nativity only as we love all other lands." [1]

This hostility to political action, and Garrison's
general disposition to combine other causes and reforms with anti-slavery, and to insist that genuine
abolitionists must accept them all, were distasteful
to both middle state and western abolitionists, and
hastened a split in the national organization. In
1839 an attempt was made to oust Garrison from
his position of leadership by excluding women from
committee positions. It failed, but both parties
girded up their loins for the next annual meeting in
1840. Every abolitionist present had a vote, and,
as Garrison boasted, an "anti-slavery boatload . . .
saved our society from falling into the hands of the
new organizers." A test vote of 560 Garrisonians

[1] Garrisons, *Garrison*, II., 230.

to 450 dissidents was the signal for the formation
of a new national society under the name of the
"American and Foreign Anti-Slavery Society." Garrison declared that the new society was a mere mask
for Lewis Tappan, who drew up its annual report
and bore the expenses of its single meeting.[1] The
old society disclaimed any attempt to make non-
resistance a test for abolitionists; but it adhered to
its women memberships and emphasized its anti-
clerical principles by voting that "the American
church, with the exception of some of its smaller
branches, has given its undisguised sanction and
support to the system of American slavery."[2]

The effect of the split was shown by the treasurer's report of the original American society, the
annual income dropping immediately from $47,000
to $7000, and for fifteen years it did not rise above
$12,000. The number of local societies and of mem-
bers also at once diminished and was never recovered. The new society never had any such galaxy
of journalists and speakers, and was unable to concentrate the western societies, which, by this time,
were changing into political organizations; and,
after 1840, abolition as a national force was giving
way to the anti-slavery movement stirred by the
efforts to annex Texas.[3]

[1] Garrisons, *Garrison*, III., 35; Goodell, *Slavery and Anti-Slavery*, 447–462.

[2] Garrisons, *Garrison*, II., 349; defence of Garrison in Chap-
man, *Right and Wrong in Massachusetts*.

[3] See Garrison, *Westward Extension* (*Am. Nation*, XVII.), chap. v.

CHAPTER XIV

THE ABOLITION PROPAGANDA

(1830–1840)

IF we are to accept the statement of the motives and purposes of the abolitionists put forward by their adversaries, they were among the worst of mankind: "Prurient love of notoriety," "envy or malignity," an intention to "excite to desperate attempts and particular acts of cruelty and horror," to bring about "a complete equalization of blacks and whites," to "scatter among our southern brethren firebrands, arrows and death"—such are some of the amenities applied to the abolitionists.[1] Even the gentle Emerson said of them: "If an angry bigot assumes this bountiful cause of Abolition, and comes to me with his last news from Barbadoes, why should I not say to him, 'Go love thy infant; love thy wood-chopper; be good-natured and modest; have that grace; and never varnish your hard, uncharitable ambition with this incredible tender-

---

[1] Harper, in *Pro-Slavery Argument*, 93; Von Raumer, *America*, 121; Garrisons, *Garrison*, I., 495–500; cf. Bledsoe, *Liberty and Slavery*, chap. ii.

ness for black folk a thousand miles off. Thy love afar is spite at home!'" [1]

These charges can hardly be thought a self-evident statement of the objects of the abolitionists, which may be gathered in part from their private character, partly from their own public statements, and partly from the methods which they employed to influence public opinion. As for their character, the abolitionists in general were people who paid their debts, attended divine service, and had the reputation of an orderly life. Some of them were one-sided men, such as Garrison and Phillips, who held a brief for liberty and did not trouble themselves to look at the case of the other side—indeed, they did not admit that there was another side. There were some impostors and some demagogues among them, but Whittier in New England, the Tappans in New York, and Birney in the west, were characteristic abolitionists of their sections, and none of them was false, self-seeking, or bloodthirsty.

In their spoken and printed statements the abolitionists justified Jay's admonition : "They will address arguments to the understanding and the consciences of their fellow-citizens"; and Lundy, an uncompromising foe of slavery, held that "the language of cutting retort or severe rebuke, is seldom convincing, and it is wholly out of place in persuasive argument." Most of them also held

---

[1] Emerson, *Essay on Self-Reliance.*

that the use of force was not part of their pro-
gramme.[1]

Then how and where was the slave to be freed?
In the first number of the *Liberator*, Garrison abjured the doctrine of gradual emancipation, and all
his societies declared unhesitatingly for immediate
emancipation, the American society adding that
"No compensation should be given to the planters
emancipating their slaves."[2] Yet, outside of New
England, the societies and leaders would have cheer-
fully accepted gradual emancipation acts from the
neighboring slave states. Among the known opponents of immediacy were Evan Lewis of Philadelphia, first president of the American Anti-Slavery
Society, William Jay of New York, and Moses Brown
of Providence.[3]

Abolition meant to the abolitionists not only freedom, but the eradication of all the incidents and
results of slavery—"all the laws, discriminations,
social customs and practices which bore against the
negro race."[4] As for the slave-holder, since slavery
was an obvious evil, the abolitionists held him
morally responsible and called upon him to repent
and to show works meet for repentance by abolish-

[1] Jay, *Miscellaneous Writings*, 140; *Life of Benjamin Lundy*,
28; Garrisons, *Garrison*, I., 295.

[2] See Garrisons, *Garrison*, I., 410, in postscript. For early advocates of immediacy, see George Bourne, *Book and Slavery Irreconcilable* (1816); Elizabeth Heyrick, *Immediate vs. Gradual
Emancipation* (London, 1824).

[3] Goodell, *Slavery and Anti-Slavery*, 393.

[4] Declaration of 1833, in Garrisons, *Garrison*, I., 408.

ing slavery on his own plantation. As incident to these purposes the abolitionists claimed the fullest right of freedom of speech, both north and south.[1]

An obvious and disturbing retort by the slave-holder was that the abolitionist knew nothing of what he was discussing. "Why don't you go South?" was a taunt frequently hurled, to which Garrison, who had never been beyond Baltimore, but whose personal courage was undeniable, re-plied: "Why, then, should we go into the slave-holding states, to assail their towering wickedness, at a time when we are sure we should be gagged, or imprisoned, or put to death, if we went thither?"[2] The only New England agitators who had seen much of slavery in the south were Channing and James Freeman Clarke, a Unitarian minister in Louisville from 1833 to 1840.[3] The reproach did not apply to men born in the south, like Birney and Cassius M. Clay, Rankin and Mahan, or Elijah P. Lovejoy, who lived for a time in St. Louis. Few abolitionists were known to have attempted a propaganda in the far south.[4] The charge that the abolitionists knew nothing of slavery was not significant, for foreign and northern visitors freely reported their impres-sions, and in the columns of southern newspapers the abolitionists found unfailing material.

The argument that the abolitionists had no busi-

---

[1] Channing to Birney, *Works*, II., 161.
[2] Garrisons, *Garrison*, I., 507.
[3] Clarke, *Anti-Slavery Days*, 22.　　[4] See chap. xvi., below

ness to discuss a question which did not concern them would have been stronger had the south encouraged or even permitted discussion by its own people. A keen foreigner observed that she "scarcely ever met with a man, or woman either, who can openly and honestly look the thing in the face. They wind and turn about in all sorts of ways, and make use of every argument, sometimes the most opposite, to convince me that the slaves are the happiest people in the world." [1] The abolitionists fell back on their right to supply the deficiency. "We are told indeed by the South," said Dr. Channing, "that slavery is no concern of ours, and consequently that the less we say of it the better. What! shall the wrongdoer forbid lookers-on to speak, because the affair is a private one?" [2]

Never doubting their legal and moral right to organize northern public opinion against slavery in the south, the abolitionists worked out a thoroughgoing propaganda: they drew up petitions to the state and national legislatures; they appeared before legislative committees; they sent out travelling agents; they busied themselves with the conditions of the free colored people; above all, they held anti-slavery meetings in all sorts of places, from a stable-loft to a church or public hall. An account of one of these meetings, in Faneuil Hall in 1850, will serve as a type of all. It was addressed by escaped

[1] Bremer, *Homes of the New World*, I., 275.
[2] Channing, *Works*, VI., 61.

fugitive slaves, one of whom was a woman. Miss Lucy Stone inveighed against the pro-slavery men of the north, and especially Daniel Webster. Edmund Quincy drew down upon himself the hisses of the audience by criticising his brother, the mayor of Boston, and was cut off by calls for Wendell Phillips, who "spoke with the low voice of suppressed emotion, and a simplicity of language, yet powerful enough to incite to the utmost the human heart. . . . The assembly hung on his lips and took in every word. An excited gentleman leapt upon the platform and began to declaim at the side of Phillips. The assembly whistled, shouted, clapped, and hissed, but began to leave with the utmost calmness and composure."[1] At the regular meetings of societies and conventions reports were made, officers were elected, and appeals to the public were drawn up.

The abolitionists early learned how much paper can be covered with printer's ink at a small expense, and had a special press. Next to the *Liberator* comes the *Genius of Universal Emancipation;* the *Emancipator*, published in New York, and, in a sense, the organ for the middle states; the *Abolitionist*, under the editorship, for a time, of William Goodell; the *Philanthropist*, in Cincinnati; and, later, the *National Era*, ably edited by Dr. Gamaliel Bailey, in Washington. No great daily took up the cause of abolition previous to 1860, but the New

[1] Bremer, *Homes of the New World*, I., 192–196.

York *Tribune* and many western dailies were anti-slavery in tone.[1] These papers all had a limited circulation among the faithful, but were vigorously edited and widely quoted.

The abolitionists, east and west, stood by their principles in admitting negroes to a part in their movement; the northern free negroes subscribed for the papers, made up part of the audiences, and furnished several agitators, of whom the Rev. J. W. Loguen, of Syracuse, was the best known. An interesting delegation of southern negroes somehow found their way north to speak from their own experience of slavery; and they were a living argument for the tenet of the abolitionists that the negro was a black white man, held back simply by lack of opportunities.[2]

When Frederick Douglass made his first appearance in New England, in 1843, Garrison asked: "Have we been listening to a thing, a piece of property, or to a man?" and he followed it up with the question, "Shall such a man ever be sent back to slavery from the soil of old Massachusetts?"[3] Douglass was at once made an agent of the Massachusetts society, wrote a striking book upon his experiences, and even set up an anti-slavery paper of his own, *The North Star*. A man of extraordinary power and magnetism, a remarkable speaker, the

---

[1] See list of papers in Smith, *Liberty and Free Soil Parties*, App. B; *Life of Benjamin Lundy*, 261.   [2] See chap. xxii., below.

[3] Garrisons, *Garrison*, III., 19.

most eminent of his race in that period, he travelled widely through the country, and occasional efforts were made to lynch him.[1] A very striking negro woman was Sojourner Truth, a New York slave, set free by the emancipation act of 1827, who preached wherever she could find hearers, made short journeys through the north, and was a frequent figure at anti-slavery meetings. Tall, very black, crowned with a bandanna turban, she looked like a sable princess, and had a shrewd and homely wisdom exemplified in her dictum on woman's rights: "Ef women want any rights, mor'n dey's got, why don't dey jes' take 'em, an' not be talkin' about it?"[2]

A similar character was the heroic Harriet Tubman, who went time after time into the southern states, made up companies of discontented slaves, and brought north to freedom about three hundred of her folk. Her extraordinary power of statement was illustrated in her description of a battle in the Civil War: "And then we saw the lightning, and that was the guns; and then we heard the thunder, and that was the big guns; and then we heard the rain falling, and that was drops of blood falling; and when we came to git in the craps, it was dead men that we reaped."[3]

The New England abolitionists sought co-opera-

---

[1] Monroe, *Lectures and Addresses*, 57–94; May, *Recollections*, 293–296; Garrisons, *Garrison*, III., 18–20.
[2] Mrs. Stowe, in *Atlantic Monthly*, XI., 473–481; *Sojourner Truth*.   [3] Heard by the author of this book.

tion with the English, and Garrison three times visited England to detach Clarkson and other veterans from the colonization movement. In 1840, Garrison, at a world's convention of anti-slavery people in London, refused to sit because women delegates from Massachusetts were not received.[1] One result of this co-operation was an address of sixty thousand Irish people to their countrymen and countrywomen in America, urging them to become abolitionists, which had little or no effect except to intensify the feeling that foreigners were meddling in our concerns.[2]

In every part of this agitation the abolitionists stood for a despised cause. The few men like Wendell Phillips, Edmund Quincy, and Thomas W. Higginson, who came out of the agreeable circle of New England aristocracy, were made to feel that it was a choice between the slave and the friends of their youth. When Harriet Martineau attended an anti-slavery meeting she found that she had given offence to the best society in Boston. Theodore Parker found his clerical brethren refusing to exchange pulpits with him, and he wrote: "My life seems to me a complete failure socially; here I am as much an outcast from society as though I were a convicted pirate."[3] The eastern colleges, almost

---

[1] Garrisons, *Garrison*, II., 353, 373; III., 159.
[2] *Ibid.*, 343–360; *Daniel O'Connell upon Am. Slavery.*
[3] May, *Recollections*, 159; Frothingham, *Parker*, 158, 347; Pierce, *Sumner*, III., 119–121.

without exception, were strongholds of pro-slavery feeling; when the appointment of Charles Follen as professor in Harvard College expired, somehow he was not reappointed.   In 1848, Charles Sumner, a graduate of Harvard, spoke to the students of the college; Longfellow said: "The shouts and the hisses and the vulgar interruptions grated on my ears.   I was glad to get away."   When Emerson spoke on the fugitive-slave law at the Cambridge city-hall, in 1851, he was hissed and hooted by young law students.[1]

That those who profited by slavery would be against them had been expected by the abolitionists, but they were sorely disappointed in the clergy and churches, especially in New England.   When Garrison began his work, he thought nothing was more like the spirit of Christ than to relieve the oppressed, to preach the gospel to the benighted, and to bring a whole race of people out of sin and debasement; but he soon found that neither minister nor church anywhere in the lower south continued to protest against slavery; that the cloth in the north was arrayed against him, and that many northern divines entered the lists against abolition, especially Moses Stuart, professor of Hebrew in Andover Theological Seminary, who justified slavery from the New Testament; President Lord, of Dartmouth College, who held that slavery was an institution of God, according to natural law;[2] and Hopkins,

---

[1] Longfellow, *Longfellow*, II., 127, 194.
[2] Clarke, *Anti-Slavery Days*, 109.

Episcopal bishop of Vermont, who came forward as a thick-and-thin defender of slavery.[1] The positive opposition of churches soon followed. Lewis Tappan and others were tried by their own churches for their abolition activity.[2] The Methodist General Conference of 1836 passed a resolution of censure on two of its members who had spoken in favor of abolition; and the New York Methodist Conference of 1838 warned all members not in any way to patronize the *Zion's Watchman*, an anti-slavery paper.

The controversy was carried into the benevolent and missionary societies. The American Board of Commissioners for Foreign Missions, a Congregational body, permitted its agents among the Indians to hold slaves. The American Home Missionary Society helped to support churches in slave-holding states, in all of which slave-holders were allowed membership. The American Bible Society permitted, without protest, the arrest of one of its agents for furnishing a Bible to a colored person.[3] The Protestant Episcopal church refused to admit to orders a colored candidate otherwise qualified. The Baptists had no authoritative general body, but its missionary and Bible societies employed slave-holders.

---

[1] Hopkins, *Scriptural View of Slavery*.
[2] Goodell, *Slavery and Anti-Slavery*, 434.
[3] Garrisons, *Garrison*, III., 30; Jay, *Miscellaneous Writings*, 661–664; Goodell, *Slavery and Anti-Slavery*, 193, 211.

On the abolition side ranged many individual clergymen of weight and ability, especially in New England. Channing's deliberate and hearty adhesion to abolition, in 1836, gave to the cause a writer of high literary skill and a leader in the conservative and fashionable Unitarian church, to which also belonged James Freeman Clarke. Theodore Parker, of the same denomination, was a radical and suspected by his brethren, but an unyielding abolitionist. Thomas Wentworth Higginson later entered the arena as a militant clerical. In the middle states, the strongest anti-slavery minister was Albert Barnes, of Philadelphia, a great light in the Presbyterian church.[1] In the west, Finney, the eccentric evangelist, carried the weight of his immense power as an exhorter; and many ministers took their congregations with them into the movement.[2]

Neither neglect nor repression could keep the question down. Two of the great national churches were, in this period, split from top to bottom. The General Assembly of the Presbyterian church was, from 1835 to 1837, engaged in an exciting discussion upon the subject, ending by laying on the table addresses by the abolitionist members.[3] Then, after expelling four synods especially affected by the

[1] Barnes, *Church and Slavery*, passim.
[2] Von Holst, *United States*, II., 226–231; May, *Recollections*, 329–345, 365–373; Fairchild, *Oberlin College*, 66, 79.
[3] Goodell, *Slavery and Anti-Slavery*, 153–155.

abolition heresy, it was divided in 1838 into the so-called New School and the Old School upon doctrinal questions.[1]   The Old School Assembly, which included some of the southern Presbyterians and a large proportion of the northern, subsequently voted that the church could not condemn slavery without condemning the apostles for conniving with it.   The New School attempted to relegate the matter to the local presbyteries, and avoided taking action upon it.   Upon this issue a small branch broke off about 1850, under the leadership of Rev. John Rankin, and formed the Free Presbyterian church, with a few thousand adherents, who made it a tenet that no slave-holder should be admitted to membership.   The great Methodist church divided, in 1844, squarely upon the question whether a bishop could hold slaves, and all the southern members withdrew and organized the Methodist Episcopal Church South.   As in the case of the Presbyterians, some smaller fragments set themselves off into out-and-out anti-slavery churches.[2]   Clearly, the impassioned agitation of the abolitionists had made it impossible for a great number of northern anti-slavery men who were not abolitionists, to remain on terms of friendship with their southern brethren.

[1] *Bibliotheca Sacra*, XX., 563–571; Baird, *History of the New School*, 506–558.
[2] Buckley, *History of the Methodists*, 403–405.

CHAPTER XV

THE ABOLITIONIST AND THE SLAVE
(1830–1840)

HOW far was it possible for the abolitionist to reach the negro and to affect the slave? So far as their own direct influence went they practised their own doctrine of equal rights ostentatiously: their negro adherents travelled with them, sat upon the same platforms with them, ate with them, and one enthusiastic abolitionist white couple adopted a negro child. Garrison, in the *Liberator*, urged the negroes to send their children to school, to build up their own trade, to stand by and protect the fugitives, to get on the voting lists, and in every way to make themselves a part of the community.[1]

These relations profoundly stirred the south, partly because they went counter to the conventional belief that if both races were free, "one race must be driven out by the other, or exterminated, or again enslaved";[2] partly because southerners sin-

---

[1] Garrisons, *Garrison*, II., 255–258.
[2] Hammond and Harper, in *Pro-Slavery Argument*, 88–90, 147–149.

cerely believed that the object of the abolitionists was an amalgamation of the two races. On the contrary, Jay demanded whether any person "in the possession of his reasoning faculties can believe it to be the duty of white men to select black wives," [1] though Channing said of amalgamation: "Allowing that amalgamation is to be anticipated, then, I maintain, we have no right to resist it. Then it is not unnatural." [2] The southern born abolitionists agreed with John Rankin: "We entirely disclaim any desire to promote or encourage intermarrying between the blacks and whites." [3] It was a fair inquiry, which the abolitionists did not hesitate to put—who was responsible for the only amalgamation that had so far taken place?

The free negroes of the south the abolitionists could not reach except by mailing publications to them, a process which fearfully exasperated the south without reaching the persons addressed. The slave was even further from any direct help; yet it was the belief of the slave-holders that efforts were made by incendiary publications to acquaint the slaves with the fact that they had friends in the north and to arouse their passions against their masters. Abolitionists were accused of slipping printed handkerchiefs, bearing anti-slavery cuts, into bales designed for the southern markets, and

[1] Jay, *Miscellaneous Writings*, 146.
[2] Channing, *Works*, V., 57.
[3] *Niles' Register*, XXXVI., 461.

of mailing prints and pictures depicting the cruelties of slavery and the delights of emancipation. The south could not understand that the annual anti-slavery almanac, with its crude wood-cuts of floggings and kidnappings, was meant to reach and educate the children of northern people. The pictures would undoubtedly have been suggestive had they reached the slaves, but there is no well-authenticated case in which such materials were found in the hands of slaves. The nearest approach was the discovery of a copy of *Uncle Tom's Cabin* in the house of a free negro in Maryland just before the Civil War, and the danger was then and there stopped by sending him to the penitentiary.[1]

The abolitionists were also charged with trying to bring about slave insurrections. In September, 1829, a southern free negro in Boston issued a pamphlet called *Walker's Appeal*, of which the tone was unmistakable. "For although the destruction of the oppressors God may not effect by the oppressed, yet the Lord our God will bring other destructions upon them—for not unfrequently will he cause them to rise up one against another, to be split, divided, and to oppress each other, and sometimes to open hostilities with sword in hand." [2]

Walker's pamphlet is known to have reached Virginia, and may possibly have influenced the Nat

[1] Brackett, *Negro in Maryland*, 226.
[2] Garrisons, *Garrison*, I., 159–162; *Walker's Appeal*, 5.

Turner insurrection of 1831, the most dangerous incident in the history of that period. Nobody had any suspicion of Nat Turner, an obscure slave in Southampton County, Virginia, though he was a preacher, and could read and write. For several years Nat was making preparations to ravage the country, raise the slaves, and take refuge in the Dismal Swamp. August 21, 1831, with six desperate companions, he rose and spared not a white soul on the plantations that were visited; his force quickly increased to sixty men, and would have probably spread like wildfire but for poor generalship on Nat's part. Before the insurrection could be headed, sixty white people had been killed. Within forty-eight hours militia were raised and United States troops were called.[1] On the first day of resistance over a hundred blacks were killed, and the bloody work continued for some time. Besides unnumbered floggings, 53 negroes in all were put on trial, of whom 21 were acquitted, 12 convicted and sold out of the state, and 20, including Nat Turner and one woman, were convicted and hanged. For a long time the excitement and lawlessness continued. Charity Bowery said: "The brightest and best men were killed in Nat's time. Such ones are always suspected. All the colored folks were afraid to pray, in the time of the Old Prophet Nat. There was no law about it; but the whites reported it round among themselves, that if

[1] *Federal Aid in Domestic Disturbance*, 56.

a note was heard, we should have some dreadful punishment." [1]

The Nat Turner insurrection shook slavery to its foundations; the fact that Nat, though he bore some marks of ill-usage, had not been treated with special cruelty proved that kindness did not bring content; since the plot went on for months without suspicion, similar movements might be pending in any community. Turner had been joined by slaves not previously recruited, so that no one could tell how far a rising, once started, might sweep. The heavy destruction of property and of innocent life, both white and black, suggested some new form of protection, more severe laws against the assembling of negroes, against their learning to read and write, and against any form of anti-slavery agitation by white people. Though negroes thereafter were occasionally whipped, shot, or burned on suspicion of a plot, no other serious rising occurred until the John Brown raid at Harper's Ferry in 1859.[2] Inasmuch as the *Liberator* became known in the south at the time of the Nat Turner insurrection, the cry was raised that the two things had a connection, although in the prison confession of Nat Turner there is not the slightest reference to either

[1] Child, *Letters from New York* (2d series), 55; Cutler, *Lynch Law*, 92–96; Higginson, *Travellers and Outlaws*, 276–326; Drewry, *Slave Insurrections in Virginia*.

[2] *Life of Benjamin Lundy*, 246; *Liberator*, 1831, 1832, passim; Olmsted, *Back Country*, 473; Olmsted, *Texas Journey*, 503; Chambers, *Am. Slavery and Colour*, 205.

the *Liberator* or *Walker's Appeal*. Garrison himself absolutely denied any relation with the insurrection,[1] and there is neither direct proof nor indirect reference which fixes on the abolitionists any share in that insurrection.

Warned by the Vesey and Turner insurrections, the militia in several states was reorganized; and special precautions were taken at fires, because it was commonly believed that discontented slaves often set them.[2] To be sure, the apologists for slavery attempted to minimize a terror which might be considered out of keeping with the argument that the slaves were happy and contented. Professor Dew declared that "the population of our slaveholding country enjoys as much or more conscious security than any other people on the face of the globe! . . . A negro will rob your hen-roost or your stye, but it is rare, indeed, that he can ever be induced to murder you. Upon this subject we speak from experience."[3] This confident assertion was out of harmony with the frequent alarms and consequent resort to lynch law, with the tenor of the statutes intended to prevent and suppress risings, and with the utterances of southerners themselves. A lady in Georgia said that "there was not a person on her plantation she dared trust her life with; and . . . she never retired at night without an axe so

[1] Garrisons, *Garrison*, I., 251.
[2] Simms, in *Pro-Slavery Argument*, 202–207.
[3] Dew, in *Pro-Slavery Argument*, 481.

near her pillow she could lay her hand upon it instantly"; and Buckingham notes that in no part of the south "did the whites seem to be in a great-er dread of the rising of the slaves than here in Louisiana." [1]

How far did abolition indirectly tend to excite insurrections? May, in 1835, said, rather as a proph-ecy than a suggestion: "If we do not emancipate our slaves by our own moral energy, they will eman-cipate themselves and by a process too horrible . . . to contemplate"; [2] but many of the abolitionists expressly disclaimed any such purpose, and Chan-ning even declared that it was the duty of the north to aid the south against such a rising. [3]

The abolitionist seemed to the south capable of any wicked course, because he systematically helped the slaves to run away. The federal fugitive-slave law of 1793 [4] was never popular in the north, and the abolitionists by turns derided its validity and ignored it—though a kind-hearted Boston clergy-man, Dr. Gannett, publicly declared that if a fugitive slave came to his door, he should feel it his duty to turn him over to the authorities. [5] Dr. Channing, for himself, held that it was his duty, if applied to, to shelter the fugitive, though he said he drew back at reaching down to the south and

[1] Burke, *Reminiscences*, 156; Buckingham, *Slave States*, I., 375.
[2] *Liberator*, V., 59.
[3] Tappan and Rankin, in *Niles' Register*, XLVI., 360; Jay, *Miscellaneous Writings*, 148–152; Channing, *Works*, V., 28.
[4] See chap. xix., below.   [5] May, *Recollections*, 367.

persuading the slave to become a fugitive.[1] Some abolitionists did not stick even at that dangerous undertaking. In 1841, Thompson, Burr, and Work, Illinois abolitionists, were captured red-handed when they "made a tour of mercy into Missouri" by trying to persuade slaves to escape from the town of Palmyra; for this crime they served several years in the Missouri penitentiary. Even there, however, they lost no opportunity to talk with the slaves who drifted into that place on the question of liberty, and even to make plans with them for running away north.[2]

The fugitives not only gave the abolitionists pleasure—they gave pain to the slave-holder. In a thinly settled and wooded region like the south, with mountains in the neighborhood, it was not difficult for a slave to slip away from the plantation into the woods or the swamps. An altercation with the overseer, the promise of a whipping, or a mere love of his own way started many a slave into this practice. Most of such runaways simply "lay out" in the woods or swamps for a time,[3] where it was easy for a fugitive in a few minutes to be beyond the reach of immediate recovery. These "outlying slaves" were likely to come back at night to the negro quarters, where they got food and comfort;

[1] Channing, *Works*, II., 77, V., 23–28, 319–322.
[2] Thompson, *Prison Life*, 159, 168, 335, 344, 348, 367.
[3] Edwards, "Two Runaways," in *Century*, X., 378–387; Burke, *Reminiscences*, 163–168.

but most of them were forced by hardships and hunger to yield at last and "take their whipping." The Dismal Swamp, in eastern North Carolina, was a favorite rendezvous for such runaways; there they brought up their children, and even got employment from negro lumbermen or the neighboring poor whites.[1]

Nothing was more common in the southern newspapers than advertisements of runaways; the rude wood-cut of a negro with a bundle slung over his shoulder from a stick was a part of the country printing-office, and many interesting details of slave life are recorded by this unconscious evidence. For example:

"Ran away, a negro girl, called Mary; has a small scar over her eye, a good many teeth missing. The letter A is branded on her cheek and forehead."

"Ran away, negress, Caroline; had on a collar with one prong turned down."[2]

"Ran away! Billy is twenty-five years old, and is known as a patroon of my boat for many years; in all probability he may resist; in that event, $50.00 will be paid for his head."[3]

Very little attempt was made to find a runaway

[1] Olmsted, *Seaboard Slave States*, 159.

[2] Jay, *Miscellaneous Writings*, 484; many such advertisements in Child, *Patriarchal Institution;* Olmsted, *Seaboard Slave States*, 162.

[3] From the *Charleston Courier*, February 20, 1836; similar incidents in the *Life of Benjamin Lundy*, 53; Chambers, *Am. Slavery and Colour*, 200–202.

through his friends; for the negroes almost universally aided their own race. If advertising failed, the next step was to hunt with dogs, and professional slave-catchers advertised blood-hounds that "can take the trail twelve hours after the negro has passed and catch him with ease." The use of the "nigger dogs" was distasteful to the north, but was not in itself an inhuman method of finding the fugitive, though some slave-holders looked on it as "a kind o' barbarous sport." The difficulty was that the dogs were sometimes allowed to tear their captures (not sufficiently to injure their market value) when taken, and that the fury of the pursuers and the despair of the quarry sometimes led to resistance and to shooting.[1] When brought back, it was usual to make an example, especially if the slave had been out a long time; and the annals of the time are full of cases where slaves carried for the rest of their lives the record of the master's resentment; they were then put in heavy iron shackles or collars, partly as a punishment and partly to prevent escape, and sometimes they suffered more direct tortures, such as drawing out the toe-nails.[2]

Perhaps one in twenty of the slaves who broke away was so well informed or so bold as to set forth

[1] Olmsted, *Seaboard Slave States*, 163; Olmsted, *Back Country*, 55, 474.

[2] Pickard, *Kidnapped and Ransomed*, 192–195, 308–310; narratives of slaves, enumerated in chap. xxii., below.

with the purpose of never seeing the plantation again. In a very few cases, such fugitives, were incited or aided by northern men who went south for that purpose. Besides Burr, Work, and Thompson, sent to the penitentiary,[1] one John L. Brown was sentenced to death, in 1846 (a sentence commuted to whipping), for aiding fugitives; and the Shaker abolitionist, Concklin, carried off the Still family of four persons from Florence, Alabama, into Indiana.[2] In a later period, John Brown, of Ossawatomie, crossed into Missouri and helped fugitive slaves away.[3] Slaves carried into the northern states by their masters as personal attendants some imes slipped away and never returned, unless the master had taken the precaution to keep some of the slave's children behind.

The fugitive slaves were surrounded by a host of watchful enemies; unless provided with a forged pass for this occasion, most of them were stopped within ten miles of home and turned back by the patrollers.[4] This danger escaped, every unknown negro found wandering about the country was subject to being taken up and imprisoned, until his captors could advertise him and find his people. If he got clear away from his country or state, he was still far from liberty; he might find his way to some southern

---

[1] See above, p. 222.

[2] Pickard, *Kidnapped and Ransomed*, 280–305, 398–409.

[3] Chadwick, *Causes of the Civil War* (*Am. Nation*, XIX.), chap. v.   [4] See above, chap. viii.

town or city and there set up as a freeman, but every
negro perfectly knew the danger of recapture under
such circumstances, and most of the determined
fugitives directed their footsteps north. "We saw
the North Star," said Harriet Tubman, "and that
told us which way to go." Many escaped by sea;
most of the coasters had negro cooks or stewards
who could often be induced by sympathy or for a
bribe to receive the fugitive and deliver him in a
northern port. In the interior, the negro must
make his own way from place to place, ignorant of
geography and of distance, and chiefly dependent
upon the aid of members of his own race: and he
found the great belt of wooded mountains stretching
from northern Alabama to Pennsylvania a natural
highway.

Once across the border, and sometimes before he
reached it, the negro entered upon a concealed and
intricate system of routes, to which the name "Underground Railroad" was commonly applied. The
term suggests not only a route, but termini, train-
men, and general officials. There was, however,
never any general association, hardly so much as a
definite understanding between the abolitionists who
carried on this forbidden traffic; nor did the con-
ductors and station-masters know all the links in
the routes which ran past, or rather into, their doors.
The "U. G." can be traced back to informal committees formed in several of the northern cities; and
two veterans in this service—Still, in Philadelphia,

and the Quaker, Levi Coffin, in Cincinnati—kept a record of the business that went through their stations.[1]

The Underground Railroad had an advertising agency in the understanding, which somehow permeated the slaves in the southern states, that if they once crossed into the free states they would find friends who would forward them from place to place, until they were free from pursuit or arrived at the haven of Canada. To reach these friends every possible method was employed: Henry Box Brown permitted himself to be nailed up in a packing-case and sent by freight to Philadelphia; another hid himself under the guards of a coasting steamer, enduring days of hunger and chill. Ellen Crafts, a very light woman, impersonated a white planter, while her husband played the rôle of personal attendant. As she expected, she was called upon at the Baltimore station to make a written statement as to her companion, but she could not write, and had bound up her arm on the pretence that it was injured. In a few hours they not only escaped, but were entertained as heroes, and their freedom was soon purchased for them. In one instance, three slaves who had some money associated themselves together, hired a travelling coach, bribed a white man to act as their master, and actually drove in state from slavery into freedom.[2]

[1] Still, *Underground Railroad;* Coffin, *Reminiscences;* Siebert, *Underground Railroad.*   [2] McDougall, *Fugitive Slaves,* §§ 67–69.

The Underground Railroad was not a route, but a net-work; not an organization, but a conspiracy of thousands of people banded together for the deliberate purpose of depriving their southern neighbors of their property and of defying the fugitive-slave laws of the United States. The geographical area of these operations extended from Maine to Kansas; the routes north of New York began at the seaports and trended towards Canada; in the neighborhood of Philadelphia there was a complexus of routes diverging from two trunk lines, one through Baltimore and the other through Gettysburg. West of the mountains the Underground Railroad was much more flourishing, both because of the hundreds of miles of contiguity between the free and slave states, and because the Ohio River was a highway from one part of the south to another much used by masters and slave-dealers. More than thirty points have been traced on the line of the Ohio and Mississippi rivers where fugitives were received and forwarded. Once on the road, they were carried, commonly at night, by short stages from house to house, concealed during the day, and sent to sure places of refuge.[1]

In some cases the master himself followed; in other cases he "sold his nigger running"—that is, transferred the title to a person, often a professional slave-catcher, who had never seen the slave before, and had no other interest than to get him back and

[1] Siebert, *Underground Railroad*, passim.

sell him at a profit. This practice, with its cold, commercial calculation, in which there was so little of the patriarchal and dignified aspect of slavery, accented the law - breaking spirit of the abolitionists.

Though hundreds of people were perfectly well known to harbor slaves,[1] in order to throw suspicion off the scent, younger members of the family, boys or girls, were often employed to drive through the woods with a fugitive. The Underground Railroad was manned chiefly by orderly citizens, members of churches and philanthropical societies. To such law-abiding folk what could be more delightful than the sensation of aiding an oppressed slave, exasperating a cruel master, and at the same time incurring the penalties of defying an unrighteous law? The Underground Railroad furnished the pleasures of a hunt in which the trembling prey was saved from his brutal pursuers; the excitement of a fight in which there was little personal danger; and the joy of the martyr's crown without the faggot. Hundreds of people deliberately engaged in this work who were not enrolled as abolitionists, and thousands of other people would not lift a hand to help a master recover a slave within a free state. After the British abolition act took effect, in 1840, the soil of Canada became absolutely free, and the British government would not take the slightest

[1] For instance, the author's grandfather and aunt kept stations on the " U. G.," in northern Ohio, and his father was a conductor.

pains to assist in returning fugitives. Canada, therefore, was a sure refuge, and many of the routes of the Underground Railroad terminated on the Canadian border or on the Great Lakes, across which there were secret ferries. The nucleus of a negro settlement was made here by an exodus of negroes from Ohio, about 1821, and in Canada West, between Lake Erie and Lake Huron, four or five negro settlements sprang up, to which recruits were sent from cities in the states as well as from the fugitives.[1]

The number of persons aided by this system can only be guessed. Official figures in the census of 1850 and 1860 showed a loss of about a thousand slaves a year; but twelve to thirteen hundred a year passed through the Underground Railroad in Ohio alone, and three to four hundred through Philadelphia. In the thirty years from 1830 to 1860, an average of perhaps two thousand slaves a year got away from their masters, of whom perhaps a tenth lost themselves in the south and another tenth got to Canada. This would leave about fifty thousand negroes who, in the fifty years, took to themselves wings and flew away to the free states. As most of the fugitives were grown people, the money loss to the south was, first and last, perhaps thirty million dollars. Nevertheless, it did not seriously affect the value of the slaves except in the

[1] *Life of Benjamin Lundy*, 240, 251–254; May, *Recollections*, 303–305; S. G. Howe, *Refugees from Slavery*.

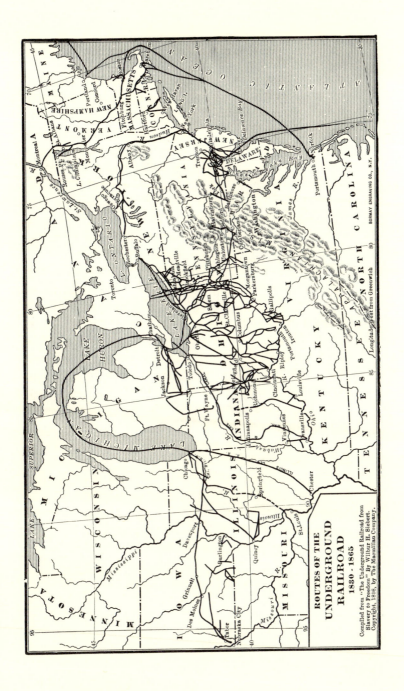

ROUTES OF THE
UNDERGROUND RAILROAD
1830 - 1865

Compiled from "The Underground Railroad from
Slavery to Freedom." By Wilbur H. Siebert.
Copyright, 1898, by The Macmillan Company.

BORMAY ENGRAVING CO., N.Y.

border counties of the border states. The Underground Railroad, therefore, was calculated not so
much to weaken slavery as to strengthen the anti-
slavery feeling throughout the northern states.[1]

[1] On interstate difficulties, arising out of slavery, see chap. xix.,
below.

CHAPTER XVI

THE ABOLITIONIST AND THE SLAVE-HOLDER
(1830–1860)

ALL the relations of the abolitionist to the negro were intended to bear upon the one purpose of affecting the master either by "moral suasion" or by arousing public sentiment against him. Garrison deliberately chose the latter method, and asked, "What has been so efficacious as this hard language? . . . its strength of denunciation bears no proportion to the enormous guilt of the slave system."[1] Although not one planter in a thousand ever heard an abolitionist speak, and not one in a hundred ever read an abolitionist book or paper, this habitual harshness aroused the fiercest resentment; the rank and file of the abolitionists were "silly enthusiasts led away by designing characters"; the leaders were "mere ambitious men . . . who cloak their designs under vile and impious hypocrisies, and unable to shine in higher spheres, devote themselves to fanaticism as a trade."[2] Calhoun said of them: "It is against this relation between the two races that the blind and criminal zeal of the Abolitionists is directed

[1] Garrisons, *Garrison*, I., 336.
[2] Hammond, in *Pro-Slavery Argument*, 173.

—a relation that now preserves in quiet and security more than 6,500,000 human beings."[1]   Even so
moderate a slave-holder as Henry Clay wrote, "Abolition is a delusion which cannot last . . . in pursuit
of a principle . . . it undertakes to tread down and
trample in the dust all opposing principles however
sacred.   It arrays state against state.   To make the
black men free it would virtually enslave the white
man."[2]

Though "moral suasion" had been going on ever
since the days of Justice Sewall, slavery was gaining
ground steadily; and Garrison scored a point when
he drew up a roll of abolitionists known for their
habitual moderation of tone, and asked, "Of the
foregoing list, who is viewed with complacency or
preferred over another by slave holders or their
apologists?"[3]   No arguments against slavery pleased
the southerners, and no mildness of statements could
reconcile them to an habitual questioning of the
justice of their practice.   A champion of slavery
wrote, "Supposing that we were all convinced and
thought of slavery precisely as you do, at what era
of 'moral suasion' do you imagine you could prevail
on us to give up a thousand millions of dollars in the
value of our slaves, and a thousand millions of dollars more in the depreciation of our lands?"[4]

[1] Calhoun, *Works*, V., 205.
[2] Clay to Gibson, July, 1842, Colton, *Private Corresp. of Clay*,
464.   [3] Garrisons, *Garrison*, I., 461.
[4] Hammond, in *Pro-Slavery Argument*, 141.

Perhaps a stronger argument for the abandonment of moral suasion was that the south would have none of it from its own people, who could speak from experience, and could appreciate the difficulties of the slave-holder. To prevent discussion in print the legislatures enlarged the existing press laws of the south against anything which might have a tendency to cause dissatisfaction among slaves. By the Georgia code of 1835, publications which tended to incite insurrections were punishable by death.[1] The Virginia code of 1849 provided that, "If a free person by speaking or writing, maintain that owners have no right of property in their slaves, he shall be confined in jail not more than one year and fined not exceeding $500."[2] Cassius M. Clay's anti-slavery paper, *The True American*, was driven out of Lexington by an organization of citizens.[3] The religious societies of the north found it impossible to carry on their work in the south except through southern men; and northern, and even English books containing criticisms were not allowed to circulate. In 1856 a member of a Texas legislature was threatened with "consequences to which we need not allude" for saying, in his place in the house, that the "Congress of the United States had the constitutional right to legislate on the subject of slavery in the territories."[4]

---

[1] *Niles' Register*, XLVIII., 441.
[2] *Virginia Code*, 1849, chap. cxcviii., § 22.
[3] *Niles' Register*, LXVIII., 408; Clay, *Memoirs*.
[4] Olmsted, *Texas Journey*, 504–506.

Threats of dire punishment if abolitionists showed themselves in the south were frequent. An Alabama minister wrote: "Let your emissaries dare to cross the Potomac, and I cannot promise you that your fate will be less than Haman's." A very few abolitionists from the north tested these threats. In 1835, Dr. Reuben Crandall, of New York, received some copies of the *Emancipator* and other anti-slavery papers at Washington, which he lent to a white friend. He was thereupon arrested and imprisoned on the charge of attempting to excite insurrection and riot among the slaves. After eight months in jail he was tried and found not guilty. Charles T. Torrey, a graduate of Yale and Andover Theological Seminary, and an abolitionist speaker and writer, went to Annapolis in 1842 to report a "Slave-holders' Convention," for which he was arrested and obliged to give bail. Subsequently, Torrey was convicted of assisting slaves to escape, and died a prisoner in a Virginia penitentiary.[1]

Seldom did such offences come to trial: they were prevented by threats of punishment or dealt with by a mob violence. The *Liberator* claimed that from 1836 to 1856 about three hundred white people were mobbed and killed in the south on suspicion of being abolitionists. No such number of authenticated cases can be traced; and those that did occur were usually of people suspected of trying to run off

[1] Goodell, *Slavery and Anti-Slavery*, 411, 437, 441–443; Buckingham, *Slave States*, I., 531.

slaves, a very different offence.[1] The principal cases which attracted attention were the following. Robinson, an English travelling bookseller, was whipped and driven out of Petersburg, Virginia, in 1832, for saying that "the blacks, as men, were entitled to their freedom and ought to be emancipated." John Lamb was tarred and feathered, badly burned, and whipped for taking the *Liberator*. Amos Dresser, a student of Lane Seminary and of Oberlin, in 1835, while on a colporteur trip to the south, wrapped a copy of the *Emancipator* around a Bible which he left at an inn in Nashville, and was found in possession of an anti-slavery paper with one of the so-called incendiary pictures, for which he was severely whipped and expelled from the south.[2]

Not satisfied with denunciation or legislation or the quieting effect of enlightened public opinion combined with mob violence, the south came outside of its breastworks and set up a new principle of federal responsibility by demanding that the northern states find means to stop the odious movement; and a succession of public meetings, executive messages, and reports of legislative committees emphasized these demands. Thus the legislature of South Carolina, in 1835, "announces her confident expectation and she earnestly requests, that the government of these [non-slave-holding] States will promptly and effectually suppress all those associations within

---

[1] Cutler, *Lynch Law*, 100–103, 115–124.
[2] *Life of Benjamin Lundy*, 255–259; Amos Dresser, *Narrative*

their respective limits purporting to be abolition societies"; and the North Carolina legislature called for "penal laws prohibiting the printing within their respective limits all such publications as may have a tendency to make our slaves discontented."[1]

To make these requests effective, demands were repeatedly put for a boycott against northern cities which permitted abolition meetings.[2] The *Charleston Patriot* recommended its citizens to trade with Philadelphia as "the only Northern city which has responded in a proper spirit to the call of the South on the North for energetic action."[3] The highest point in these demands was reached in a message of Governor McDuffie to the South Carolina legislature in 1835, in which he inveighed against the abolition literature, expressing it as his "deliberate opinion, that the laws of every community should punish this species of interference by death without benefit of clergy."[4]

Though abolition was tabooed in the south, the American Colonization Society, with a large clientèle of state and local branches, supported by the churches, and receiving indirect money aids from the national government, was put forth as the real and only practicable measure for ameliorating African slavery, and had adherents and support

---

[1] Goodell, *Slavery and Anti-Slavery*, 413.
[2] Von Holst, *United States*, II., 111–113.
[3] *Niles' Register*, XLIX., 74.
[4] Von Holst, *United States*, II., 118.

there till the Civil War. To be sure, in the second decade of colonizing activity, from 1831 to 1840, only 2403 emigrants were actually sent to Africa;[1] but the idea of colonization captivated both slave-holder and reformer: the former by the assurance that the despised free negro was to disappear, the latter by declarations that the colonizationists de-sired "to hasten as far as they can the period when slavery shall cease to exist."[2] The same contra-diction was carried into Africa: the degraded free negro, when settled in Liberia, was to stop the slave-trade and to be the centre of a movement of civilization and of missionary activity.[3] So alluring was this idea of giving the negro an opportunity to develop a community of his own, that Benjamin Lundy, from 1832 to 1836, was constantly engaged in plans of a negro colony in Texas,[4] and actually carried over to Haiti a small number of negroes, who founded an unsuccessful colony.

The African settlements did not flourish: one after another the agents succumbed to disease; the various little settlements united into the "Common-weath of Liberia," at first governed by the Ameri-can Colonization Society; but in 1847 it took on it-self the form of an independent government, which received the few colonists sent out by the society.

---

[1] *African Repository*, XLIII., 110–112; Alexander, *History of Colonization*, passim.

[2] Maryland Society, in McPherson, *Liberia*, 53.

[3] McPherson, *Liberia*, 53–59.

[4] *Life of Benjamin Lundy*, 30–168, passim.

It was never prosperous, and furnished a stock argument that under the most favorable conditions negroes could not keep up a government of their own.

At home, the society encountered the most determined opposition from the abolitionists. Garrison, in his pamphlet *Thoughts on African Colonization*, published in 1832, criticised their colonies, accused them of trying to maintain slavery, and declared that the society "imperatively and effectually seals up the lips of a vast number of influential and pious men."[1] The attack came at a critical time, when a plan had been formed to secure an annual appropriation of $240,000 from Congress, by which it was estimated the negroes could all be carried out of the country in twenty-eight years; but when the project was presented to Congress, the southern members almost unanimously objected.[2]

Colonization never really approved itself either to north or south. The south pooh-poohed at its small results, predicted its failure, and abjured federal aid to help them out of the difficulty;[3] and impartial observers thought the Colonization Society contained too many slave-holding members and did not accomplish anything for its ostensible object.[4] Throughout the period the two organizations were at war with each other. The colonizationists gave

[1] Garrisons, *Garrison*, I., 290–302.   [2] *Ibid.*, 261, 303.
[3] Dew, in *Pro-Slavery Argument*, 391–420.
[4] Reed and Matheson, *Narrative*, II., 258.

blow for blow, publicly attacked Garrison, and intimated that he ought to be turned over to the civil authorities of some southern state; and the abolitionists scoffed at the fruitlessness of their rivals' efforts.[1]

As for general emancipation, immediate or remote, its difficulties and its dangers were clearly realized by many impartial observers. Some calculated the immense sums that would be necessary to compensate the owners for their slaves.[2] The planters themselves foresaw nothing but ruin for both races: the cultivation of cotton would cease; race war would break out; emancipation could not last, for "the law would make them freemen, and custom or prejudice, we care not which you call it, would degrade them to the condition of slaves"; when the slaves were gone the land would be worthless; the free negroes would rapidly increase, and the white population correspondingly decrease.[3] These objections applied with equal strength to gradual emancipation; for when the slave property "is gone, no matter how, the deed will be done, and Virginia will be a desert."[4] Hence, emancipation of any kind would be fatal unless the negroes were all to be deported, for the free negroes would be driven out by white competition.[5] The argument

---

[1] Garrisons, *Garrison*, I., 324.

[2] Von Raumer, *America*, 125.

[3] Harper and Dew, in *Pro-Slavery Argument*, 85–88, 357–376, 433–436, 444; Adams, *Southside View*, 119–122.

[4] *Ibid.*, 384.   [5] Lyell, *Travels*, 1st series, I., 191.

focuses in the conclusion that "every plan of emancipation and deportation . . . is totally impracti-
cable."[1]

Against this battery of argument the abolitionists
were conscientiously obtuse: they saw no loss to
the community from employing free negroes in fields
where they had labored as slaves, except the power
of exchange into other forms of property; the experience, on a smaller scale, of the northern states convinced them that it was perfectly possible to get rid
of slavery without disturbance of the business or
safety of the community; and they did not for a
moment believe that the negroes would cut the
throats of their former masters and mistresses. As
for the invective of the south, the abolitionists were
of the mind of Major Jack Downing: "I met a man
from Georgia there, 6 feet 9 inches high, a real good
fellow. Most all these Southern folks are good fellows, if you don't say nothin' about the tariff, nor
freein the niggers; but they talk pretty big — I
know how to manage them, the Gineral tell'd me a
secret about that—says he 'Major, when they say
they can hit a dollar, tell 'em you can hit a four-
pence hapenny.'"[2]

[1] Dew, in *Pro-Slavery Argument*, 292, 379–384.
[2] Davis, *Letters of Major J. Downing*, 35.

CHAPTER XVII

ABOLITION AND GOVERNMENT

(1830–1840)

THE abolitionist leaders did not depend on a moral agitation alone; they began at once to use the ordinary methods of appeals to their state governments, secured the early personal liberty laws,[1] and agitated with some success against the black codes. Though eventually some extremists arrived at the point of denying that any process of law could make a man another man's chattel, most of the abolitionists accepted the principle laid down in their declaration of 1833—"the sovereignty of each state to legislate exclusively on the subject of the slavery which is tolerated within its limits."[2] Any other principle would limit the right of the northern states to maintain their freedom.

To their own state governments the abolitionists looked also for the protection which "causes" of every kind received. Prison reformers, prohibitionists, and Mormons argued, published, and declaimed; why not abolitionists? But as soon as they attracted the attention of the south, they found en-

---

[1] See chap. xix., below.　　[2] Garrisons, *Garrison*, I., 411.

emies at home: the community was shocked by
what they thought the antics of the abolitionists,
their loud and violent speeches, the association of
women, the exaltation of the negroes, who were the
most despised element in the northern as well as
the southern states. And in financial and manufacturing circles a pocket nerve was touched by the
outcries of people who had cotton to sell and heavy
orders to give.

For a time people proposed to draw the fangs of
abolition by showing that good people disliked it.
John Quincy Adams records in 1835 that "Mr.
Abbott Lawrence told me that they were going to
have a very great meeting at Boston to put down
the anti-slavery abolitionists";[1] and great lawyers like Rufus Choate, statesmen like Van Buren
and Buchanan, frontier leaders like Lewis Cass,
alternately pooh-poohed and scolded at the abolitionists.

The demand of southern legislatures for action
by their northern brethren caused an effort to discover, in existing law, a means of shutting off this
unwelcome discussion. Governor Edward Everett,
of Massachusetts, intimated to the legislature that
"whatever by direct and necessary operation is calculated to excite insurrection among the slaves,
has been held, by highly respectable legal authority,
an offence against the peace of this Commonwealth,
which may be prosecuted as a misdemeanor at com-

[1] Garrisons, *Garrison*, I., 487.

mon law." [1] And a rural grand jury in New York made a presentment to the effect that those who joined in an abolition society were guilty of sedition. [2]

To maintain such a position was impossible in the face of the bills of rights in all the state constitutions, protecting liberty of speech and of the press; and in no northern state would the courts hold general utterances against slavery and slave-holders outside that state to be libellous. Hence several efforts to secure new laws which would cover the case. In New York, under a hint from Governor Marcy, a legislative report was made promising the desired legislation; [3] in Rhode Island a bill was introduced, but failed. In Massachusetts a committee, headed by George Lunt, which had a restrictive measure in charge, was compelled by public sentiment to hold a hearing, in which the abolitionists made it evident that they had a right and an intention to express their opinions even in the presence of a legislative committee. [4]

So far as the laws of the northern states went, not a single abolitionist seems to have laid himself liable to prosecution at any time. The opposition nevertheless expressed itself without law and in opposition to law, especially by interfering with schemes for the education of the free negroes. In June, 1831, when an attempt was made to plant a

[1] Goodell, *Slavery and Anti-Slavery*, 415.   [2] *Ibid.*, 409.
[3] Garrisons, *Garrison*, II., 75.   [4] *Ibid.*, II., 102–105.

kind of manual - training school in New Haven, a
public meeting declared that "the founding of colleges for educating colored people is an unwarrantable and dangerous interference with the internal
concerns of other states, and ought to be discouraged." [1] The school had to be given up, as did a
similar attempt at Canaan, New Hampshire, where
three hundred men appeared with a hundred yoke
of oxen and pulled the school-house into a neighboring swamp.[2]

Miss Prudence Crandall, at Canterbury, Connecticut, admitted colored girls into her school.   Her
neighbors attempted to boycott her, and then to
arrest her pupils as vagrants.   As she still persisted,
they procured a special act of the legislature, May
24, 1833, prohibiting, under severe penalties, the
instruction of any negro from outside the state
without the consent of the town authorities, under
which Miss Crandall was indicted and imprisoned.
The abolitionists at once assumed her defence, but
she was convicted, and though the higher courts
quashed the proceedings on technicalities, she gave
up the contest and the school was closed.[3]

The years from 1834 to 1836 were fateful for the
abolitionists; throughout the country, from east to
west, swept a movement of mob violence, intended
to silence them by terror.   About twenty-five ef-

[1] *Niles' Register*, XLI., 88.
[2] *Boston Morning Post*, August 18, 1835.
[3] May, *Recollections*, 39–72.

forts were made within a few years to break up anti-
slavery meetings, and the cry was raised that unless
the abolitionists were silenced the Union could not
continue.[1] In New York the trouble began with
appeals from the newspapers to show that New
York was not infested with abolitionists, leading
directly to a riot at Clinton Hall, October, 1833,
when the place selected for an abolitionist meeting
was stampeded by opponents; then from July 7 to
11, 1834, a succession of riots led to the sacking of
the house of Lewis Tappan and the destruction of
other houses and churches.[2]

In Boston the trouble was brought to a head by
the arrival, in September, 1834, of George Thompson, a powerful and refined speaker, experienced in
the English abolition agitation,[3] assisted by Garrison, who expected the visitor to work, through
public sentiment, upon state legislatures and Congress.   Thompson at once showed his ability as a
speaker, but several of his meetings were disturbed,
and, returning to Boston, he found that he was one
of the worst-hated men in the country,[4] a state of
things hard to understand in these days of international comity and world congresses of philanthropy. The announcement that George Thompson was to speak at a meeting of the Female Anti-

[1] B. R. Curtis, in Garrisons, *Garrison*, I., 501.
[2] Greeley, *Am. Conflict*, I., 126.
[3] Garrison, *Lectures of George Thompson* [in England], 1836;
George Thompson, *Speech delivered at . . . Broadmead* (1851).
[4] Garrisons, *Garrison*, I., 434–453; II., 59.

Slavery Society, in 1835, brought out a handbill as follows:

"Thompson — the abolitionist.   That infamous foreign scoundrel Thompson will hold forth this afternoon at the *Liberator* office, No. 48 Washington Street.   The present is a fair opportunity for the friends of the Union to *snake Thompson out!* It will be a contest between the abolitionists and the friends of the Union.   A purse of $100. has been raised by a number of patriotic citizens to reward the individual who shall first lay violent hands on Thompson so that he may be brought to the tar-kettle before dark.   Friends of the Union be vigilant!" [1]

Thompson did not attend, but Garrison did, and found the room beset by an uproarious crowd, whom the mayor harangued in vain; that functionary finally informed the ladies that he could no longer guarantee their safety, and when they were gone the crowd surged in, gutted the office, and then began a man-hunt for Garrison.   They put a rope around his body, dragged him through the streets, where, an eye-witness says, "The man walked with head erect, flashing eyes, like a martyr going to the stake, full of faith and manly hope." The mayor sallied forth, sheltered him in the city hall, and then, to save his life, sent him to the Charles Street jail, in which he was with difficulty lodged, out of the hands of the howling mob.[2]

[1] *Niles' Register*, XLIX., 145.   [2] Garrisons, *Garrison*, II., 1-37.

This outrage overdid itself. Thereafter abolition meetings were sufficiently protected in Boston; but on the very same day came the culmination of a series of riots at Utica, New York, intended to prevent the formation of an abolition society. As in Boston, an anti-slavery press was wrecked; but Gerrit Smith received the four hundred abolitionists in his own house, where they completed their organization.[1]

In 1836 a similar scene was witnessed in Cincinnati, where the office of the *Philanthropist* was gutted and desperate efforts were made to kill its editor, James G. Birney. The infection still further spread, in 1837, to Alton, Illinois, to which place Elijah P. Lovejoy, editor of a little abolition paper in St. Louis, had recently been driven for criticising a mob which had burned a negro at the stake. The people of Alton warned him to be silent; they twice destroyed his press; a third time he fitted out a printing-office, and went on building up abolition societies, and a company of volunteers was formed to protect him. On the night of November 7, 1837, a mob of people attacked the building in which his press was stored and fired upon it; the fire was returned, and one of the assailants was wounded; the mob returned to burn the building, and deliberately watched for and shot Lovejoy. In due time twelve of them were tried for the offence, and after ten minutes' deliberation the jury brought them in not

[1] Frothingham, *Gerrit Smith*, 164–166.

guilty. Lovejoy was honorable and high-minded, and his only offence was a determination to criticise slavery in a state where it was illegal, and to defend his property and life when assailed.

The list of pro-slavery riots was enlarged by Philadelphia, a turbulent and ill-policed city. In one such affair, in 1834, forty-four houses were injured or destroyed.[1] Finding it difficult to obtain a suitable place for abolition meetings, the anti-slavery people of the city in 1838 constructed a building called Pennsylvania Hall. May 16, 1838, Garrison and others addressed an audience there, and the next day it became known that the mob proposed to destroy the building. The mayor attempted to check them by good counsel, but they broke open the doors, set a fire, and staved off the firemen who came to put it out. The city authorities gave no sort of protection to property, and barely to life; so far as the commonwealth and city were concerned, the abolitionists were outlaws.

Nothing could have been more favorable to the abolitionists than this succession of outbreaks, which flashed public attention upon Garrison and Birney and Lovejoy, and placed their personal character in the strongest contrast to the means employed to silence them. Mob violence emphasized the fact that the abolitionists were not acting contrary to law, and it aroused the fighting spirit of thousands of people who knew very little about the controversy

[1] *Life of Benjamin Lundy*, 272.

except that the abolitionists had something to say so important that it must be prevented by violence and murder. These were the days of triumph for the abolitionists, who increased in numbers and resources, and had a happy sense of shaking the whole institution of slavery to its centre by their impassioned utterances.

In none of the state legislatures, previous to 1840, did abolitionists make much impression as members, and only one anti‑slavery man was sent to Congress — William Slade, from Vermont. Thomas Morris, United States senator from Ohio, about 1835 joined an abolition society and defended the cause in Congress.[1] In 1838 Slade was joined by the first out-and-out western abolitionist — Joshua R. Giddings, from a district in the Western Reserve; and before long the abolitionists founded a political organization.[2]

So far as the influence of their best-known leader went, the abolitionists would never have elected a representative to Congress, for Garrison was infuriated by the power of the slave-holders in the national government, and worked out a theory to get rid of their domination. It was the custom of the time to look to the federal Constitution as a kind of political Bible, a cyclopædia of public and moral law, from which the rightfulness or unrightfulness of slavery

---

[1] Garrisons, *Garrison*, I., 455 (northeast); cf. Von Holst, *United States*, II., 289; Smith, *Liberty and Free Soil Parties*, 23-26 (west).　　　[2] See chap. xx., below.

could infallibly be inferred. When the abolitionists insisted that the word "slave" nowhere occurs
in the Constitution, the other side pointed to the
phrases "free persons or other persons," and "importation of . . . persons," and argued that the Constitution was not only compatible with slavery, but
recognized slavery, and even gavé sanction to slavery.

Granting that the Constitution did recognize the
existence of slavery where it existed in 1789, and
that the statutes for admitting new states into the
Union with slavery constitutions recognized its
extension, the abolitionists could fall back on the
clauses by which Congress could "exercise exclusive
legislation in all cases whatsoever" over the seat of
government, and could "make rules for" the territories, and to several acts of Congress actually
prohibiting slavery in the territories—the act of
1789, reaffirming the ordinance of 1787; the statutes
organizing free territories in the northwest; and the
compromise of 1850. Congress seemed to have the
same authority over slavery in a territory that the
state governments had within a state; nevertheless,
the south denied any constitutional right to prohibit
slavery in the District of Columbia, because it was
created out of cessions made by Virginia and Maryland; they discovered an unwritten principle of the
Constitution that the south must not be humiliated
by abolishing slavery in a district which would thus
become a centre of abolition propaganda in the heart
of a slave - holding area. They insisted that the

southern states had adopted the Constitution only under tacit compact that slavery should not be disturbed by the general government.

To offset the doctrine that the federal Constitution maintained slavery, some of the abolitionists admitted that the Constitution was a pro-slavery document, and therefore abjured the Constitution. The moderate Channing declared, in 1836, that "a higher law than the Constitution protests against the act of Congress on this point.   According to the law of nature no greater crime against human being can be committed than to make him a slave";[1] an argument which, perhaps, suggested Seward's later plea, "There is a higher law than the Constitution." [2]

Garrison, in 1835, called God to witness that "we are not hostile to the Constitution of the United States,"[3] but was soon carried by his non-resistance principles into the extreme doctrine that abolitionists must withdraw themselves from a government which they believed to be cruel and oppressive.   In January, 1843, he came to the point where he placed at the head of his paper the statement that "the compact which exists between the North and the South is a covenant with death, and an agreement with Hell—involving both parties in atrocious criminality and should be immediately annulled." [4]   He

[1] Channing, *Works*, II., 10, V., 291.
[2] Hart, *Contemporaries*, IV., 58.   [3] *Liberator*, V., 134.
[4] Garrisons, *Garrison*, III., 88; the reference is to the Hebrew prophet's " Your covenant with death shall be disannulled, and your agreement with hell shall not stand " (*Isaiah*, xxviii., 18).

even went to the point, in 1850, of offering a resolution against Longfellow's appeal to the Union:

> " Thou too, sail on, O ship of state;
> Sail on, O UNION, strong and great." [1]

In 1854 he publicly burned a copy of the Constitution, crying out, " So perish all compromisers with
tyranny!" [2]

These violent phrases have been quoted a thousand times as stating the position of "the abolitionists." Actually not one abolitionist in twenty for
a moment accepted either the dogma that the Constitution was pro-slavery or the consequence that
it ought to be destroyed. William Jay, the most
active writer among the middle-states abolitionists,
in express terms disavowed these extreme theories. [3]
Salmon P. Chase, the most notable of the western
abolitionists, was one of the main defenders of the
precisely opposite theory that the Constitution is
an anti-slavery document, which nowhere mentions,
approves, or protects slavery, and which, like the
Declaration of Independence and the Ordinance of
1787, laid down principles incompatible with slavery.
To say that the Constitution did anything more than
to recognize that for the time being some of the
states had slavery was, in his mind, "morally speaking, a black forgery." [4] As for the seat of govern-

---

[1] Garrisons, *Garrison*, III., 280.   [2] *Ibid.*, 412.
[3] Jay, *Miscellaneous Writings*, 161–166.
[4] *Letter to O'Connell*, November 30, 1843; *Argument in the Van
Zandt Case*, 1848.

ment, Chase went so far as to say that "slavery exists in the District of Columbia by virtue of unconstitutional acts of Congress, and may be abolished at any time by the simple repeal of those acts"; [1] and he found in the Fifth Amendment, by which "No persons shall be deprived of their liberty or property without due process of law," an absolute prohibition upon establishing slavery in the territories, and thereby depriving free negroes of their liberty.

If, as Chase believed, the Constitution could be invoked against slavery; or if, as most of the abolitionists believed, the Constitution was neutral as to slavery in the states, but positive in the powers it conferred over the slave-trade, slavery in the District of Columbia, and slavery in the territories, there was every reason for standing by the Union. Garrison's violent language, which simply put a weapon into the hands of his opponents, was no more characteristic of abolition than the violent disunion talk of Thomas Cooper, president of the College of South Carolina. [2] And nothing can be found in the *Liberator* more antagonistic to union than the message of Governor McDuffie, of South Carolina, in 1835, when he declared that "the refusal of a state to punish these offensive proceedings against another, by its citizens or subjects, makes

---

[1] *Chase MSS.*, in Library of Congress, *Diary*, May 27, 1848, June 15, 1848, December 15, 1853.

[2] Marryatt, *Diary in America*, 1st series (Am. ed.), 200.

the state so refusing an accomplice in the outrage, and furnishes a cause of war." [1]   From that time on the threat or the prediction of disruption of the Union was the *delenda est Carthago* of extreme speeches on both sides.

[1] *American History Leaflets*, No. 10, p. 12.

CHAPTER XVIII

ANTI-SLAVERY IN CONGRESS

(1831–1840)

FOR a long time the abolition controversy little disturbed the great clearing-house of public opinion at Washington. Not that Congress at first considered slavery outside of its functions or unsuitable for its deliberations; but from 1829 to 1835 the country was absorbed in other questions. The abolitionists, however, were a folk who pressed into every opening where they could affect public sentiment, and they adopted a system of sending petitions for emancipation in the District of Columbia to members of Congress good-natured enough to present them.

For some years such petitions were few in number and excited little interest. December 12, 1831, John Quincy Adams presented fifteen petitions, but deprecated a discussion which "would lead to ill-will, to heart-burning, to mutual hatred . . . without accomplishing anything else." [1] These petitions were referred to committees who reported against granting the prayer. In February, 1835, the House

[1] Adams, *Memoirs*, VIII., 434, 454.

laid upon the table such a petition, for reasons expressed by Wise, of Virginia: "Sir, slavery, inter-woven with our very political existence, is guaran-teed by our Constitution and its consequences must be borne by our Northern brethren as resulting from our system of government, and they cannot attack the institution of slavery, without attacking the institutions of the country, our safety, and welfare." This was the first clear notice that discussion of slavery in Congress was thought to be dangerous to the institution.[1]

Meanwhile, the number of abolitionist petitions steadily increased; and in the House there was at last a member who would not only present but defend them. December 16, 1835, Slade, of Ver-mont, insisted, as a constitutional right, that an abolition petition should be printed, and he warned the House that the signers included many people not directly connected with the abolitionists. A week later he went into a long argument affirming the power of Congress to prohibit slavery in the District, and protesting against the increasing power of the south in national affairs. "The progress of aboli-tion," said he, "was necessary to preserve the bal-ance of the Constitution or rather to restore it."[2]

A few days later, January 7 and 11, 1836, the

---

[1] Tremain, *Slavery in Dist. of Col.*, 71; *Debates of Congress*, XI., 1399.

[2] *Cong. Globe*, 24 Cong., 1 Sess., 48; Slade, *Speech* (reprint from *National Intelligencer*).

same question arose in the Senate through a motion of Calhoun to lay upon the table petitions for the abolition of slavery in the District of Columbia, presented by Morris, of Ohio, and by Buchanan, of Pennsylvania. The Pennsylvania petition, drawn up by a quarterly meeting of Quakers, set forth: "That, having long felt deep sympathy with that portion of the inhabitants of these United States which is held in bondage, and having no doubt that the happiness and interests, moral and pecuniary, of both master and slave, and our whole community, would be greatly promoted if the inestimable right to liberty was extended equally to all, we contemplate with extreme regret that the District of Columbia, over which you possess entire control, is acknowledged to be one of the greatest marts for the traffic in the persons of human beings in the known world, notwithstanding the principles of the Constitution declare that all men have an unalienable right to the blessing of liberty. We therefore earnestly desire that you will enact such laws as will secure the right of freedom to every human being residing within the constitutional jurisdiction of Congress, and prohibit every species of traffic in the persons of men, which is as inconsistent in principle, and inhuman in practice, as the foreign slave trade." [1]

The text of this petition is a sufficient comment on Calhoun's declaration that it was "a foul slander

[1] Curtis, *Buchanan*, I., 336.

on nearly one half of the states of the Union"; and
to his demand that it be not received, in order "that
a stop might be put to that agitation which had pre-
vailed in so large a section of the country and which
unless checked would endanger the existence of the
Union." [1] March 9, 1836, Calhoun's motion was
rejected by 36 to 10, and instead was adopted an
ingenious compromise offered by Buchanan: "That
the prayer of the petition be rejected." This vote,
which became the practice of the Senate, avoided
the issue of refusing consideration of respectful petitions, while giving opportunity for an emphatic
denial of the relief desired. [2]

The House was not disposed to accept this method
of both doing and not doing; and on February 8,
1836, a special committee was appointed, under the
chairmanship of Pinckney, of South Carolina, which
accused the abolitionists of dangerous agitation tend-
ing to break up the Union, and recommended a
resolution: "That all petitions, memorials, resolutions, propositions or papers relating in any way
or to any extent whatever to the subject of slavery
or the abolition of slavery shall, without being
either printed or referred, be laid upon the table
and that no further action whatever shall be had
thereon." [3] This so-called "gag resolution" was

[1] Debates of Congress, XII., 73.
[2] Tremain, Slavery in Dist. of Col., 76–80; Von Holst, United
States, II., 238, 242; Curtis, Buchanan, I., 315–338.
[3] Niles' Register, L., 241–248.

duly adopted, May 26, by a vote of 117 to 68; and
the principle was thus laid down that no petitions
on slavery should be brought to the attention of
the House.[1] When the name of John Quincy
Adams was called, he cried: "I hold the resolution
to be a direct violation of the Constitution of the
United States, of the rules of this House, and of
the rights of my constituents."[2]

Pinckney, in support of his resolution, developed
a new kind of reasoning, that Congress had "exclusive jurisdiction in all cases whatsoever" over
the District only if it was agreeable to the neighboring states; that action by Congress would arouse
the south and "endanger the Union itself"; and
that therefore "the agitation of such questions in
either branch of Congress" shook the confidence of
the south in the security of their most important
interests.[3]

The issue thus presented was by no means so
simple as Pinckney thought. Under the general
phrase of the Constitution, "Congress shall make
no law . . . abridging the freedom of speech, or . . .
the right of the people peaceably to assemble, and
to petition the government for a redress of griev-
ances,"[4] the right to petition had always been
held to include the right to bring the petition to
the notice of Congress, unless disrespectful in tone,

[1] Tremain, *Slavery in Dist. of Col.*, 76; Von Holst, *United
States*, II., 245.   [2] Adams, *Memoirs*, IX., 287.
    [3] *Niles' Register*, L., 245–248.   [4] *Amendment* I.

or praying for unconstitutional action. Under the Pinckney resolutions, it was practically held disrespectful to Congress to mention slavery at all; and unconstitutional to assume that Congress had power of any kind with regard to slavery.

Under the practice of the House at that time the rules expired at the end of every session, but the gag resolution was easily renewed in January, 1837, by a vote of 129 to 69.[1] When the new Congress assembled in December, 1837, resolutions of the Vermont legislature were presented asking their representatives and senators to use their influence to abolish slavery in the District of Columbia. By the doctrine of state sovereignty such resolutions had a different footing in Congress from the memorials of individuals; nevertheless, most of the southern members thereupon withdrew from the House to concert measures against further discussion of slavery in Congress. To this so-called "Memorable Secession" Rhett, of South Carolina, proposed a special committee to report on the best way of peaceably dissolving the Union; but it finally agreed upon a more stringent gag resolution, which was passed next day by a vote of 122 to 74.[2]

This policy of non-action, this attempt to ignore the political existence of abolitionists, required an equal silence on the part of the south. Nevertheless, Calhoun, who had now come out as the great

[1] *Niles' Register*, LI., 336.
[2] *Cong. Globe*, 25 Cong., 2 Sess., 41, 45.

champion of the slave power, December 27, 1837, brought forward in the Senate a series of resolutions intended to fix upon the abolitionists the crimes of inspiring slave insurrections and endangering the Union. After premising that the states are "free, independent and sovereign states," Calhoun's resolutions condemned "any intermeddling of any . . . states or a combination of their citizens with the domestic institutions and police of the others"; declared it "the solemn duty of the government to resist all attempts by one portion of the Union to use it as an instrument to attack the domestic institutions of another"; asserted that abolition was a "manifest breach of faith and a violation of the most solemn obligations, moral and religious"; and that "the intermeddling of any state or states or their citizens to abolish slavery in this district or any of the territories . . . would be a direct and dangerous attack on the institutions of all the slave-holding states." [1]

These resolutions laid down several novel doctrines of constitutional law: they declared agitation in free states or attempts to influence Congress against slavery to be breaches of the Constitution, and, if persisted in, sufficient ground for secession. One of Calhoun's colleagues protested that the resolutions "allowed ground for discussion and that the subject ought not to be allowed to enter the halls of

[1] *Cong. Globe*, 25 Cong., 2 Sess., 55.

the Legislative Assembly."[1]   Morris, of Ohio, and Swift, of Vermont, were the only members of the Senate to press hard against these resolutions, of which the essentials were adopted by test votes of 31 to 13.

Adams's protest against the gag resolutions was significant; for no other member of Congress had so lively a sense of the political power of the north. After leaving the presidency, he was, in 1830, somewhat to his own surprise, elected to Congress for the district in which he lived, on the anti-Masonic ticket. He was quite unaware of his power in debate, and up to 1835 had been distinctly a proslavery man; as senator, in 1807, he voted against the prohibition of the slave-trade; as negotiator of the treaty of Ghent, he insisted on compensation for slaves taken away by the British; as secretary of state, he turned an unfriendly ear to the overtures of Great Britain for a slave-trade treaty; as president, he never showed any personal interest in the anti-slavery cause. To the day of his death he was never especially interested in the negro slave; his defiant protest against the gag resolution was aroused by his sense that the rights of white freemen were involved.

That he was no abolitionist is clear from Garrison's complaint that Mr. Adams had been "zealous in protesting against an effect, and yet was resolved not to strike at the cause."[2]   And on June 25, 1836,

---

[1] *Cong. Globe*, 24 Cong., 1 Sess., 57.
[2] Garrisons, *Garrison*, II., 325.

in a letter to a Philadelphia abolitionist, Adams says, "You will perceive how far short my opinions on the subject of American slavery fall of the standard which you believe to be that of the true faith."[1] It was not slavery as an unjust and demoralizing system that Adams disliked so much as slavery as an influence paralyzing free speech and endangering the Union. The importance of Adams's position was to show that others than abolitionists could join in resisting what they believed to be the encroachments of the south; and his position as the leader and defender of the right of free criticism of slavery, in and out of Congress, was never disputed.

In 1838 Adams was joined in the House by Joshua R. Giddings, a big, burly, and fearless man, an energetic speaker, especially skilful in answering questions and parrying interruptions. On entering Congress he at once set himself deliberately to evade the gag resolutions and to bring slavery questions before Congress; he began a series of attacks against the slave-trade in the District of Columbia; he somehow introduced petitions for abolition in the District. February 13, 1839, on the apparently harmless question of building a bridge in the District, he found an opportunity to discuss the slave-trade, slavery, and the right of petition. The Seminole War, which broke out about this time, also furnished him ammunition for de-

[1] Mass. Hist. Soc., *Proceedings*, 1902, p. 457.

bates on the question of payment for fugitive slaves who had taken refuge with the Indians; and he wrote a book which proved to his own satisfaction that the war was waged for the sole purpose of re-enslaving these fugitives.[1]

Giddings complained that "our Northern friends are, in fact, afraid of these Southern bullies."[2] Slade, of Vermont, and Gates, of New York, were the only House members who stood by Giddings and Adams. Daniel Webster was the leading northern Whig, and upon nullification vigorously represented his section. Upon another subject Webster publicly expressed an opinion in 1830: "I regard domestic slavery as one of the greatest evils, both moral and political."[3] In the Senate debates on petitions, in 1836, he held that it was the duty of Congress "to take care that the authority of this government is not brought to bear upon it [slavery] by any in-direct interference"; but that the north was unan-imous in believing that Congress had power over slavery in the District.[4] A little later he more boldly announced as to slavery that he would "do nothing . . . to favor or encourage its further exten-sion"; and with regard to abolition, that the subject "has taken strong hold on the consciences of men— to coerce it into silence. . . . I know nothing, even in the Constitution or in the Union itself which would

[1] Julian, *Giddings*, 29, 52–101, passim, 365–369.
[2] *Ibid.*, 53.   [3] Webster, *Works*, III., 279.
[4] *Ibid.*, IV., 231–233.

not be endangered by the explosion which might follow." [1]

The abolitionists got very little aid and comfort out of this negative attitude; and they got still less from Henry Clay, who as a young man had advocated emancipation in Kentucky, and was conspicuously mild in his theories of slavery. February , 1839, he took occasion to make a speech on abolition. A man of strong humanitarian feeling, he could not forbear saying: "I am, Mr. President, no friend of slavery; the Searcher of all Hearts knows that every pulsation of mine beats high and strong in the cause of liberty;" but he added, "I prefer the liberty of my own country to that of any other people, and the liberty of my own race to that of any other race." He criticised the refusal to receive the petitions, preferring to have them referred to a committee, which should report against their object; but held up the abolitionists to odium as demanding a course in the District of Columbia which would be a "great practical inconvenience and annoyance," although he would not squarely say that it was unconstitutional. He scored them also for asking for the prohibition of the domestic slave-trade, which he considered entirely out of the power of Congress; he accused them of standing against the beneficent prospect of colonization, of preaching the amalgamation of the white and black races, of trying to deprive their

[1] Webster, *Works*, I., 356.

neighbors of twelve hundred millions of dollars in slave property, of carrying on an agitation which, unless stopped, would break up the Union.[1] This sentiment was well received in the south, and at the close of his speech Calhoun rose and expressed his pleasure: "The work is done! abolition is no more! the South is consolidated!"[2]

One of Calhoun's resolutions of 1837 declared that "to refuse to extend to the Southern and Western States any advantage which would tend to strengthen or render them more secure, or increase their limits of population by the acquisition of new territory or states . . . under the plea that the institution of slavery . . . is immoral or sinful—would be contrary to that equality of rights and advantages which the Constitution was intended to secure." This was an allusion to the new sectional issue of the annexation of Texas, which Jackson strongly desired and vigorously urged in the last hours of his administration.[3] The farthest point that he could reach was to send a diplomatic agent in the last hours of his administration.[4] When Van Buren became president, therefore, Texas was still independent, and he saw to it that no progress was made towards annexation during his administration. The tension in Congress was for a time relieved.[5]

[1] Cong. Globe, 25 Cong., 3 Sess., App., 354–359.
[2] Buckingham, Slave States, I., 147.
[3] Richardson, Messages and Papers, III., 278.   [4] Ibid., 281.
[5] Garrison, Westward Extension (Am. Nation, XVII.).

In this issue, as in many others, the chief apostle
of slavery was John C. Calhoun, senator from South
Carolina, who had been once a foremost champion
of nationalization, and was now the great leader in
state rights; who was at the same time the advocate
of democratic government among a favored few, and
the author of abstruse reasoning to bolster up slavery. Himself a slave-holder, though known as a
just master, as early as 1820 he came to think slavery indispensable; and when the rising importance
of cotton gave the large planters a steady and profitable crop, and at the same time his illusions as to
employing slaves in manufactures were dissipated,
he defended slavery for exactly the reason that
John Quincy Adams opposed it, because of what
each thought to be the interests of the whites of his
own section. Stern, inflexible, and reasoning from
selected bases of argument in true scholastic fashion,
it was Calhoun's function on slavery, as on nullification, to marshal a body of well-drilled arguments.

In a formal speech on the subject, March 9, 1836,
he took the ground that "Congress has no legitimate
jurisdiction over the subject of slavery, either here
or elsewhere," the germ of the later doctrine of
non-interference, which culminated in the Kansas-
Nebraska bill and led to the Civil War: if Congress
had really no authority, then the abolitionists had
no right to petition. This is assuming the ground
of controversy, but Calhoun made inroads on his
other favorite principle of state rights by holding

that the abolitionists had no right to discuss slavery
at all; and he demanded of Congress (which in his
other view had no jurisdiction over slavery) that it
pass affirmative laws for the protection of the slave-
holding communities against abolition mail; and he
insisted, as a constitutional right, as the moral duty
of sister states, and as the condition of a continued
union, that the agitation in the north should cease.
"The conflicting elements would burst the Union
asunder; powerful as are the links that hold it together. Abolition and the Union cannot co-exist. . . .
Come what will, should it cost every drop of blood and
every cent of property we must defend ourselves."[1]

While Calhoun's resolutions of 1837 were still
pending in the Senate, Adams, as was his wont,
presented a batch of petitions to the House, and
then remarked that "he had in his possession a
paper upon which he wished to have a decision of
the speaker; the paper, he said, came from twenty
persons declaring themselves to be slaves." Was
such a petition covered by the gag resolution? The
chair left it to the House to decide whether the
petition should be received. Instantly the southern
members took alarm, called for the punishment of
Adams, and threatened that otherwise "every member from the slave states should immediately in a
body quit this House and go home to their constituents."[2] Resolution after resolution was intro-

[1] Calhoun, *Works*, II., 488, 629.
[2] *Cong. Globe*, 24 Cong., 2 Sess., 165.

duced in censure of the Massachusetts member. Adams at last obtained the floor long enough to say that the petition was against the abolition of slavery; but he would "be willing the petition should be received and considered." The next step was a resolution to the effect that Adams should be censured "for creating the impression and leaving the House under such impression that said petition was for the abolition of slavery when he knew it was not." If, as seems likely, this extraordinary petition was contrived to put Adams in a dilemma, it missed its aim, for, after several days' debate, it was recognized that "creating an impression" was hardly a parliamentary offence; it was impossible to pass any resolution reflecting on Adams, and the whole controversy was dropped.[1]

The unwisdom of efforts by gag resolution or by censure to check the flow of abolition petitions was shown by the constant increase in the number of those inflammable documents, which, in 1838, had three hundred thousand signatures; the legislatures of Massachusetts and Vermont both voted that the gag resolutions were unconstitutional;[2] and at the beginning of every session there was a fight against them. In December, 1838, a third gag resolution, introduced by a northern man, passed;[3] and January

---

[1] *Cong. Globe*, 24 Cong., 2 Sess., 164–176.
[2] Von Holst, *United States*, II., 284.
[3] Tremain, *Slavery in Dist. of Col.*, 87; Schouler, *United States*, IV., 307.

8, 1840, wearied with bickerings, the House, by the fifth gag resolution, made it a standing rule that no memorial on slavery in the District of Columbia or in any state or territory, or the domestic slave-trade, should be entertained in any way whatsoever. When the rules of the House were revised, Adams for days fought against the inclusion of this rule; and on December 2, 1844, by a vote of 108 to 80, it was abandoned.[1]

The possibility of servile war for years lay in the mind of John Quincy Adams, and he could not be restrained from uttering it. As early as 1820 he entered in his diary, "If slavery be the destined sword in the hand of the destroying angel, which is to sever the ties of this Union, the same sword will cut in sunder the bond of slavery itself."[2]

May 23, 1836, Adams made a speech of five hours, in which he predicted that in case of a general slave insurrection Congress must interfere or foreign powers would interfere, and he took quick advantage of an admission by Wise, of Virginia, that Congress had "the right to interfere for the support and protection of slavery in the states." The sting of Adams's suggestion lay first in the allusion to the possibility of a servile war—for, to the mind of the south, mentioning such a possibility aloud was the same as advocating it; and second, in its clear statement of the doctrine that circumstances might arise

---

[1] Julian, *Giddings*, 171; Schouler, *United States*, IV., 481.
[2] Adams, *Memoirs*, V., 210.

under which the federal government must interfere to emancipate the slaves. This idea Adams never forgot; again, April 14, 1842, he announced in Congress that "when a country is invaded and two hostile armies are set in hostile array, the commanders of both armies have power to emancipate all the slaves in the invaded territory. . . . I lay this down as the law of nations"; and his own comment upon this speech was, "My speech of this day stung the slavocacy to madness." [1]

After four years of a kind of armed truce, President Tyler's renewal of the plans for the annexation of Texas again aroused Congress. In January, 1842, Adams gave the desired opportunity for a conflict by presenting to the House a petition of citizens of Haverhill, Massachusetts, asking Congress to adopt measures for the breaking up of the Union; Adams moved that this petition be referred to a select committee with instructions to prepare a report showing why the petition could not be granted. To silence this inveterate defender of the sanctity of petitions, a conference of southern members agreed to stand by each other, in a resolution of censure that: "A proposition . . . to dissolve the organic law . . . is a high breach of privilege, a contempt offered to this House, a direct proposition to the legislature and each member of it to commit perjury, and involves necessarily in its execution and its consequences

[1] See Charles Francis Adams, in Mass. Hist. Soc., *Proceedings,* January, 1902, pp. 439–478.

the destruction of our country, and the crime of high treason"; that Adams had "disgraced his country . . . might well be held to merit expulsion from the national councils, and the House deem it an act of grace and mercy when they only inflict upon him their severest censure." [1] Wise, of Virginia, made it a personal matter and accused Adams of being in league with British abolitionists.

Considering that Adams had neither signed, advocated, nor approved the petition, this was a strong resolution; and when Adams took the floor, he called for the reading of the constitutional definition of treason and for the clause of the Declaration of Independence which asserts that "whenever any form of government becomes destructive to these ends it is the right of the people to alter it or to abolish it." The excitement rose from hour to hour, and after eleven days of this extraordinary debate, when Adams offered to drop the subject if the resolutions were laid upon the table, the House so voted by 106 to 93; and the Haverhill petition was then refused by 116 to 40. The attempt to silence Adams was never again renewed, to the day of his death on the floor of the House in 1848.

Adams had behind him the prestige of a great name and long experience in parliamentary law. Giddings was still an Ishmaelite, his hand against every man and every man's hand against him; and within two months a similar effort was made to

[1] *Cong. Globe*, 27 Cong., 2 Sess., 168, 169.

silence him. The cause was the introduction, March 21, 1842, of a series of resolutions brought about by the Creole slave case,[1] in which he asserted that "slavery being an abridgment of the natural rights of man can exist only by force of positive municipal law." Having accomplished his purpose of calling public attention to the case and of disturbing his fellow-members from the south, Giddings withdrew his resolutions without bringing them to a vote. But Botts, of Virginia, at once offered a resolution to the effect that "this House hold the conduct of said member altogether unwarranted and unwarrantable, and deserving the severe condemnation of the people of this country and of this body in particular." Giddings was thus put upon the defensive, but the House had tied itself up with its own procedure to such a degree that Giddings found he had no parliamentary status. A second resolution of censure was adopted by 125 to 69, and nothing was left for Giddings but to send in his resignation.[2] A special election was held and his district promptly returned him, and with this increased prestige he at once renewed his tactics of exasperation.

Between Slade's first abolition speech of 1835, and the attempts to censure Adams and Giddings in 1842, less than seven years had elapsed; but the

[1] See p. 294, below.
[2] Julian, *Giddings*, 113–125; *Cong. Globe*, 27 Cong., 2 Sess., 342–346.

attitude of the anti-slavery men was totally changed, and every effort to prevent the introduction of abolition petitions had brought about a debate on slavery. The gag resolutions rested on a principle which might be applied to any other subject unpleasant to a majority of the members of Congress, and therefore had to be abandoned. No greater mistake was made throughout the struggle than the assumption that slavery was a subject of such peculiar sanctity that it must not be discussed on the floor of Congress. The debates of the House went abroad, and might, perhaps, reach the eyes of slaves; but they equally reached the eyes of freemen, who could appreciate the gibe of the abolitionists, that a subject which could not be safely discussed in the Congress of the United States was an institution harmful to the country; and that, if public discussion was damaging to slavery, the proof was complete that discussion was needed.

CHAPTER XIX

INTERSTATE AND INTERNATIONAL RELATIONS
OF SLAVERY

(1822–1842)

IN the debates of Congress the point of view of the
south was that the power of the federal government over slavery was negative; the use of federal
machinery was disclaimed. At the same time it was
expected that through the clauses of the Constitution on interstate relations affirmative support should
be given to slavery. "Full Faith and Credit shall be
given in each State to the public Acts and judicial
Proceedings of every other State "[1]—that is, statute-
books and judicial records are to be accepted as evidence of legal status and of legal proceedings, under the laws of the state issuing them; the state
courts were to apply the laws and decisions of other
states, as of foreign countries.

When part of the states swept away all their
previous legislation on slavery, the degree of effect
which either side would give to the law of the other
became a disputed question. For instance, did the
clause on "privileges and immunities of citizens"

[1] Article IV., sec. i.

give a master a right to carry his slaves into another state? Did it give negro citizens in one state the right to go into another state? Indiana and Illinois forbid their entrance, but when Missouri, in 1821, tried to do the same thing, a compromise had to be contrived to get around the difficulty.[1]

After the unsuccessful Denmark Vesey insurrection of 1820, suspicion was strong against every negro. South Carolina passed a series of laws, commonly called the "negro seamen acts," which provided in effect that whenever a ship arrived in port any negroes on board must go to jail, there to stay till the vessel was ready to sail again. Northern states at once protested that their citizens were thus deprived of their "privileges and immunities"; and the British government made similar remonstrances.[2] After an opinion of Attorney-General Wirt that the law was unconstitutional, South Carolina relaxed the measure as against England, but continued it against the northern states.[3]

Under pressure from the anti-slavery people, the Massachusetts legislature, in 1844, sent Samuel Hoar as a commissioner to Charleston, to make a test case of a negro citizen of Massachusetts deprived of rights in South Carolina, to be brought to the supreme court. A committee of the South Carolina legislat-

---

[1] Turner, *New West* (*Am. Nation*, XIV.), chap. x.
[2] *Niles' Register*, XXVII., 242.
[3] *Opinions of Attorneys-General*, I., 659–661.

ure thereupon voted that "this agent comes here not as a citizen of the United States, but as an emissary of a foreign Government hostile to our domestic institutions and with the sole purpose of subverting our internal police." The legislature passed resolutions demanding the exclusion of Mr. Hoar, and he was notified that his life was in danger, and left Charleston—an example of how little state comity could be relied upon in any measure against slavery.[1]

The southern states were inclined to claim the principle that the status of a slave, created only by the law of his domicile, might under some circumstances follow him into a free state. This principle was tested in various ways. When a master deliberately took a slave into a free state, freedom suits were occasionally brought; though the northern courts sustained the state emancipation provisions they sometimes gave validity to so-called "indentures" or written agreements by negroes to serve a master for life. As to temporary residence of slaves, in Massachusetts the law in terms forbade it for any cause.[2] In other states the courts held that the anti-slavery clauses of the constitutions did not apply to such cases.[3] If they voluntarily returned with their masters, southern courts, especially

[1] Greeley, *American Conflict*, I., 180–185; *Niles' Register*, LXVII., 226.

[2] Commonwealth *vs*. Aves, 18 Pick., 193.

[3] Supreme Court of Illinois, in Willard *vs*. the People, 4 Scammon, 461; Hurd, *Law of Freedom and Bondage*, II., 359.

in Missouri and Louisiana, frequently held that they reverted to slavery.[1]

Complications also came over the claim to a "right of transit" from one place in a slave-holding state to another, or from a slave-holding state to a foreign country, through free territory, or along the Ohio and Mississippi rivers, lying between free and slave states. The claim was that interstate or international comity, and the "privileges and immunities" clause, gave the slave-owner protection during the few hours or days of travel. The laws of Indiana permitted such transit provided no purchases were made amounting to "location." [2]

Not so those of Pennsylvania. In 1855, John H. Wheeler, of North Carolina, on his way to New York and thence to Nicaragua, to which country he had been appointed minister, brought a slave woman named Jane to Philadelphia. While sitting on board the boat in which they had arrived, she was informed by Passmore Williamson, secretary of the Pennsylvania Abolition Society, that under the laws of the state she was free to go where she would, and she left the boat against the express will of her master. Frantic efforts were made to recover Jane by *habeas corpus*, and Williamson was charged with abducting her; whereupon she appeared in court

---

[1] Collins *vs*. America, 9 B. Monroe, 565; Rachael *vs*. Walker, 4 Mo. Supreme Court, 350; Goodloe, *Southern Platform*, 73.

[2] Several interesting cases in Coffin, *Reminiscences*, 195–202, 534–541, 554–557.

and testified that she had always desired to be free and had the intention to escape in New York. Williamson was then charged with contempt of court for asserting that Jane was free and desired her freedom, but the state courts upheld Jane's status as a free woman, and Williamson was eventually released.[1]

The only class of southern negroes in northern states for whom the federal government took responsibility was the "fugitives from service or labor."[2] Though the act of 1793 permitted the claimant of a fugitive to carry him before either a federal or a state magistrate for decision as to whether he was the person described in the claimant's documents, state officials were usually called upon to render judgment. When the abolitionists came upon the scene they began to stir up their legislatures to pass what came to be known as "personal liberty laws," intended to protect free colored people from kidnapping and from unfounded claims under the federal statute. Some of these laws were hardly compatible with the national act; for instance, Pennsylvania passed, in 1826, a law which prohibited the carrying away of negroes to be enslaved, but which also protected persons claimed as fugitives. A series of similar acts was passed by half a dozen northern states between 1824 and 1840:

[1] Still, *Underground Railroad*, 86–97.
[2] Extracts from accounts of fugitives, in Hart, *Contemporaries*, IV., §§ 29–33.

Indiana and Connecticut provided a jury trial for alleged fugitives, an example followed by Vermont and New York, and Connecticut also forbade state officials to take part in fugitive-slave cases. New York and Vermont provided that state attorneys should act as legal advisers for the negroes in such cases. One state, Ohio, in 1839, passed a fugitive law of its own, giving the master more privileges than under the federal statute.

The irritation at the capture of fugitives shown by the personal liberty bills soon took the form of defiance of the federal law. In 1836 occurred a damage suit against abolitionists for aiding fugitives to escape, and of violent rescue of a fugitive.[1] In 1837 the field of such interference was extended to the west, where the slave Matilda, who was being taken by her master (and father) down the river, walked ashore from the steamer at Cincinnati and found employment with the family of James G. Birney, who asked no questions about her. When her whereabouts were discovered, she was claimed and surrendered as a fugitive, though Chase, as counsel, insisted that she had been voluntarily brought within the jurisdiction of the state by her master.

A test case of intentional breach of the law was that of John Van Zandt, a former Kentuckian, but an abolitionist and official of the Underground Railroad, who was driving a market wagon in the neighborhood of Cincinnati very early one morning

[1] *Niles' Register*, L., 423; McDougall, *Fugitive Slaves*, § 42.

in 1840, and, by a coincidence which was never explained, fell in with a party of nine slaves who had escaped from the other side of the river that night. While carrying them out into the country, they were stopped by two people who had no legal authority, and all the slaves except one were returned to the owners.[1]

Such incidents showed the determination of the abolitionists that the fugitive-slave law should not be carried out. A supreme court decision now both strengthened and weakened the force of the act of 1793. A woman named Margaret Morgan, a fugitive from Maryland, in 1837 was discovered in Pennsylvania by Edward Prigg, an agent of her master, who seized her without the simple process provided by the law, and thereby violated the Pennsylvania statute of 1826 against the kidnapping of negroes. Prigg was convicted of this latter offence in the Pennsylvania courts, but appeal was brought to the supreme court of the United States, which in 1842[2] reached a decision to the effect that the owner of the slave had a right to recover him under the federal statute without restraint by any conflicting state acts; at the same time it held that the act of 1793 could not be construed to create any obligation of the state authorities to take part in the administration of the law.

Just at this time a fugitive named Latimer was

---

[1] Hart, *Chase*, 75; Schuckers, *Chase*, 53.
[2] Prigg *vs.* Pennsylvania, 16 Peters, 539.

seized in Boston. On the basis of the Prigg decision, Chief-Justice Shaw refused to issue the *habeas corpus* provided by the state liberty bill so as to take the custody of Latimer from the federal authorities. The abolitionists held a succession of public meetings to protest, and if possible to prevent the return of Latimer, and finally ended the excitement by raising the necessary four hundred dollars to buy his freedom.[1] This experience aided the abolitionists, for, so far from putting an end to the personal liberty bills, the Prigg case suggested a new crop, some passed simply with the purpose of taking advantage of the right to withdraw the use of the state machinery of magistrates and jails and prosecutors; other states set out with the deliberate intention of avoiding or interfering with the act of 1793. Hence, the personal liberty laws were felt to be a burning grievance by the south, especially after the second federal law of 1850.[2]

The authority of the federal statute was further shored up through a damage suit against Van Zandt for the value of the slave who had escaped in 1840 through his means. Chase, as couusel, did his best, but judgment was obtained against Van Zandt for twelve hundred dollars. In 1847 the case came before the supreme court on appeal, and Seward and Chase made arguments. Chase's point was that the

---

[1] McDougall, *Fugitive Slaves*, § 44.
[2] See later statute, Smith, *Parties and Slavery (Am. Nation.* XVIII.), chap. xix.; Parker, *Personal Liberty Laws*.

fugitive-slave law was contrary to the ordinance of 1787 and to the Constitution of the United States, and that the states and not the nation were intended to legislate on the subject: the court squarely and thoroughly affirmed the constitutionality of the federal fugitive-slave law.[1]

The tide of anti-slavery feeling had now risen to a point where, law or no law, decision or no decision, the return of fugitives was openly resisted. In the decade from 1840 to 1850 came a dozen or more exciting seizures, though in only one instance, the Walker case (1844), did the fugitive escape. The Kennedy case in 1847 made a great noise, because the owner, a Maryland man, tried to seize his fugitive without the usual process of the law, was resisted, and broke his knee-cap. The riot caused the trial of thirty-six people, and Kennedy, who does not appear to have been seriously injured in the scrimmage, died during his convalescence— to many minds this seemed a clear case of the murder of a master by his slave.[2]

Another part of the act of 1793 provided that persons charged with a crime in one state and fleeing to another state might be returned on a requisition made by one governor upon the other governor. Slave stealing, including assisting fugitives to escape, was a crime known to the statute-books of all the southern states, but impossible to commit in com-

[1] Jones vs. Van Zandt, 5 Howard, 215; Hart, Chase, 76–80.
[2] Cong. Globe, 36 Cong., 2 Sess., 801.

munities where there was no legal slavery—was it an offence extraditable under the statute? This question was raised when, in May, 1837, the officers of the schooner *Susan*, bound from Georgia, allowed a negro stowaway to escape on reaching port in Maine. The governor of Georgia sent a requisition for them on the charge of slave stealing in Georgia; but Governor Dunlap took the rather narrow ground that the officers of the *Susan* had not "fled from justice," inasmuch as they left Georgia before they were charged with the crime.[1] The governor of Georgia thereupon proposed to his legislature to consider all sailor citizens of Maine, who came to Georgia, "as doing so with the intent to commit the crime of seducing negro slaves from their owners."[2]

A similar case occurred in 1839, when three sailors on a vessel bound to New York encouraged a slave to escape from Norfolk. The fugitive was recaptured, but Governor William H. Seward, who had travelled through the south, and had a personal dislike of slavery, twice declined to grant a requisition for the sailors, because the extradition clause "applied only to those acts which, if committed within the jurisdiction of the state in which the accused is found, would be felonious . . . or criminal, by the laws of that state . . . or by the laws of all civilized countries." The controversy lasted several years: the legislature of New York backed their governor up

---

[1] *Niles' Register*, LIII., 71; *Senate Docs.*, 26 Cong., 1 Sess., No. 273.　　[2] Von Holst, *United States*, II., 540.

by passing a personal liberty law, under which every person claimed as a fugitive was entitled to a jury trial; Virginia replied by a statute requiring a special inspection of all vessels bound to New York from Virginia; while Mississippi offered to unite with "other states in any mode or measure of resistance or redress." [1]

The uproar was resumed in 1860 when the commonwealth of Kentucky appealed to the federal supreme court for a mandamus to compel the governor of Ohio to surrender one William Lago, a free negro under indictment in Kentucky for assisting a fugitive to escape. The supreme court took the ground that there was a legal right to demand extradition for an offence not defined by the statute-book of the state to which he had fled, and that it was a "moral duty" of the governor of Ohio to give up Lago; but that "there is no power delegated to the general government, either through the judicial department or any other department, to use any coercive means to compel him." [2]

Whether it was possible for a person in one state to commit a crime of which other states could take cognizance, without the alleged criminal leaving his own domicile, was a question raised when abolition newspapers and other controversial material was sent to people in the southern states. These papers

[1] Bancroft, *Seward*, I., 101 – 104; Lothrop, *Seward*, 39 – 42; McDougall, *Fugitive Slaves*, § 47.
[2] Kentucky *vs*. Dennison, 24 Howard, 103–110.

contained rude wood-cuts illustrating the cruel treatment of slaves, and many allusions to the injustice
and illegality of slavery. In several southern cities
such papers were seized in July, 1835, by self-con-
stituted guardians of the peace, and burned before
thousands of spectators. The postmaster of Charleston appealed to the postmaster of New York to stop
sending such matter; and he asked the anti-slavery
societies to discontinue their use of the mails—a
request which they refused to consider. The postmaster-general, Amos Kendall, himself a slave-
holder, declined to issue any official order to exclude matter duly mailed, but added the significant
hint: "We owe an obligation to the laws, but a
higher one to the communities in which we live."
With this statement, which bears a singular kinship
to the "higher law" principle of the abolitionists,
the postmaster was well enough contented, and no
more abolition mail was delivered in Charleston.

In this virtual approval of a search and censor-
ship of the mail, Kendall was supported by President
Jackson,[1] who, in his annual message of 1835, suggested action by Congress. Calhoun introduced a
Senate bill in 1836 providing that any mail matter
(other than letters) touching the subject of slavery
should not be delivered in any state prohibiting the
circulation of such matter;[2] and he got nineteen

[1] *Niles' Register*, XLVIII., 402, 447; Kendall, *Autobiography*,
648; Richardson, *Messages and Papers*, III., 175.
[2] *Debates of Congress*, 24 Cong., 1 Sess., 383.

votes in favor of his proposal against twenty-five. Congress was held back by constitutional objections: it was to enact in advance laws not yet made by the states, and also to make as many different kinds of federal law as there were varieties of state legislation on the subject. Nevertheless, in our day the disputed principles have been conceded; the federal government excludes from the mails matter which the post-office authorities deem dangerous to morals, such as obscene literature and lottery mail; and by the original package act, Congress in a sense re-enacts the state statutes prohibiting the sale of liquor, and thereby makes a federal law in some states which does not apply to others.

If the agitators could not be silenced, might they not be punished? Some efforts were made to indict and then to extradite leading abolitionists; and in 1831 it was publicly suggested that Garrison should be "prosecuted in the place where he had procured his incendiary paper to be distributed "—that is, in the south.[1] The only serious attempt to carry out this method was set forth by the grand jury of Tuscaloosa County, Alabama, September, 1835, in the following indictment: "Robert G. Williams, late of said county, being a wicked, malicious, seditious and ill-disposed person, and being greatly disaffected to the laws . . . of said state, and feloniously, wickedly, maliciously and seditiously contriving, devising and intending to produce conspiracy, insurrection and

[1] Garrisons, *Garrison*, I., 239

rebellion among the slave population of said state, ... did cause to be distributed, circulated and published, a seditious paper called The Emancipator [containing the expression] 'God commands and all nature cries out that man should not be held as property.'" [1] Governor Gayle, of Alabama, thereupon called upon Governor Marcy, of New York, to surrender Williams. But Marcy was unable to see how a crime could be committed in Alabama by a man who was at the moment in New York, and how a man could "flee" from a state in which he had never set foot.

In several instances rewards were offered for the delivery of particular abolitionists, especially Arthur Tappan, of New York; and by an official statute of Georgia, December 26, 1831, five thousand dollars was appropriated "to be paid to any person or persons who shall arrest, bring to trial and prosecute to conviction, under the laws of this state, the editor or publisher of a certain paper called the *Liberator*." [2]

The difficulty of appealing to the good - will of neighbors and to the general principles of comity between nations was manifested in the foreign relations of the country after 1840, when all the neighboring countries except Cuba and Porto Rico, some of the French colonies and the empire of Brazil, were free; while the United States stood in the eyes

---

[1] *Niles' Register*, XLIX., 358.
[2] Garrisons, *Garrison*, I., 247; Goodell, *Slavery and Anti-Slavery*, 410.

of the world as a slave-holding country. Flanked north and south by the free territory of Canada and Mexico, the slave-holders lost live property across both borders. The strength of the British emancipationist party was so great that it was useless to revive projects for a treaty for the surrender of fugitive slaves from Great Britain. On the other hand, the slave states refused to accept foreign negroes as citizens on the same footing as whites; and in 1831 Attorney - General Berrien gave the opinion that the South Carolina seaman act was a police regulation, against which the British government had no reasonable right of complaint.[1]

The slave-trade continued after 1830, as before, to disturb the friendly relations between the United States and her neighbors. Notwithstanding the severe statutes between 1820 and 1830, very little effort was made to enforce them; the greater part of the trade to Brazil and the Spanish colonies was under the United States flag; and several thousand slaves were shipped into the United States every year.[2] Unless a vessel could be overhauled on the high seas and required to show her papers, it was impossible to stop the slave-trade, and Great Britain had an active navy and was fitted to be the policeman of the seas; but the United States would admit

---

[1] *Opinions of Attorneys-General*, II., 426–442.
[2] DuBois, *Suppression of the Slave-Trade*, 143; cf. President Tyler's message, February 20, 1845, in Richardson, *Messages and Papers*, IV., 362–364.

no "right of search" even to find out whether a vessel was entitled to fly the American flag,[1] and the trade by Americans was little disturbed.

A "right of visit" to ascertain the charter of the ship was conceded by France and several of the smaller European powers; and in 1841 England secured the so-called "Quintuple Treaty," signed by Great Britain, Austria, Prussia, and Russia, to recognize this practice among them. Without instructions, Lewis Cass, the American minister to France, published a pamphlet intended to prove that the purpose of Great Britain was to set up a new principle of international law which would eventually be forced upon the United States, and he lodged an effective protest against the ratification of the treaty by France.[2] The method was harsh and unusual, the danger remote, but it turned the discussion into another channel, and in the Ashburton treaty of 1842 the United States and Great Britain entered into a "cruising convention" by which they agreed to maintain a joint squadron for the suppression of slavers on the coast of Africa.

It remains to notice a group of difficulties arising out of the appearance in the ports of other countries of American vessels lawfully carrying slaves. In

---

[1] Schuyler, *Diplomacy*, pt. ii., 248–252; Channing, *Works*, VI., 363–368.

[2] DuBois, *Suppression of the Slave-Trade*, 143–146; Schuyler, *Diplomacy*, pt. ii., 252; McLaughlin, *Cass*, 175–182.

1831 the ship *Comet*, with slaves bound from an Atlantic to a Gulf port, was wrecked upon the Bahamas and the slaves on board were brought to Nassau and set free, on the ground that the British law did not recognize slavery on the high seas. In 1833 the *Encomium*, in 1835 the *Enterprise*, and in 1840 the *Hermosa* were brought within the British jurisdiction in about the same way. The United States demanded an indemnity for all these slaves, and asserted that the accidental presence of the vessels in British waters did not dissolve the relations of master and slave which existed under the law of the place from which they set sail. It was easy to point out that the ports of the United States as such were neither slave-holding nor free; that the status of slavery was created by commonwealths which could claim no jurisdiction of any kind on the high seas, and which had no direct diplomatic relations with any foreign country. Nevertheless, it was inequitable that England should set these cargoes of slaves free while slavery was not completely extinguished in her own colonies. After long negotiations, in 1840 Great Britain allowed an indemnity of one hundred and fifteen thousand dollars for the slaves on board the *Comet* and *Encomium*, because these cases occurred previous to completion of the West India emancipation; but notice was given that no further payments of that kind would be made. The Senate, by resolution, then claimed that the *Enterprise* case was a violation of international law, but no redress could be had.[1]

While these negotiations were pending arose the case of the ship *L'Amistad*, which, in June, 1839, left Havana bound to another Spanish port, having on board certain persons described in a certificate held by two of the passengers as "slaves." In reality they were persons imported from Africa contrary to Spanish law, and therefore legally free. On the voyage the Africans rose, killed the officers, and compelled one of the ship's company to navigate the vessel, as they supposed towards Africa; in reality he edged towards the coast, where in August they were picked up by Lieutenant Gedney in a federal revenue-cutter.[2]

The affair gave rise to unexampled complications: Gedney claimed salvage; Ruiz and Montez, the masters, claimed their slaves; the negroes, in whom the abolitionists took great interest and who were well defended, claimed their liberty; the Spanish minister, under the treaty of 1795, claimed the restoration of both ship and cargo as "property rescued from pirates,"—the negroes having the double distinction of being pirates and booty, President Van Buren was ready to surrender them, but the federal courts took jurisdiction and the supreme court, on appeal, gave judgment that the papers were not prima-facie evidence of the status of the

[1] Moore, *International Arbitrations*, I., 408–412.
[2] Wharton, *Digest of American International Law*, § 161.

negroes, who in law were free when they left Havana, and, as freemen, were entitled to kill those who attempted to carry them into slavery; and the United States was under no obligation to interfere. The captives were allowed to go free and remained in the United States.[1]

The shock to the south caused by this decision was increased in November, 1841, by the case of the American ship *Creole*, bound from Hampton Roads to New Orleans with a cargo of slaves. Perhaps inspired by the *L'Amistad* incident, the slaves rose, killed one person, and carried the vessel into the port of Nassau, where they were discharged by the British government. Although Webster, as secretary of state, demanded their return for "mutiny and murder," a claim which virtually made them out to be subject to the officers of the ship, Charles Sumner took the ground that "they became free men when taken, by the voluntary action of their owners, beyond the jurisdiction of the slave states."[2]   Had they been white men they would have been surrendered; had they escaped without a fight they could not have been demanded as criminals; but Webster held that, inasmuch as slaves were recognized as property by the Constitution of the United States in those states in which slavery existed, that status continued at sea.[3]

[1] Baldwin, in New Haven Hist. Soc., *Papers*, IV., 341–371; *Opinions of Attorneys-General*, III., 484–492; 15 Peters, 518.

[2] Pierce, *Sumner*, II., 200.

[3] Moore, *International Arbitrations*, I., 410–412.

The case was different from the *L'Amistad* in that the slaves were legally held at the time of departure; and it was stretching British emancipation a long way to apply it to such a circumstance. Ten years of negotiations brought about no agreement, and in 1853 the question was submitted to the arbitration of Joshua Bates, an English banker, American born, who decided that an indemnity was due, and a hundred and ten thousand dollars was paid by the British government to extinguish this obligation.[2]

[1] Moore, *International Arbitrations*, I., 417.

CHAPTER XX

PANIC OF 1837

(1837–1841)

LOOKING back through the Civil War and the steps which led up to it, the most important question before the country in 1837 seems now to have been the abolition controversy; but though it occupied a large place in men's minds, people were chiefly interested in every-day commercial and financial questions and the manœuvrings of the two national parties, which now began to take distinct form.

In his inaugural address, March 4, 1837, Van Buren said, "I tread in the foot-steps of illustrious men." As he hinted, his administration was to be a conscientious attempt to carry into effect the principles which Jackson with such masterful blows had hammered into shape as the basis of the Democratic party.[1] On slavery, Van Buren declared himself the "inflexible and uncompromising opponent of every attempt on the part of Congress to abolish slavery in the District of Columbia against the

[1] Cf. MacDonald, *Jacksonian Democracy* (*Am. Nation*, XV.), chap. xvii.

wishes of the slave-holding states"; and also equally determined "to resist the slightest interference with it in the states where it exists"; mob violence against the abolitionists he condoned because a "reckless disregard of the consequences of their conduct . . . has exposed individuals to popular indignation." [1]

As a kind of third term of Andrew Jackson, Van Buren carried over the cabinet that he found in office, except that Poinsett, of South Carolina, was made secretary of war. With the exception of Levi Woodbury, of New Hampshire, secretary of the treasury, and Amos Kendall, postmaster-general, it was an inconspicuous cabinet; and three changes were made in the course of the administration. To the supreme court Jackson appointed a new justice in the last days of his administration, and Van Buren made two appointments.

Although Jackson in his own mind was a reformer, the post-offices throughout the country were made political machines, the treasury was ill-managed, no proper effort was made to secure prompt settlements from financial officials or to deal with embezzlements when discovered, and national currency was demoralized. The accounts of Samuel Swartwout, for seven years the collector of the port of New York, were known to be in arrears; but not until seven months after Swartwout had finally retired from office did Van Buren take steps to compel a settle-

---

[1] Richardson, *Messages and Papers*, III., 318.

ment, and it was then discovered that he owed a million and a quarter, which was never paid.[1]

The business of the country had never seemed so flourishing as at the beginning of 1837. When the federal charter of the United States Bank expired, March 1, 1836, it continued under a state charter with the same capital of $35,000,000, but of course without the privilege of branches in other states, the place of which was taken by new state banks. The United States still owned seven millions of stock, which it sold out to advantage in 1838. Banking in all its forms was therefore turned over wholly to banks created by the states, which, in 1837, numbered 788, with a capital of $291,000,000, a circulation of $150,000,000, and disproportionate loans of $525,000,000.[2] Several of the states later abandoned the old system of special charters for the banks, and passed general banking acts, fixing conditions upon which any person who could bring together the necessary capital might receive a charter; but no less than fourteen states of the Union were engaged in the business of public banking, the most noticeable being Kentucky, Indiana, and Illinois.[3] In about half of the states of the Union the laws adequately protected the note-holder under ordinary conditions, but there were numerous wildcat banks; for instance, the Essex Bank, incorpo-

[1] *House Exec. Docs.*, 25 Cong., 3 Sess., No. 13.
[2] Dewey, *Financial Hist. of the U. S.*, 225.
[3] *Sound Currency*, II., Nos. 1, 10, V., Nos. 9, 16.

rated in Vermont in 1833, which put out a large amount of currency on no capital whatever, except the notes of stockholders for $2000.[1]

In 1834 there was a stringency, amounting almost to a crisis, but from that time on the state banks seemed prosperous, and there were few bank failures. This prosperity was apparently not disturbed by the passage of the distribution act of 1836, by which $37,468,859, arising from the unexpected receipts of public lands during 1835 and 1836, was to be drawn in four quarterly instalments from the state banks in which the money was on deposit, and to be paid over to the states for such uses as they saw fit; the smallest payment was to be $382,000 to Michigan and Delaware, and the largest, over $5,000,000, to New York.[2] The first instalment of $9,367,000 was duly called for on January 1, 1837, and the states proceeded to decide what use should be made of this sum. Some used it to pay off old debts; others appropriated it to running expenses; some of the New England states appropriated it for public schools, and distributed it among the counties and towns; or the money was deposited with the towns and used according to their discretion; in a few cases the money was distributed and paid in cash to the voters. The states of Illinois, North Carolina, Delaware, and Michigan used the whole of

[1] Brothers, *United States*, 451.
[2] MacDonald, *Jacksonian Democracy* (*Am. Nation*, XV.), chap. xvi.

their allotment for internal improvements; in some other states it went to pay debts on such improvements.[1]

The call for the second instalment, April 1, 1837, was honored by the banks, but it now became evident that the deposits had unduly accumulated in the northern and western banks; for instance, against Michigan's share of $382,000 there were deposits in Michigan banks of almost a million; Mississippi, which was to receive about $500,000, had over $17,000,000 on deposit; while Pennsylvania, with claims of nearly four millions, contained on deposit only a quarter of a million.

The surplus was only one element in a period of extraordinary speculation. The government deposits in the weak frontier banks gave them funds which they could employ profitably only in local loans to purchasers of government land. The country was filling up rapidly, improved farms were worth many times the government price of $1.25 an acre in cash, and a vicious circle was initiated under which the proceeds of the loans were paid to the land offices for lands and redeposited in the banks by the land offices, where they became the basis for renewed transactions. The credit of the banks was thus tied up with the speculative value of the lands; if the time came when they could not be sold at a large advance over the cost price, somebody stood to lose immense sums.

[1] Bourne, *Surplus Revenue*, passim.

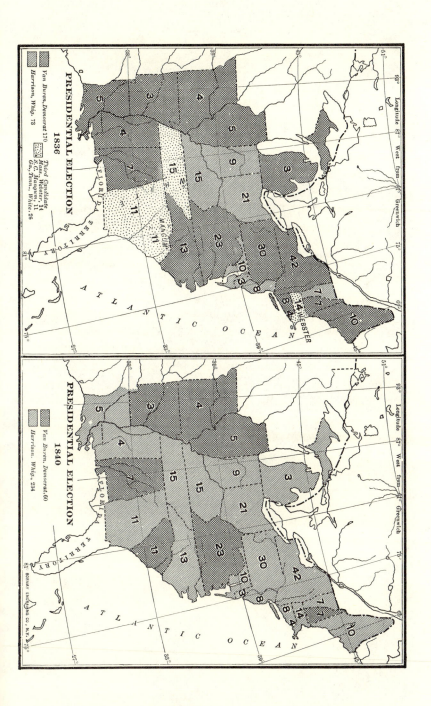

PRESIDENTIAL ELECTION
1836

Van Buren, Democrat 170
Harrison, Whig, 73

Third Candidate
Mass., Webster, 14
N. C., Mangum, 11
Ga., Tenn., White, 26

PRESIDENTIAL ELECTION
1840

Van Buren, Democrat, 60
Harrison, Whig, 234

Another extension of business beyond the needs of the country was in railroad building; between 1831 and 1837, 1274 miles were constructed,[1] most of which was still drawn from American capital, inasmuch as American railroads as yet had no credit abroad. About this time the states discovered that there were large masses of capital in Europe seeking investment, and millions of dollars was placed in state loans, intended chiefly for the construction of canals; the eastern banks also had foreign correspondents who were willing to place large sums indirectly through their instrumentality. The total amount of these foreign loans, nearly all incurred after 1830, was estimated at $200,000,000.[2] The southern states alone appear to have borrowed about $50,000,000,[3] and in May, 1838, the aggregate state debt, foreign and domestic together, was stated at $170,000,000.[4]

All the conditions were ripe for a crash: an artificial and reckless system of private and public finance; the United States government expecting the unusual sales of public lands to go on indefinitely; the states plunging into debt out of all proportion to their means and needs, and incurring interest charges which would require higher taxes than their people had ever known; private banking expanded,

[1] Poor, *Railroad Manual*, 1869–1870, p. 24.
[2] Richardson, *Messages and Papers*, III., 552.
[3] *Democratic Review*, 48–101.
[4] Lalor, *Cyclopædia*, I., 728, III., 604.

from the ease of raising funds abroad and of placing
them at home; the country merchant stretching his
credit to buy new stocks of goods, and giving credit
to his farming customers; real estate soaring upward, so that in New York City the appraisal rose
from $104,000,000, in 1832, to $253,000,000 in 1836.[1]
Men were willing, even in financial centres, to pay
ruinous discounts. In seven years a balance of
trade of $140,000,000 was created against the United
States, for which the foreigners practically received
the obligations of states and banks.[2] Cotton was
very high in 1835, rising to sixteen cents; and thousands of southwestern planters bought negroes on
credit, expecting to pay for them out of their cotton
crop. If anything occurred to check this feeling of
buoyant confidence, a crash must come. The specie
circular of July 11, 1836, requiring payment for land
in specie, was really an effort to check this alarming
tide of speculation, which extended into business of
every sort.[3]

In November, 1836, the failure of the "three
W's"—Wilkes, Wilde, and Wiggins—large English
houses engaged in American trade, was the premoni-
tion of the crash.[4] The panic began in the south,
where cotton broke to ten cents; in March, 1837, the
calamity extended to the New York banks. All but

[1] *Niles' Register*, LI., 167.
[2] Dewey, *Financial Hist. of the U. S.*, § 96.
[3] MacDonald, *Jacksonian Democracy* (*Am. Nation*, XV.), chap.
xvi.   [4] Von Holst, *United States*, II., 194.

four of the deposit banks were obliged to suspend
specie payments. The Dry-Dock Bank, one of the
government deposit banks, showed cash resources of
$15,000 and outstanding loans of $313,000. Throughout the Union most of the banks ceased to redeem
their notes in specie over their counters; and two
failures of crops, one in 1835, and again in 1837,
greatly reduced the recuperative power of the
country. In a few weeks, in New York alone, the
value of real estate and stocks declined at least
$100,000,000. Amid this excitement and distress
the third instalment was called from the banks, on
July 1, 1837. About four out of nine millions of
this call was received at the time, and then, later,
the loss to the government from insolvent banks
seems to have been only about fifty thousand dollars.

Out of a treasury balance of $46,000,000, on
January 1, 1837, only $28,000,000 was turned over
to the states, but the balance of $18,000,000 disap-
peared in the expenses of the government, so that,
in October, Congress, summoned in special session,
was obliged to suspend the call for the fourth instalment and to authorize the temporary issue of treasury notes; and in the next six years $47,000,000 of
such notes were put forth to tide over temporary
stringencies. In 1841 a bonded debt was authorized, and from that day to the present the United
States has always had a public debt. In every year
between 1837 and 1843, with the one exception of
1839, there was a deficit. The sale of the public

lands fell from 20,000,000 acres, in 1836, to 3,500,000 in 1838. Imports shrank in two years from $190,-000,000 to $113,000,000, with a corresponding diminution of the customs duties to less than half their previous figure.[1]

The treasury notes were simply a palliative. What could the federal government do to relieve the community in this serious crisis? Van Buren summoned Congress in special session, September 4, 1837, and the powerful Democratic party found itself in a majority of only three for the choice of James K. Polk as speaker. Van Buren reported not only a deficit in the treasury, but serious embarrassment in some of the deposit banks and the suspension of others; and he suggested vaguely a scheme for replacing public funds in the state banks by "the establishment by law at a few important points of offices for the deposit and disbursement of . . . portions of the public revenue."[2] He not only criticised the state banks, but he inveighed against their notes, and insisted that the country ought to have a specie currency.

Whether sound or unsound, these measures could not arrest the panic, which, after six months of terrible distress, in which a large part of all the firms that had been in business suspended payment, gradually spent its force. Notwithstanding the immense losses of 1837, the greater part of the

[1] Dewey, *Financial Hist. of the U. S.*, §§ 99–105.
[2] Richardson, *Messages and Papers*, III., 336.

banks resumed, the number actually increased by more than one hundred and the bank capital by $27,000,000, while the loans were somewhat reduced. In August, 1838, specie payments were resumed by all the banks, the United States Bank of Pennsylvania being the last. In the state elections of 1838 the Democrats were in general more successful, but in the congressional elections the Whigs and Democrats were about evenly balanced.

Van Buren's plan of relief, which came to be called the Independent Treasury or the Sub-Treasury, was first suggested in 1834,[1] and it met the immediate danger of loss to the government by the failure of banks, and prevented speculation in money derived from government deposits. It was, furthermore, a party measure intended to prevent a return to the national bank, to which Van Buren was absolutely opposed. A bill embodying the suggestion was presented to Congress in 1837, debated for several weeks, passed by the Senate, but failed in the House; the Whigs, under the leadership of both Webster and Clay, uniting upon a revival of the United States Bank. The Democratic party was itself divided upon the currency question; the "Loco-Focos," or hard-money branch, supporting the president, the "conservative" Democratic leaders uniting with the Whigs. The Whigs took advantage of this split in 1838 to elect as governor of New York the brilliant young statesman William H. Seward.

[1] *Debates of Congress*, 23 Cong., 1 Sess., 4640.

The need of a new system was emphasized by a second crash in 1839, memorable for its effect on the United States Bank, which had financed certain unfavorable cotton speculations.   October 10, 1839, the bank suspended payments; drafts on Paris to the amount of several million francs were protested; the stock fell sixteen per cent. in a day, and eventually the whole capital of $35,000,000 was a total loss.   The crisis of 1839 was, however, rather a bank than a commercial panic, and the country speedily revived.

When the new Congress met in 1839 it was found that there were two sets of returns from the state of New Jersey; if the certificate of the Whig governor was accepted, a Whig speaker would be elected; and if the Democratic candidate were seated, the Democrats would control the House.   The clerk of the previous House refused to insert the names of either delegation, and also refused to put any motions until the House had accepted that decision. After four days' tumult, John Quincy Adams suggested a way out of the imbroglio, and when the cry was raised, "Who will put the question?" replied, "I intend to put the question myself."   The final result was that the Democratic contestants were seated, and that Hunter, a Whig, who favored the Independent Treasury, was elected speaker.[1]

This organization made it possible to pass the Independent Treasury bill, and thus to fulfil the

[1] Follett, *Speaker of the House*, 52.

promise that the Democratic administration would do something to relieve the country. The president backed the project up with long and patient messages in which he again urged that nothing but specie be received and paid in public transactions. After long debates, July 4, 1840, an act was secured under which the treasurer of the United States was directed to "keep all the public monies which shall come to his hands in the Treasury of the United States"; in addition to which the mints and some of the custom-houses were also made places of local deposit. A hard-money clause was included, to take gradual effect, so that until 1843 part of the government payments could be made in bank-notes. After three years of controversy the Independent Treasury was at last realized.[1]

Nevertheless, the state of the government finances made a profound impression upon the people. The total revenues in 1840 were $19,000,000, as against $51,000,000 in 1836, while the expenditures were only $6,000,000 less than in that year; and when the compromise tariff should take full effect in 1842, the income would be further diminished. The general sensation of poverty was reflected in a series of startling repudiations of their debts by the states. The amount of those debts has already been stated as about $170,000,000; but six states for a time ceased to pay interest on their debts, and three states made no further provision either for interest or

[1] Kinley, *Hist. of Independent Treasury*, chap. ii.

principal.[1] The rich commonwealth of Pennsylvania owed about $41,000,000, of which two-thirds was held in England; after the crash of 1837 the state paid its interest out of borrowed money, and in 1841 absolutely suspended.[2] It was this experience which caused Sydney Smith to say that he never met a Pennsylvanian without a desire to "strip him of his clothes and boots for division among the guests, most of whom had probably suffered by his state's dishonesty." Mississippi had loaned $5,000,000 to a bank, and when it failed the state government insisted that there had been an informality in the issue, and that therefore the state, which had received the proceeds, was not liable. It was in this episode that Jefferson Davis first came to the front, in 1843, as an advocate of repudiation.[3]

So serious was the crisis that application was made to Congress to assume the state debts, and a committee, in March, 1843, reported that the outstanding state debts were then $208,000,000, carrying an interest charge of $10,000,000 a year. Pennsylvania resumed payment in 1845, and returning prosperity enabled all the states that so desired to meet their just debts; but $11,000,000, subscribed by creditors of the states previous to 1840, have never been paid to this day.

[1] Scott, *Repudiation of State Debts*, passim.
[2] Lyell, *Travels*, 1st series, 217–226.
[3] Lalor, *Cyclopædia*, III., 605; Shields, *Prentiss*, 327; R. Davis, *Recollections*, 166.

CHAPTER XXI

THE EFFECTS OF ABOLITION

(1830–1860)

THE question still remains, how far did the abolitionists accomplish what they set out to do? After thirty years of agitation, suddenly slavery ceased to be, through the use of that military power which John Quincy Adams had foreseen and almost invoked.[1] The abolitionists naturally believed that they had pulled down the heavens and let the freedmen escape through the cracks. Are they entitled to the credit for this tremendous result?

The work of the abolitionists can be estimated only in contrast with their aims, motives, and results, up to the breaking out of civil war. So far as the effect upon the conditions of the slave was concerned, the abolitionist accomplished little of what he set out to do: the slave codes were more severe in 1860 than in 1830; the national fugitive-slave act was more drastic; the law of the territories was more favorable to slavery; the square miles open to slavery had doubled in the thirty years; the

[1] See chap. xviii., above.

number of slaves had increased from two millions to nearly four millions; even the bulwark against the African slave-trade seemed weakening, under the vigorous demands of the lower south for cheaper slaves.[1]

As for the attempt to affect the slave-holder by moral suasion or by hard language, it was a total failure. A few slave-holders, like John S. Wise, shocked by the brutality of the system as they saw it, privately put their heads together and "agreed that a system in which things like that were possible was monstrous; and that the question was, not whether it should be abolished and abolished quickly, but as to the manner of its abolition"[2]; but the community in general defended slavery in all its ramifications, accepting the worst features of it as disagreeable but inevitable incidents.

The insurmountable difficulty in the whole controversy over slavery was that the two sides were not dealing with the same thing. The starting-point in the north was the individual, his inborn God-given right to make the best of himself, no matter what his race or color. As Lincoln put it, "in the right to eat the bread, without the leave of anybody else, which his own hand earns, he [the negro] is my equal, . . . and the equal of every living man."[3]

---

[1] See Smith, *Parties and Slavery* (*Am. Nation*, XVIII.), chap. xx.

[2] Wise, *End of an Era*, 87; cf. Smedes, *Memorials of a Southern Planter*, 190–192.   [3] Lincoln, *Works*, I., 289.

From that stand-point all arguments of social or
economic advantage to the whites seemed foreign
to the subject. On the other hand, the slave-
holders were thinking of their community, of its
vested rights, of the superiority of favored men
backed up and supported by a powerful social
system which protected them in their hold on the
resources of their section, both natural and human.
The basis of slavery was the conviction that the
negro was put into the world for the benefit of the
white man, and his highest glory and advancement
was in serving the superior race well. As for the
mulattoes, they bore the mark of their sinful origin
in their complexions, and their white blood must be
submerged in their negro blood for the protection of
the white race.

With two such widely differing conceptions of the
basis of society and of the right and wrong in human
life, the contestants might have argued for a century without convincing each other. Contradiction
stood out of every phase of the discussion. With
the same breath the pro-slavery advocates declared
that the negro was a barely human creature, saved
from barbarism only by his contact with the whites;
and that he was a docile, affectionate, and faithful
servitor, a friend of his master and a fit companion
and playmate of his master's family. The negro
was incapable of political organization because sunk
in sloth and licentiousness; and at the same time a
dangerous conspirator, who was kept from cutting

his master's throat only by unceasing watchfulness. Doubtless some negroes were bad and some negroes were good, but as a race the negro could not be at the same time a brute and a happy serf, a criminal and a family friend.

This confusion, which can be traced in almost every southern book dealing with the subject, was combined with a tactical error which gave the north a great advantage in the discussion; and that was the prohibition after 1835 of all open criticism of slavery in the lower south. The reason given was the danger of such discussion before slaves; but it went on habitually in almost every house in the south, for people somehow forgot that those standing behind their chairs had ears to hear and tongues to repeat. To assure the world that slavery was God-given, hallowed by the experience of mankind, enjoined by Scripture, the foundation of republican government, the source of all southern blessings,—and then to insist that it could be overthrown by the mere wind of doctrine,—was a confession that it was really unstable and iniquitous. No great institution contributing to human enlightenment has ever needed to be protected by silence.

Another advantage of the abolitionists throughout the controversy was that nobody was able to suggest a remedy for slavery that was any more acceptable to the slave-holders than outright emancipation. Southside Adams's naïve remedy was for the northern people to invite slave-holders to come up and bring

their slaves with them, so as to prove how mild the
system was.   Some visitors suggested that slaves
be paid small wages, encouraged to thrift and saving, and taught to read and write; but this seemed
to the south absolutely incompatible with safety.
Channing proposed that in the slave states every
slave should have a guardian for his protection and
should be encouraged to buy himself and his family;
then, if the free negroes should be educated and up-
raised, the whole problem would be solved.[1]   Another proposition was to restrict the sale of slaves,
as by forbidding the sale of a slave for debt or the
separation of a young child from its mother; another
was to fix a time beyond which fugitives could not
be recoverable.[2]

Had any of these minor remedies been taken up
in good faith by the south, the abolition movement
would have lost much of its force.   A trial on a
small scale of the slave-wages scheme was considered
to be a total failure.[3]   Not a single state took action
to facilitate self - purchase; a few ineffective acts
were passed to limit the sale of little children from
their mothers—and that was all.   The south had
an instinctive feeling that to admit that anything
was wrong in slavery was to give up the principle

[1] Adams, *Southside View*, 147–156; Buckingham, *Slave States*,
I., 168; Channing, *Works*, II., 109–111; Bremer, *Homes of the
New World*, 328, 443–448.
[2] Adams, *Southside View*, 135, 151; cf. Nott, *Slavery and the
Remedy*, passim; T. S. Clay, *Detail of a Plan*, passim.
[3] Dew, in *Pro-Slavery Argument*, 426–428.

that it was a beneficent institution; and it seemed to the southern people craven to yield anything to the undistinguishing abolition attacks.[1]

In fact, the only plan that had any adherents in the south was gradual emancipation, combined with the expatriation of all the free negroes, a plan set forth in detail by Henry Clay, in a letter of 1849;[2] but even that plan was based upon the theory that the negro race should somehow pay for its own transportation, and the history of the Colonization Society showed the lack of interest in the south and the hopelessness and the futility of any attempt to carry all the negroes away.[3] In forty years of activity, from the first emigration in 1820 to the end of the year 1860, the Colonization Society, with an expenditure of $1,806,000, succeeded in carrying over to Africa 10,586 negroes (besides about a thousand sent by state societies); of these about 4500 were born free, 344 purchased their freedom, and about 6000 were emancipated to go to Liberia; the largest number transported in any late year was 783, in the year 1853. Out of this whole number the seven cotton states furnished less than 4000; and the customary surplus of births over deaths in those states filled up this thirty years' depletion in a single month.[4] Colonization was a hopeless suggestion: first, and finally, because it would have cost

[1] Dew, in *Pro-Slavery Argument*, 426–428.
[2] Colton, *Clay*, III., 346–352.   [3] See chap. xvii., above.
[4] Am. Colonization Soc., *Fiftieth Annual Report*, 1867, p. 65.

seven hundred million dollars to remove the four millions of people whose labor alone could earn the seven hundred million dollars, provided they remained in America.

It must never be forgotten that the whole theory of abolition depended upon accepting the negro as a brother American, who had as good a right to his place in the community as his master; and after a few years of agitation the abolitionists realized that the only means to secure their end was by arousing the north.   In this result their enemies co-operated by their gag resolutions and appeals for silence, but on the northern people the movement, after 1840, seemed to have spent its force. Agitators, funds, and public interest diminished. Other reforms— woman suffrage, the care of the insane, temperance —seemed more to interest the public. At this point two questions arose, neither of which primarily involved abolition, and both of which gave the abolitionist a new opportunity: one was the annexation of Texas;[1] the other was fugitive slaves.[2] On both these questions the attitude of the abolitionists did much to arouse the northern mind, although the two movements outran them and were taken up by the non-abolitionist anti-slavery people.

Long before this point was reached the abolitionists had organized a political movement, which was destined to have far greater effects than their

[1] Garrison, *Westward Extension* (*Am. Nation*, XVII.), chap. ix.
[2] Smith, *Parties and Slavery* (*Am. Nation*, XVIII.), chap. v.

philanthropic propaganda. The entry of the abolitionist into politics was cautious and timid. Channing, in 1836, complained that "by assuming a political character they lose the reputation of honest
enthusiasts. . . . Should they in opposition to all
probability become a formidable party, they would
unite the slave-holding states as one man. . . . No
association like the abolitionists . . . can, by becoming a political organization, rise to power." [1]
The uproar in Congress from 1835 to 1837 put a
different face upon the whole question of political
action. The very sensitiveness of the pro-slavery
leaders showed that here was a good point of attack;
and there were too many questions upon which the
federal government could take action for anybody
convincingly to assert that slavery was wholly outside the jurisdiction of the federal government.

In vain did Garrison inveigh against an abolition
party or abolitionist votes. In 1843 he proposed
to read out of the abolitionist ranks any man who
would take an oath to the Constitution or vote for
its support.[2] The next year his Massachusetts Anti-
Slavery Society, as a body, accepted this dogma, set
forth in extravagant speeches by Wendell Phillips;
and they made an effort to fix a stigma upon every
abolitionist who should vote in the election of that
year.[3]

So far from accepting Garrison's dictum, the

[1] Channing, *Works*, VI., 69.
[2] Garrisons, *Garrison*, III., 90.   [3] *Ibid.*, 96–112, 117–119.

middle states and western abolitionists began to use
their votes directly and to some purpose. Exasperated at the failure of members of the legislature
to carry out their pre-election promises, the Ohio
abolitionists, in the state election of 1838, used their
balance of power to elect a Democratic governor,
and they sent Giddings to Congress. When the
legislature turned its back upon them and enacted
a state fugitive-slave act in 1839, the abolitionists
began to put up independent candidates. Mean-
time, Holly, a New York abolitionist, and Torrey,
a New-Englander, were organizing like movements
in the east; and in November, 1839, while many of
the New England abolitionists were breaking away
from Garrison, a convention of abolitionists at War-
saw, New York, nominated James G. Birney for
president. This action, repeated by a formal Liberty
convention in 1840, was followed by state Liberty
conventions in Ohio and then in northwestern states;
and thus the first abolitionist national political party
was born, in defiance of Garrison's teachings and a
protest against his leadership.

The movement was still feeble: though in 1840
the societies included probably 50,000 voters, only
7100 votes were cast for Birney, of which about
a third came from New England. But the change
in method was startlingly significant: it gave a new
impulse to the flagging spirits of the abolitionists;
it formed a new centre for the open discussion of
slavery; it was one method of organizing opposi-

tion to the annexation of Texas; above all, in the next two national elections the political abolitionists proved to have the balance of power in decisive states, and thus gained an importance and consideration vastly greater than their scanty numbers would warrant.

The Liberty party, in all its ramifications, was substantially an abolitionist movement, at which the anti-slavery men in both Whig and Democratic parties looked askance. Nevertheless, it swept into its ranks two of the most conspicuous men in the struggles of the next quarter - century. In 1841, Salmon P. Chase, a former Whig, came over into the little Ohio Liberty party, became its leader, and with voice and pen tellingly set forth its principles. Thus, in a printed address in 1845, he prophesies the destruction of slavery by the following methods: "By repealing all legislation, and discontinuing all action, in favor of slavery, at home and abroad; by prohibiting the practice of slaveholding in all places of exclusive national jurisdiction, in the District of Columbia, in American vessels upon the seas, in forts, arsenals, navy yards: by . . . declaring that slaveholding, in all states created out of national territories is unconstitutional, . . . and by electing and appointing to public station such men, and only such men as openly avow our principles, and will honestly carry out our measures." [1]

The other man was Charles Sumner, of Massachu-

[1] Hart, *Chase*, 60.

setts, a man of high education, who, from his first interest in the cause in 1835, objected to Garrison's pronunciamentos against voting. Sumner matured slowly, and did not enter public life until 1845, but in the next year he broke away from the Whigs because they supported the Mexican War, and thenceforward was a power in the abolition councils and a noted anti-slavery orator.

A writer of great weight, in discussing the election of 1840, has said that the "Liberty Party in running Birney, simply committed a political crime, evil in almost all its consequences; they in no sense paved the way for the Republican Party, or helped forward the anti-slavery cause, or hurt the existing organizations." [1] This criticism proceeds upon the assumption that the abolitionists expected eventually to elect a president or a majority of Congress. Such a platform as Chase's was a counsel of perfection: its author for more than ten years was animated by the hope of compelling the Democratic party to take over principles which he thought akin to its genius. Old Whigs like Giddings had similar hopes for the Whig party. The abolitionist use of their balance of power to defeat Clay, an opponent of the annexation of Texas, in 1844, and Cass, a northern man, in 1848, was not a childish freak: they wanted to convince the Whig and Democratic parties that unless they made concessions to the anti-slavery feeling they would lose the election; and they hit hardest

[1] Roosevelt, *Benton* (ed. of 1887), 295.

at those men who seemed to them to owe most respect to their feelings. The anti-slavery party, in its various forms of Liberty men in 1840 and 1844, Free-Soilers in 1848, and Free Democrats in 1852, shaped the principles, forged the arguments, and trained the leaders who, in 1856, formed the combination of anti-slavery Whigs and anti-slavery Democrats which the abolitionists had so long desired.[1]

It is this political movement which most conclusively shows how little Garrison is entitled to be taken as the typical or the chief abolitionist. The power and force of the abolitionists diverged from Garrison upon that issue, and attempted ends of which Garrison strongly disapproved.[2] Abolitionists like Chase adhered to the Union cause, and appealed to the Constitution as an anti-slavery document. Yet many of the most moderate abolitionists foresaw a terrible end to the discussion. Said Channing, "The blow that would sever the Union for this cause, would produce an instantaneous explosion to shake the whole land. The moral sentiment against slavery, now kept down by the interests and duties which grow out of union, would burst its fetters, and be reinforced by the whole strength of the patriotic principle."[3] Indeed, some of the most sagacious southerners recognized the fact that sla-

[1] Hume, *The Abolitionists;* Smith, *Liberty and Free Soil Parties in the Northwest*, chaps. xvii., xix.; Hart, *Chase*, chaps. iv., v.
[2] See chap. xii., above.   [3] Channing, *Works*, V., 71.

very and the free discussion of slavery could not exist within the same federation. To say that the abolitionists revealed the contradiction between a free republic and human bondage does not throw upon them the responsibility of the catastrophe.

For, with all their one-sidedness and intensity, and the vituperation indulged in by many of their number, the abolitionists laid hold of a principle without which the republic could not exist—the principle, namely, that free discussion is the breath of liberty; and that any institution which could not bear the light of inquiry, argument, and denunciation was a weak and a dangerous institution. If the slave-holders could have sat quietly behind their own boundaries and invited the critical world to come and see for themselves how good slavery was, if they had pruned away the worst excrescences of the institution, if they had been able to show by superior refinement and wide - spread culture that slavery made even the white man's lot more enviable, the abolitionists would have had no fighting-ground.

Another immense advantage of the abolitionists was that the evil which they were attacking was localized. In the contemporary movement against the use of strong drink, the defenders were in every state and in every community, and the agitators had to confront and attack their own neighbors; while the abolitionists were dealing with something which every state in the north by its own statutes repro-

bated.   Hence the main function of the abolitionist movement was to convince the northern people
that slavery was not only harmful to the south but
contrary to their own interests.   This process put
a terrible torsion on the federal government, but it
was in the end effective.

Perhaps, after all, the main reason for the eventual spread of anti-slavery, till it became the tenet
of a considerable majority of the northern people,
was that the abolitionists were taking hold of the
"great wheel going up hill," that they were march-
ing with modern civilization, while the defenders of
slavery were standing for the obsolete, the abnormal,
and the impossible.   This difference was not ob-
scured by the intemperate language so plentiful on
both sides of the controversy, or the prejudice and
violence of extremists of the two opposite schools,
who stretched the principles of the Constitution to
the utmost, or threw them to the winds.   The
breaking strain in the argument for slavery was its
underlying assumption that a minority of the community was entitled to compel the services of the
majority.   Nobody ever more clearly brought out
that paradox than Abraham Lincoln in a memo-
randum of 1854: "If A can prove, however conclusively, that he may of right enslave B, why may
not B snatch the same argument and prove equally
that he may enslave A?   You say A is white and
B is black.   It is color, then; the lighter having the
right to enslave the darker?   Take care.   By this

rule you are to be slave to the first man you meet with a fairer skin than your own. You do not mean color exactly? You mean the whites are intellectually the superiors of the blacks, and therefore have the right to enslave them? Take care again. By this rule you are to be slave to the first man you meet with an intellect superior to your own. But, you say, it is a question of interest, and if you make it your interest you have the right to enslave another. Very well. And if he can make it his interest he has the right to enslave you." [1]

This was the argument that most affected the plain, common people of the north; the workingman, however slight his sympathy with the slave, had an instinctive apprehension that the liberty of the white laborer was somehow at stake. He did not understand the economic reasons why slavery was a profitless method of organizing labor; he did not comprehend how it weakened the community in which it existed; but he did see clearly that slavery depreciated the lot of the man who had nothing but his own strong arm. As Lowell put it:

" God works for all. Ye cannot hem the hope of being free
 With parallels of latitude, with mountain-range or sea.
 Put golden padlocks on Truth's lips, be callous as ye will,
 From soul to soul, o'er all the world, leaps one electric thrill." [2]

[1] Lincoln, *Works*, I., 178, 179.
[2] Lowell, *Poems* (Riverside ed.), VII., 224.

CHAPTER XXII

CRITICAL ESSAY ON AUTHORITIES

BIBLIOGRAPHICAL AIDS

THE best formal bibliography of slavery and of the slavery question is W. E. B. DuBois, *A Select Bibliography of the Negro American* (*Atlanta University Publications*, No. 10, 1905). Bibliographical data arranged in much the same order as the chapters of this book will be found in Channing and Hart, *Guide to the Study of American History* (1896), §§ 148, 152, 161, 186–189, 198, 214; J. N. Larned, *Literature of American History, a Bibliographical Guide* (1902), 181–213, 375–383, each book being briefly criticised; Albert Bushnell Hart, *Handbook of the History, Diplomacy, and Government of the United States* (1903), §§ 19h, 47, 55. Three recent bibliographies deal with the Negro and his status: W. E. B. DuBois, *A Select Bibliography of the American Negro for General Readers* (1901); A. P. C. Griffin, *Select List of References on the Negro Question* (Library of Congress, 1903); Walter L. Fleming, *Documents Relating to Reconstruction* (1904), 156–163. See also Samuel May, Jr., *Catalogue of Anti-Slavery Publications in America* (1863). See also the foot-notes to the secondary writers and biographies below.

Very serviceable bibliographies on both slavery and abolition are to be found in appendices to the following monographs: Mary S. Locke, *Anti-Slavery in America, 1619–1808* (1901); Marion G. McDougall, *Fugitive Slaves, 1619–1865* (*Fay House Monographs*, No. 3, 1891); Alice D. Adams, *The Neglected Period of American Anti-Slavery*,

1808–1831 (not yet published); Mary Tremain, *Slavery in the District of Columbia* (University of Nebraska, *Seminary Papers*, No. 2, 1892); Wilbur H. Siebert, *The Underground Railroad from Slavery to Freedom* (1898); W. E. B. DuBois, *Suppression of the African Slave-Trade* (*Harvard Historical Studies*, No. 1, 1896); Winfield H. Collins, *The Domestic Slave-Trade of the Southern States* (1904); and the special monographs on slavery in particular communities enumerated below.

GENERAL SECONDARY WORKS

Four formal political histories of the period 1830–1860 include the slavery controversy: John B. McMaster, *History of the People of the United States* (5 vols., published 1883–1900)—as yet reaches only to 1830; James Schouler, *History of the United States* (6 vols., rev. ed., 1895–1899)—touches on social conditions at II., chap. vii., III., 507–531, IV., 1–31, 199–221; Herman E. von Holst, *Constitutional and Political History of the United States* (Lalor's transl., 7 vols. and Index vol., 1877–1892)—really a history of the slavery contest, with a strong anti-slavery slant; James Ford Rhodes, *History of the United States from the Compromise of 1850* (5 vols. published, 1893–1904)—especially vol. I., chap. iv., one of the best brief accounts of the conditions of slavery. Henry Wilson, *History of the Rise and Fall of the Slave Power in America* (3 vols., 1872–1877) —by an actor in the slavery drama, but uncritical, diffuse, and devoid of references. On the legal aspects of the struggle, George Ticknor Curtis, *Constitutional History of the United States* (2 vols., 1889–1896), II., chap. ix.

Of specific histories of the struggle: William Henry Smith, *A Political History of Slavery* (2 vols., 1903)—ambitious but superficial; Horace Greeley, *The American Conflict* (2 vols., 1864–1866), includes brief extracts from contemporary documents and newspapers, and is serviceable, though partisan; George W. Williams, *History of the Negro Race in America from 1619 to 1880* (2 vols., 1883)—diffuse and uncritical; vol. II., chaps. iv.–viii., deals with the heat of the controversy; George S. Merriam, *The Negro and the Nation* (1906)—makes numerous slips on the history of slavery; George Lunt, *Origin of the Late War* (1866)—a pro-slavery discussion; John F. Hulme, *The Abolitionists* (1905)—a defence of the abolitionists; Friedrich Kapp, *Die Sklavenfrage in den Vereinigten Staaten; geschichtclich entwickelt* (1854)—strongly anti-slavery.

BIOGRAPHIES

General lists may be found in Channing and Hart, *Guide to the Study of American History* (1896), § 25; and Albert Bushnell Hart, *Handbook of the History, Diplomacy, and Government of the United States* (1903), §§ 130a, 130b. Most of the public men of the time are included in the *American Statesmen Series* (rev. ed., 1899). For the public men of the period, see MacDonald, *Jeffersonian Democracy* (*Am. Nation*, XV.), chap. xix.

Among special biographies of anti-slavery men, first and foremost is Wendell P. Garrison and Francis J. Garrison, *William Lloyd Garrison, the Story of His Life Told by His Children, 1805–1879* (4 vols., 1885–1889), a storehouse of significant material, in a large degree made up of extracts from the *Liberator;* Edward L. Pierce, *Memoir and Letters of Charles Sumner* (4 vols., 1877–1893); William Birney, *James G. Birney and His Times* (1890); F. B. Sanborn, *Life and Letters of John Brown* (1885); William H. Channing, *Memoir of William Ellery Channing* (3 vols., 1848); J. W. Schuckers, *Life and Public Services of Salmon P. Chase* (1874); Charles Francis Adams, *Richard Henry Dana, a Biography* (2 vols., 1890); Charles W. Chesnutt, *Frederick Douglass* (1899); Frank B. Sanborn, *Ralph Waldo Emerson* (1901); A. H. Grimke, *William Lloyd Garrison the Abolitionist* (1891); Oliver Johnson, *William Lloyd Garrison and His Times* (1881); George W. Julian, *Joshua R. Giddings* (1892); Catherine H. Birney, *Sarah and Angelina Grimké* (1885); Lydia Maria Child, *Isaac T. Hopper, a True Life* (1853, 2d ed. 1860); Bayard Tuckerman, *William Jay and the Constitutional Movement for the Abolition of Slavery* (1893); Samuel Longfellow, *Life of Henry W. Longfellow* (2 vols., 1886); J. G. Nicolay and John Hay, *Abraham Lincoln, a History* (12 vols., 1890); J. C. and O. Lovejoy, *Memoir of the Rev. Elijah P. Lovejoy* (1838); H. E. Scudder, *James Russell Lowell* (2 vols., 1901); Anna D. Hallowell, *James and Lucretia Mott, Life and Letters* (1884); T. S. Perry, *Life and Letters of Francis Lieber* (1882); Thomas J. Mumford, *Memoir of Samuel Joseph May* (1873); O. B. Frothingham, *Theodore Parker, a Biography* (1874); Thomas Wentworth Higginson, *Wendell Phillips* (1884); O. B. Frothingham, *Gerrit Smith, a Biography* (1878); Lewis Tappan, *Life of Arthur Tappan* (1870); Clarence W. Bowen, *Arthur and Lewis Tappan* (1883); S. T. Pickard, *Life and Letters of John Greenleaf Whittier* (2 vols., 1894); A. G. Riddle, *Life of Benjamin F. Wade* (1886).

COLLECTIONS OF SOURCES

Special collections of anti-slavery material exist in the Cornell Library (May Collection, see Library of Cornell University, *Bulletins*, I., 229); Boston Public Library (Parker Tracts); Harvard College Library (Sumner Tracts, Higginson Tracts, set of the *Liberator*); Providence Public Library (Harris materials); Library of Congress (a variety of rare sources).

Some of the general collections on the period include cogent material, as: Albert Bushnell Hart, *American History Told by Contemporaries* (4 vols., 1897–1901); Albert Bushnell Hart, *Source Book of American History* (1900), chap. xvii.; Alexander Johnston, *American Orations* (4 vols., edited by Woodburn, 1898); Herman V. Ames, *State Documents on Federal Relations*, No. 5, *Slavery and the Constitution* (1904).

Most of the formal biographies of abolitionists and anti-slavery men abound in letters and other source material, especially the lives of Garrison and Sumner, as do the controversial works on slavery noted below. Extracts from early writers and records in William F. Poole, *Anti-Slavery Opinions before the Year 1800* (1873); Mary E. Locke, *Anti-Slavery in America* (1901); George Livermore, *Historical Research Respecting the Opinions of the Founders of the Republic on Negroes* (1862); Daniel R. Goodloe, *Southern Platform* (1855); Collections of slave advertisements and incidents in Lydia Maria Child, *Patriarchal Institution* (1860), and in LaRoy Sunderland, *Anti-Slavery Manual* (1837).

COLLECTED WORKS OF STATESMEN.—Descriptions of the collected works of Clay, Webster, Calhoun, and other public men of the period will be found in William MacDonald, *Jacksonian Democracy* (*Am. Nation*, XV.), chap. xix. For anti-slavery men: William Ellery Channing, *Works* (1st ed., 5 vols., 1841; 2d ed., 6 vols., 1843); Joshua R. Giddings, *Speeches in Congress* (1853); Abraham Lincoln, *Complete Works* (Nicolay and Hay ed., 2 vols., 1894); Wendell Phillips, *Speeches, Lectures, and Letters* (1863); William H. Seward, *Works* (5 vols., 1853–1884); Charles Sumner, *Works* (15 vols., 1870–1883); John G. Whittier, *Writings* (7 vols., 1888–1889).

AUTOBIOGRAPHY AND REMINISCENCE.—The following are the principal memoirs of people engaged in the anti-slavery contest: John Quincy Adams, *Memoirs, comprising Portions of His Diary from 1795 to 1848* (12 vols., 1874–1877)—one of the most important books; Thomas H. Benton, *Thirty Years' View, 1820–1850* (2 vols., 1854–1856)—by a western man inclined to anti-slavery; Cassius M. Clay, *Life, Memoirs, Writings, and Speeches* (1 vol. published, 1886); Reuben Davis, *Recollections of Mississippi and Mississippians* (1891); Frederick Douglass, *Life and Times, written by Himself* (1881); J. H. Fairchild, *Oberlin, the Colony and the College* (1883); Horace Greeley, *Recollections of a Busy Life* (1868); T. W. Higginson, *Cheerful Yesterdays* (1898); George W. Julian, *Political Recollections, 1840–1872* (1884); Amos Kendall, *Autobiography* (edited by William Stickney, 1872); Benjamin Lundy, *Life, Travels, and Opinions of Benjamin Lundy* (arranged by Thomas Earle, 1847); Samuel J.

May, *Memoir, consisting of Autobiography and Selections from his Diary and Correspondence* (1873); James Monroe, *Oberlin Thursday Lectures, Addresses, and Essays* (1897); B. F. Perry, *Reminiscences of Public Men* (two series, 1883, 1889)—by a southern editor; Alvan Stewart, *Writings and Speeches on Slavery* (edited by L. R. Marsh, 1860); H. B. Stanton, *Random Recollections* (2d ed., 1886); E. S. Thomas, *Reminiscences of the Last Sixty-Five Years* (2 vols., 1840); George Thompson, *Prison Life and Recollections* (1847).

FOREIGN TRAVELLERS

Among the best materials for an appreciation of life, manners, and conditions in the slavery period are the numerous travels of foreigners, of which the most important published after 1823, together with a few of the American travellers, are the following: H. T. Tuckerman, *America and Her Commentators* (1864), discusses critically some of the principal travels; E. S. Abdy, *Journal of a Residence and Tour in the United States* (3 vols., London, 1835); J. E. Alexander, *Transatlantic Sketches* (2 vols., London, 1833); J. J. Ampère, *Promenade en Amérique* (2 vols., Paris, 1855); Anonymous, *Things as They Are* (New York, 1834); C. D. Arfwedson, *The United States and Canada, in 1832, 1833, and 1834* (2 vols., London, 1834); A. F. de Bacourt, *Souvenirs of a Diplomat* [*1837–1845*] (New York, 1885); G. C. Beltrami, *A Pilgrimage in Europe and America* (2 vols., London, 1828); Bernhard, Duke of Saxe-Weimar-Eisenach, *Travels through North America during the Years 1825 and 1826* (2 vols. in 1, Philadelphia, 1828); J. R. Beste, *The Wabash* (2 vols., London, 1855); Fredrika Bremer, *Homes of the New World* (2 vols., New York, 1853); J. Boardman, *America and the Americans* (London, 1833); T. Bromme, *Reisen durch die Vereinigten Staaten und Ober Canada* (3 vols. Baltimore, 1834); Thomas Brothers, *The United States as They Are* (London, 1840); J. S. Buckingham, *America, Historical, Statistical, and Descriptive* (3 vols., London, 1841); J. S. Buckingham, *The Slave States of America* (2 vols., London, 1842); J. S. Buckingham, *The Eastern and Western States of America* (3 vols., London, 1842); W. Bullock, *Sketch of a Journey through the Western States* (London, 1827); T. Buttrick, Jr., *Voyages, Travels, and Discoveries* (Boston, 1831); Isaac Candler, *A Summary View of America* (London, 1824); William Chambers, *Things as They Are in America* (London, 1854); M. Chevalier, *Society, Manners, and Politics in the United States* (Boston, 1839, transl. from 3d Paris ed.); W. Cobbett, *A Year's Residence in the United States of America* (1st ed., London, 1818); E. T. Coke, *A Subaltern's Furlough* (2 vols. in 1, New York, 1833; London, 1833); J. F. Cooper, *Notions of the Americans* (2 vols., London, 1828); Charles Dickens, *American Notes for General Circulation* (London, 1842; many reprints); H. W. E. Eggerling, *Beschreibung der Vereinigten Staaten von Nord-Amerika* (2d ed., Mannheim, 1833); S. A. Ferrall, *A Ramble of Six Thousand Miles through the United States of America* (London, 1832); George W. Featherstonhaugh, *Excursion through the Slave States* (New York, 1844); Isaac Fidler, *Observations on Professions, Literature, Manners, and Emigration in the United States and Canada* (New York, 1833); John Finch, *Travels in the United States of America and Canada* (London, 1833); J. Fowler, *Journal of a Tour in the State of New York in the Year 1830* (London, 1831); C. von Gerstner, *Beschreibung einer Reise durch die Vereinigten Staaten von Nord-Amerika* (Leipzig, 1842); F. J. Grund, *The Americans in their Moral, Social, and Political Relations* (2 vols., London, 1837); F. J. Grund, editor, *Aristocracy in America* (2 vols., London, 1839; German ed., Stuttgart, 1839); Basil Hall, *Forty Etchings, from Sketches . . . in North America* (Edinburgh, 1829); Basil Hall, *Travels in North America in the Years 1827 and 1828* (3 vols., Edinburgh, 1829); J. Hall, *Letters from the West* (London, 1828); T. Hamilton, *Men and Manners in America* (2d Am. ed., 2 vols., Philadelphia, 1833); N. Hesse, *Das westliche Nordamerika* (Paderborn, 1838); Adam Hodgson, *Letters from North America* (2 vols., London, 1824); C. F. Hoffman, *A Winter in the West* (2 vols., New York, 1835); Frances A. Kemble, *Journal* (2 vols.,

1835); C. J. Latrobe, *The Rambler in North America, 1832–1833* (2 vols., New York, 1835); A. Levasseur, *La Fayette in America in 1824 and 1825* (2 vols., Philadelphia, 1829; French ed., 1829); F. Lieber, *The Stranger in America* (Philadelphia, 1835); Sir Charles Lyell, *Travels in North America* (2 vols., London, 1845); Sir Charles Lyell, *Second Visit to the United States* (2 vols., London, 1849); Alexander Mackay, *The Western World, or Travels . . . in 1846–1847* (2 vols., Philadelphia, 1849); Harriet Martineau, *Retrospect of Western Travel* (3 vols., London; 2 vols., New York, 1838); Harriet Martineau, *Society in America* (2d ed., 3 vols., London, 1837); James W. Massie, *America, . . . Her Claim for Anti-Slavery Sympathy* (London, 1864); Prince Maximilian of Wied-Neuwied, *Voyage in the Interior of North America* (London, 1843); B. Morrell, *Narrative of Four Voyages to the South Sea, North and South Pacific Ocean* (New York, 1832); Prince Achille Murat, *America and the Americans* (New York, 1849—French ed., *Lettres sur les États-Unis, à un de ses Amis d'Europe*, Paris, 1830); Amelia M. Murray, *Letters from the United States, Cuba, and Canada* (2 vols. in 1, New York, 1856); C. A. Murray, *Travels in North America* (2 vols., New York, 1839, 3d ed., 2 vols., London, 1854); P. Neilson, *Recollections of a Six Years' Residence in the United States of America* (Glasgow, 1830); T. L. Nichols, *Forty Years of American Life* (2 vols., London, 1864); V. Nolte, *Fifty Years in Both Hemispheres* (New York, 1854); J. K. Paulding, *John Bull in America* (New York, 1825); T. M. Pavie, *Souvenirs Atlantiques* (2 vols., Paris, 1833); T. Power, *Impressions of America* (2 vols., Philadelphia, 1836); C. S. Rafinesque, *Life of Travels and Researches in North America* (Philadelphia, 1836; Rafinesque, *Works,* V.); Frederick von Raumer, *America and the American People* (Turner's transl., New York, 1846); Reed and Matheson, *Narrative of a Visit to the American Churches* (2 vols., 1835); F. F. de Roos, *Personal Narrative of Travels in the United States and Canada in 1826* (London, 1827); P. Shirreff, *Tour through North America* (Edinburgh, 1835); Arthur Singleton, *Letters from the South and West* (Boston, 1824); James Stirling, *Letters from the Slave States* (London, 1857); J. Stuart, *Three Years in North America* (2 vols., New York, 1833); J. Stuart, *Refutation of Aspersions on "Stuart's Three Years in North America"* (London, 1834); Mrs. F. E. Trollope, *Domestic Manners of the Americans* (London, 1832); G. T. Vigne, *Six Months in America* (2 vols., London, 1832; Philadelphia, 1833); C. H. Wilson, *The Wanderer in America* (Thirsk, 1823); F. P. W. Herzog von Würtemberg, *Reise in Nordamerica während den Jahren 1822, 1823, und 1824* (2 vols. in 1, Mergentheim, 1828); Lorenzo de Zavala, *Viage a los Estados Unidos del Norte de America* (Paris, 1834).

PROCEEDINGS OF SOCIETIES

Most valuable material on the whole contest is to be found in the annual reports of the principal anti-slavery organizations, especially the American Anti-Slavery Society (beginning 1833), the American Colonization Society (beginning 1817), and the various state and local societies. The reports of the American Convention from 1808 to 1831 are widely scattered. Later material has been collected by some of the state historical societies and may be reached through A. P. C. Griffin, *Bibliography of American Historical Societies* (American Historical Association, *Report*, 1895, new ed. in preparation).

PERIODICALS

For the whole slavery contest there is a wealth of periodical material on both sides. The great arsenal of the anti-slavery men is William Lloyd Garrison's *Liberator* (1831–1865), many of the significant parts reprinted in the Garrisons, *William Lloyd Garrison*. From the southern point of view the best general authority is J. D. B. De Bow, *De Bow's Commercial Review of the South and West* (39 vols., 1846–1870). On the whole impartial, though rather inclined to pro-slavery, is Hezekiah Niles, *Niles' Weekly Register* (76 vols., 1811–1849); more general in scope is *Hunt's Merchants' Magazine and Commercial Review* (63 vols., 1839–1870). Distinctly pro-slavery is the *Southern Literary Messenger* (36 vols., 1834–1864). Of newspapers, the following are the principal distinctively abolition journals: *The Emancipator*, edited by R. G. Williams (New York and Boston, 1834–1848); *The Philanthropist*, edited by Birney and Bailey (Cincinnati, 1836–1847); *The Genius of Universal Emancipation*, edited by Benjamin Lundy (various places, 1821–1838)—complete set in the Boston Public Library, except two volumes; *Herald of Freedom*, edited by J. H. Kimball and others (Concord, New Hampshire, 1835–1846); *North Star*, edited by Frederick Douglass (Rochester, New York, 1847–1863); *National Anti-Slavery Standard*, edited bv N. P. Rogers and others (New York, 1840–1864); *Anti-Slavery Bugle* (Salem, Ohio, 1845–1861). Files of these papers are rare and imperfect. A metropolitan anti-slavery weekly of much influence was *The National Era*, edited by Dr. Gamaliel Bailey (Washington, 1847–1864). The Colonization Society issued the *African Repository*, and *The Colonizationist, a Journal of Freedom*. The only notable daily newspaper with a strong anti-slavery slant was the *New York Tribune*, edited by Horace Greeley (beginning 1841).

SOCIAL CONDITIONS OF THE SOUTH

A brief bibliography of social conditions is in Channing and Hart, *Guide* (1896), § 180. The basis for most of the statistical discussion and comparison is the publications of the United States Censuses for 1830, 1840, 1850, 1860, which are conveniently analyzed in Edward C. Lunt, *Key to the Publications of the United States Census, 1790–1887* (American Statistical Association, *Publications*, 1888)—these census figures are crude and not very well analyzed. The best contemporary on social standards in the thirties is Alexis de Tocqueville, *Democracy in America* (2 vols., Paris, 1835, 1840; also in several American translations), and some other foreign travellers, especially Buckingham,

Bremer, Bernhard of Saxe-Weimar, Kemble, Lyell, Mar
tineau, Stuart.

On the development of education, see G. H. Martin,
Evolution of the Massachusetts Public-School System (1894);
R. G. Boone, *Education in the United States* (1889); H. B.
Adams (editor), in U. S. Bureau of Education, *Circulars of
Education* (33 numbers to 1902); A. D. Mayo, *Common
Schools in the Southern States beyond the Mississippi River
from 1830 to 1860* (U. S. Commissioner of Education, *Report*,
1900–1901, pp. 357–401); Stephen B. Weeks, *Beginnings of
the Common-School System in the South* (*ibid.*, 1896–1897,
II., 1379–1474).

On literature, see W. P. Trent, *Southern Writers* (1905);
B. B. Minor, *Southern Literary Messenger* (1905).

On religion, and especially the relation of slavery to the
churches: J. M. Buckley, *History of Methodism in the
United States* (1896); S. M. Janney, *History of the Religious
Society of Friends to 1828* (4 vols., 1859–1867); Lyman
Beecher, *Autobiography* (2 vols., 1864–1865); Peter Cart-
wright, *Autobiography* (1856 and later reprints); Samuel
J. Baird, *History of the New School* (1868); Albert Barnes,
The Church and Slavery (1857); James G. Birney, *The
American Churches the Bulwarks of American Slavery* (2d
ed., 1842); Charles K. Whipple, *Relation of the American
Board of Commissioners of Foreign Missions to Slavery*
(1861); Richard Furman, *Exposition of the Views of the
Baptists relative to the Colored Population* (1833).

ECONOMIC CONDITIONS OF THE SOUTH

The general economic changes of the period are set forth
in three brief books: Carroll D. Wright, *Industrial Evolution
of the United States* (1895); Edwin E. Sparks, *Expansion of
the American People* (1900); Katherine Coman, *Industrial
History of the United States* (1905), all with maps and
charts. For material on the sections of the Union sepa-
rately, see Turner, *New West*, chaps. ii.–viii. (*Am. Nation*,
XIV.), and chap. xx., specific authorities on tariffs, com-

merce, and other economic topics.　Discussions of economic conditions are all more or less controversial: J. D. B. De Bow, *Industrial Resources, etc., of the Southern and Western States* (3 vols., 1852–1853)—made up chiefly of extracts from *De Bow's Review*, arranged in cyclopædic form; J. E. Cairnes, *The Slave Power, its Character, Career, and Probable Designs* (1863), a powerful economic argument against slavery, founded chiefly on Olmsted.　Frederick Law Olmsted, in the fifties, made long journeys through the heart of the south and embodied his observations in three volumes: *A Journey in the Seaboard Slave States* (1856, new ed., 1904); *A Journey through Texas* (1857); *A Journey in the Back Country* (1861).　Parts of these three books are reprinted in *The Cotton Kingdom, a Traveller's Observations on Cotton and Slavery* (2 vols., 1861)—although a distinct opponent of slavery, Olmsted's statements of fact have always been unquestioned.　Less-searching contemporaries are: Daniel R. Goodloe, *An Inquiry into the Causes which Retard the . . . Southern States* (1846); Thomas P. Kettell, *Southern Wealth and Northern Profits* (1861)—by a former editor of the *Democratic Review;* Hinton R. Helper, *The Impending Crisis of the South, How to Meet It* (1857 and many reprints)—an unskilled but vigorous attempt to arouse the poor whites.　The most important sources on social and economic history are *De Bow's Review* (1846–1870), *Hunt's Merchants' Magazine* (1839–1870), *Niles' Weekly Register* (1811–1849), *and* George M. Weston, *The Progress of Slavery in the United States* (1857).

Among recent books describing ante-bellum conditions, the best are: Edward Ingle, *Southern Sidelights, a Picture of Social and Economic Life in the South a Generation before the War* (1896) — well arranged and thoughtful; W. G. Brown, *The Lower South in American History* (1902); Thomas Nelson Page, *The Old South, Essays Social and Political* (1892) — perhaps too roseate; J. C. Reed, *The Brothers' War* (1905).

On cotton the best authority is Matthew B. Hammond, *The Cotton Industry, an Essay in American Economic His-*

tory (American Economic Association, *Publications*, new series, No. 1, 1897).   A modern discussion is U. B. Phillips, "Economic Cost of Slaveholding" (*Political Science Quarterly*, XX., 257 – 275).   Pro - slavery contemporaries are: David Christy, *Cotton is King* (2d ed., 1856); J. D. B. De Bow, *Industrial Resources of the Southern and Western States* (3 vols., 1852–1853), I., 114–243.

On transportation and travel, the best special books are: Milton Reizenstein, *Economic History of the Baltimore and Ohio Railroad* (*Johns Hopkins University Studies*, XV., No. 7, 1897); G. W. Ward, *Early Development of the Chesapeake and Ohio Canal Project* (*ibid.*, XVII., Nos. 9–11, 1899); Jeremiah S. Young, *Political and Constitutional Study of the Cumberland Road* (1904) — confused but serviceable; Archer B. Hulbert, *Historic Highways of America* (16 vols., 1902–1905), especially XI.–XIV.; S. A. Mitchell, *Compendium of the Internal Improvements of the United States* (1835); G. S. Callender, "Early Transportation and Banking Enterprises of the States" (*Quarterly Journal of Economics*, XVII., 111–162).   Compare the list of writers in Turner, *New West* (*Am. Nation*, XIV.), 348–350.

THE NEGRO

Recent favorable views are: Booker T. Washington and others, *The Negro Problem* (1903); William A. Sinclair, *The Aftermath of Slavery* (1905)—by a former slave; Joseph A. Tillinghast, *The Negro in Africa and America* (American Economic Association, *Publications*, 3d series, III., No. 2, 1902)—thoroughgoing and thoughtful; George W. Cable, *The Silent South, together with the Freedman's Case in Equity* (1885); T. J. Morgan, *The Negro in America and the Ideal American Republic* (1898); W. E. B. DuBois, *The Souls of Black Folk* (1903)—a plea for the largeness of negro character.

Unfavorable recent books are: Frederick L. Hoffman, *Race Traits and Tendencies of the American Negro* (American Economic Association, *Publications*, XI., Nos. 1–3, 1896); William B. Smith, *The Color Line, a Brief in Behalf of the Unborn* (1905); W. H. Thomas, *The American Negro, What He Was, What He Is, and What He May Become* (1901)—an exaggerated criticism of the race by a negro; W. Laird Clowes, *Black America, a Study of the Ex-Slave and His Late Master* (1891)—the negro under reconstruction; Philip A. Bruce, *The Plantation Negro as a Freeman* (1889) —a study of negro laborers. A significant book on negro characteristics is H. J. Nieboer, *Slavery as an Industrial System, Ethnological Researches* (Hague, 1900).

Among pro-slavery arguments that the negro was hopelessly inferior, or even a beast, see especially: George Fitzhugh, *Cannibals All* (1857); Ariel [B. H. Payne], *The Negro, What is His Ethnological Status* (1867); J. D. B. De Bow, *Industrial Resources of the Southern and Western States* (3 vols., 1852–1853), II., 315–344; and pro-slavery arguments cited below.

On the status of the free negro, see the controversial works and Ohio Anti - Slavery Society, *Report on Condition of the People of Color in the State of Ohio* (1835); William Jay, *On the Condition of the Free People of Color in the United States* (in his *Miscellaneous Writings on Slavery*, 1853). The law of the free negro and slave is set forth in four treatises: T. R. R. Cobb, *An Inquiry into the Law of Negro Slavery* (1 vol. only, 1858)—strongly pro-slavery; George M. Stroud, *Sketch of the Laws Relating to Slavery* (1856); William Goodell, *American Slave Code in Theory and Practice* (1853); Richard Hildreth, *Despotism in America* (1854)—all anti-slavery; John C. Hurd, *The Law of Freedom and Bondage* (2 vols., 1858–1862)—prepared as a lawbook, technical but searching; also James E. Cutler, *Lynch Law, an Investigation into the History of Lynching* (1905)— on mob law.

PRO-SLAVERY DISCUSSIONS

FORMAL ARGUMENTS.—Among the most thoroughgoing arguments for slavery are four books by northerners: Bishop John Henry Hopkins, *A Scriptural, Ecclesiastical, and Historical View of Slavery* (1864)—chiefly Scriptural;

Dr. John H. Van Evrie, *Negroes and Negro Slavery* (1853)—an argument on physical grounds; Rev. Nehemiah Adams, *A Southside View of Slavery, or Three Months at the South* (1854)—a roseate picture, throwing whatever blame there was on the north; Rev. Samuel Seabury, *American Slavery . . . Justified by the Law of Nature* (1861).

The most comprehensive defences of slavery are: *The Pro-Slavery Argument* (1852), by several authors, which covers the moral, political, and economic sides of the subject from various points of view; Albert T. Bledsoe, *An Essay on Liberty and Slavery* (1856); James K. Paulding, *Slavery in the United States* (1836)—fairly impartial. The Biblical argument appears in Howell Cobb, *Scriptural Examination of the Institution of Slavery* (1856); Thornton Stringfellow, *Scriptural and Statistical Views in Favor of Slavery* (4th ed., 1856).

SOUTHERN DESCRIPTIONS.—Good pictures of plantation life by members of slave-holding families or by friendly visitors are: Emily P. Burke, *Reminiscences of Georgia* (1850); Mrs. V. V. Clayton, *White and Black under the Old Régime* (1899)—a vivacious but rather superficial book; Mrs. Roger A. Pryor, *Reminiscences of Peace and War* (1904); John S. Wise, *End of an Era* (1899)—contains two critical chapters on slavery; E. A. Pollard, *Black Diamonds Gathered in the Darkey Homes of the South* (1859)—racy and suggestive; Susan D. Smedes, *Memorials of a Southern Planter* (Thomas Dabney) (1887)—a description of a slave-holding elysium.

ANTI-SLAVERY DISCUSSIONS

FORMAL WORKS.—First in interest and in detail is W. P. and F. J. Garrison, *William Lloyd Garrison* (4 vols., 1885–1889), which discusses most of the controverted questions. Samuel J. May, *Some Recollections of Our Anti-Slavery Conflict* (1869), is a lively, first-hand account by a man who was in the thick of the fight; William Goodell, *Slavery and Anti-Slavery* (1852), is rather more abstruse. William Jay wrote several monographs, especially *A View of the Action*

of the Federal Government in Behalf of Slavery (1839) and
*An Inquiry into the Character and Tendency of the American
Colonization and American Anti-Slavery Societies* (1835), both
reprinted in his *Miscellaneous Writings on Slavery* (1853);
James Freeman Clarke, *Anti-Slavery Days* (1883), is a pict-
ure of the agitation in Boston.   See also the biographies
cited above.   Southern anti-slavery sentiment is shown in
Stephen B. Weeks, *Anti-Slavery Sentiment in the South*
(Southern History Association, *Publications*, II., No. 2);
Stephen B. Weeks, *Southern Quakers and Slavery* (*Johns
Hopkins University Studies*, extra vol. XV., 1896); John
S. Bassett, *Anti-Slavery Leaders of North Carolina* (*ibid*,
XVI., No. 6, 1898).

SPECIAL ARGUMENTS.—The general books and biogra-
phies often state or summarize the arguments on slavery.
Against the Scriptural argument three books may be cited:
Rev. Albert Barnes, *An Inquiry into the Scriptural Views
of Slavery* (1846); Rev. George B. Cheever, *The Guilt of
Slavery and the Crime of Slaveholding* (1860); Augustin
Cochin, *The Results of Slavery* (transl. by Booth, 1863).
Lydia Maria Child wrote several suggestive books, espe-
cially, *An Appeal in Favor of that Class of Americans called
Africans* (1833); *Authentic Anecdotes of American Slavery*
(2d. ed., 1838); *Anti-Slavery Catechism* (1836); *The Patri-
archal Constitution as Described by Members of its Own Family*
(1860); *The Oasis* (1834).   Other useful books are: Daniel
R. Goodwin, *Southern Slavery in its Present Aspects* (1864);
J. D. Paxton, *Letters on Slavery* (1833); Harriet Beecher
Stowe, *Key to Uncle Tom's Cabin* (1853); Rev. John Ran-
kin, *Letters on American Slavery* (2d ed., 1836)—one of the
best summaries of anti-slavery argument; Rev. Charles
Elliott, *Sinfulness of American Slavery* (2 vols., 1851)—an
analytic discussion; Parker Pillsbury, *Acts of the Anti-
Slavery Apostles* (1884)—ill-arranged extracts and data;
T. D. Weld, *American Slavery as It Is*, *Testimony of a
Thousand Witnesses* (1839).

VISITORS.—Among the many unfavorable witnesses are:
Frances Anne Kemble, *Journal of a Residence on a Georgian*

Plantation (1863)—the darkest picture of slavery; William Chambers, *American Slavery and Colour* (1857)—by an intelligent foreign visitor; George W. Cable, *Strange True Stories of Louisiana* (1889)—several interesting episodes of slavery; William H. Russell, *My Diary North and South* (1863)—by a correspondent of the *London Times;* E. H. Botume, *First Days amongst the Contrabands* (1893); T. W. Higginson, *Army Life in a Black Regiment* (1870) — first-hand accounts of freedmen.

SLAVE NARRATIVES.—Many fugitives who escaped to the north told their stories, which were often put into literary form by anti-slavery friends. Such books are: Charles Stearns, *Narrative of Henry Box Brown* (1849); Freaerick Douglass, *My Bondage and My Freedom* (1855); W. G. Eliot, *The Story of Archer Alexander* (1885); *Narrative of Events in the Life of William Green* (1853); *Life of J. Henson, Formerly a Slave* (1849); *Experiences of Thomas Jones, who was a Slave for Forty-Three Years* (1850); W. G. Hawkins, *Lunsford Lane* (1863); R. Hildreth, *The Slave, or Memoirs of Archy Moore* (2 vols., 1836); Solomon Northup, *Twelve Years a Slave, Narrative of Solomon Northup* (1853); *Narrative of the Adventures and Escape of Moses Roper* (1837); L. W. Paine, *Six Years in a Georgia Prison* (1852); Kate E. R. Pickard, *The Kidnapped and the Ransomed* [Peter Still] (1846); *Narrative of Sojourner Truth* (1850); *Narrative of Henry Watson, a Fugitive Slave* (1845); Booker T. Washington, *Up from Slavery, an Autobiography* (1901).

SLAVERY IN PARTICULAR COMMUNITIES

Several carefully digested monographs deal with slavery in a particular colony or state.   In the *Johns Hopkins University Series:* J. R. Brackett, *The Negro in Maryland* (extra vol. VI., 1889), and *Notes on the Progress of the Colored People of Maryland Since the War* (VIII., Nos., 7–9, 1890); J. H. T. McPherson, *History of Liberia* (IX., No. 10, 1891); E. Ingle, *The Negro in the District of Columbia* (XI., Nos. 3, 4, 1893); B. C. Steiner, *History of Slavery in Connecticut* (XI., Nos. 9, 10, 1893); H. S. Cooley, *Slavery in New Jersey* (XIV.,

Nos. 9, 10, 1896); J. S. Bassett, *History of Slavery in North Carolina* (XVII., Nos. 7, 8, 1899); J. C. Ballagh, *White Servitude in the Colony of Virginia* (XIII., Nos. 6, 7, 1895); E. L. Whitney, *Government in the Colony of South Carolina* (XIII., Nos. 1, 2, 1895); E. J. McCormac, *White Servitude in Maryland* (XXII., Nos. 3, 4, 1904). Other similar monographs are: K. F. Geiser, *Redemptioners and Indentured Servants in Pennsylvania* (*Yale Review*, X., No. 21, supplement, 1901); Mary Tremain, *Slavery in the District of Columbia* (University of Nebraska, *Seminary Papers*, No. 2, 1892) —very useful; Edward McCrady, *Slavery in the Province of South Carolina, 1670–1770* (American Historical Association, *Report*, 1895, pp. 629–673); Edwin V. Morgan, *Slavery in New York* (American Historical Association, *Papers*, V., 1891); Charles Deane, *Letters and Documents Relating to Slavery in Massachusetts* (1877); George H. Moore, *Notes on Slavery in Massachusetts* (1866); Edward Bettle, *Notices of Negro Slavery in Pennsylvania* (Pennsylvania Historical Society, *Memoirs*, I., 1826); Edward Needles, *Historical Memoir of the Pennsylvania Society* (1848); Alexander Savine, *Bondsmen under the Tudors* (Royal Historical Society, *Transactions*, new series, XVII., 235–289); N. Dwight Harris, *History of Negro Servitude in Illinois* (1904); E. B. Washburne, *Sketch of Edward Coles and of the Slavery Struggle of 1823–1824* (1882); J. P. Dunn, Jr., *Indiana, a Redemption from Slavery* (1888); J. N. Davidson, *Negro Slavery in Wisconsin* (in Wisconsin Historical Society, *Proceedings*, 1903, pp. 82–99); Louis Pelzer, *The Negro and Slavery in Early Iowa* (*Iowa Journal of History and Politics*, II., 471–484, 1904); A. J. Northrup, *Slavery in New York* (State Library, *Bulletins, History*, No. 4, 1900); T. W. Smith, *The Slave in Canada* (Nova Scotia Historical Society, *Collections*, X., 1899); C. T. Hickok, *Negro in Ohio, 1802–1870* (Western Reserve University, 1896).

INCIDENTS OF SLAVERY

Fugitives and the Underground Railroad.—On this subject there are several excellent books: Marion G.

McDougall, *Fugitive Slaves, 1619–1865 (Fay House Monographs*, No. 3, 1891)—brief but to the point, with excellent foot-notes and bibliography; William H. Siebert, *The Underground Railroad from Slavery to Freedom* (1898)—derived from interviews and correspondence with old abolitionists; William Still, *The Underground Railroad* (1872, enlarged ed., 1883)—by a negro who was stationmaster on the U. G. in Philadelphia; Levi Coffin, *Reminiscences* (1876)—in charge of the work at Cincinnati; Daniel Drayton, *Personal Memoir, . . . including a Narrative of Voyage and Capture of Schooner "Pearl"* (1853); Joel Parker, *Personal Liberty Laws* (1861); Benjamin Drew, *North-Side View of Slavery, . . . or the Narratives of Fugitive Slaves in Canada* (1856); S. G. Howe, *Refugees from Slavery in Canada West* (1864).

COLONIZATION. — On colonization in Liberia the best brief history is John H. T. McPherson, *History of Liberia (Johns Hopkins University Studies*, IX., No. 10, 1891); a contemporary book is Achibald Alexander, *History of Colonization on the Western Coast of Africa* (1846). The standard sources are the publications of the American Colonization Society, especially their *Annual Reports;* the work of half a century is summarized in *Fiftieth Annual Report* (1867). The Society also issued *The African Repository and Colonial Journal* (1825 – 1876). A similar publication, not official, was the monthly *Colonizationist, a Journal of Freedom* (beginning 1833).

INSURRECTIONS.—The best books are: T. W. Higginson, *Travellers and Outlaws* (1889)—careful accounts of the principal insurrections; W. S. Drewry, *Slave Insurrections in Virginia* (1900); Joshua Coffin, *An Account of Some of the Principal Slave Insurrections* (1860); *Federal Aid in Domestic Disturbances (Senate Documents*, 57 Cong., 2 Sess., No. 209)—action of the federal government; James E. Cutler, *Lynch Law* (1905)—punishment of insurrections. A negro advocate of insurrection was David Walker, *Walker's Appeal, in Four Articles* (1829; 2d ed., 1830).

FOREIGN SLAVE-TRADE.—Inasmuch as the foreign slave-trade was strictly prohibited by federal law, that subject hardly enters into the anti - slavery controversy. The standard monograph is W. E. B. DuBois, *The Suppression of the African Slave - Trade to the United States of America, 1638–1870* (*Harvard Historical Studies*, No. 1, 1896)— scholarly, full, and abounding in foot-notes. A standard account of the African slave-trade and middle passage is Thomas Fowell Buxton, *The African Slave-Trade* (Am. ed., 1839). Other books: Commander Andrew H. Foote, *Africa and the American Flag* (1854); H. C. Carey, *The Slave-Trade, Domestic and Foreign* (1853); John R. Spears, *The American Slave-Trade* (1900)—a sketchy, popular book.

DOMESTIC SLAVE-TRADE.—The only monograph is Winfield H. Collins, *The Domestic Slave-Trade of the Southern States* (1904)—interesting but not very full. The subject is discussed in the monographs on slavery in particular communities noticed above, and crops out in many of the controversial writings.

INDEX

ABOLITIONISTS, religious phase of movement, 15 and literature, 31, 32; causes, 170–172; purpose compared with anti-slavery, 173–175; border-state movement, 175–179 southern leaders in north, 179; Lundy organizes, 180 Garrison as leader, 180, 194, 320; *Liberator*, 180–183 New England society, 183; national society, 183; its principles, 184 growth, 184 Garrison leaders, 184–187 New England non-Garrisons, 188 in middle states, 189; western, 190–196 Lane Seminary discussion, 190, 191 Oberlin as centre, 191–193; Ohio state society, 193; Birney's *Philanthropist*, 193; other western societies, 194; diverse sectional development, 194, 196; Chase as political, 195; in Western Reserve, 196; dissensions of eastern, 197–201 question of women agitators, 198; and church disruption, 198; non-political covenant, 200; and other isms, 200; split, 200; effect of split, 201; decay as national moral force, 201, 315; adversaries on motives, 202, 232; character, 203; method of agitation, 203, 232; and gradual emancipation, 204; and slave-holders, 204, 310; knowledge of slavery, 205; and right of discussion, 205, 234, 244, 312, 321; propaganda, 206; typical meeting, 206; publications, 207, 332; negro leaders, 208, 209; English co-operation, 209; Irish address, 210; social ostracism, 210; and eastern colleges, 210; clerical opposition, 211, 212; clerical support, 213; church split on, 213; association with negroes, 215, 315; and amalgamation, 216; incendiary publications, 216; and slave insurrections, 217–221; and fugitives, 221; southern threats against, 235; arrested in south, 235; mobbed there, 235; south demands northern suppression, 236, 237; antagonism with colonization, 239; and difficulties of emancipation, 241; appeals to state governments, 242; and slavery in states, 242; northern agitation against, 242, 243; movement for legislation against, 243, 244; within the law, 244; Massachusetts hearing, 244; attacks on their schools, 244, 245; mobbed in north, 245–249; reaction, 249; representation in Congress, 250;